ALEXANDER THE GREAT FAILURE

Alexander the Great Failure
The Collapse of the Macedonian Empire

John D. Grainger

hambledon
continuum

Hambledon Continuum is an imprint of Continuum Books
Continuum UK, The Tower Building, 11 York Road, London SE1 7NX
Continuum US, 80 Maiden Lane, Suite 704, New York, NY 10038

www.continuumbooks.com

First published 2007

British Library Cataloguing-in-Publication Data
A catalogue record for this book is available from the British Library.

ISBN 978 1 84725 188 6

Typeset by Pindar New Zealand (Egan Reid), Auckland, New Zealand

Printed in the United States of America

Contents

Maps

Genealogies

Abbreviations

Austin	M.M. Austin, *The Hellenistic World from Alexander to the Roman Conquest*, Cambridge 1981
BCH	*Bulletin de Correspondance Hellenique*
CAH	*Cambridge Ancient History*
CQ	*Classical Quarterly*
FGrH	P. Jacoby, *Die Fragmente der Griechischen Historiker*, Berlin, from 1923
IG	*Inscriptiones Graecae*
JHS	*Journal of Hellenic Studies*
Macedonia	N. G. L. Hammond *et al.*, *A History of Macedonia*, Oxford 1972–1978
OGIS	W. Dittenberger, (ed.) *Orientis Graeci Inscriptones Selectae*, Leipzig, 1903–1905
REA	*Revue des Etudes Anciennes*
SVA	*Die Staatsvertage des Altertums*, vol. 2 ed. H. Bengtson, vol. 3 by H. H. Schmitt, Munich 1962 and 1969
Tod, *GHI*	M. N. Tod, *A Selection of Greek Historical Inscriptions*, Oxford 1948

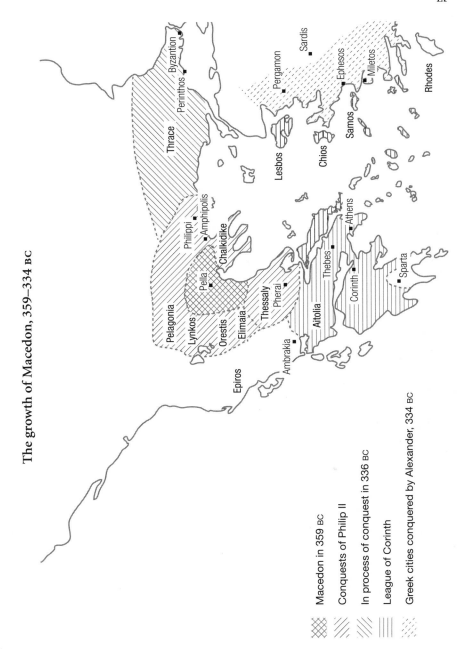

The growth of Macedon, 359–334 BC

Macedon in 359 BC

Conquests of Philip II

In process of conquest in 336 BC

League of Corinth

Greek cities conquered by Alexander, 334 BC

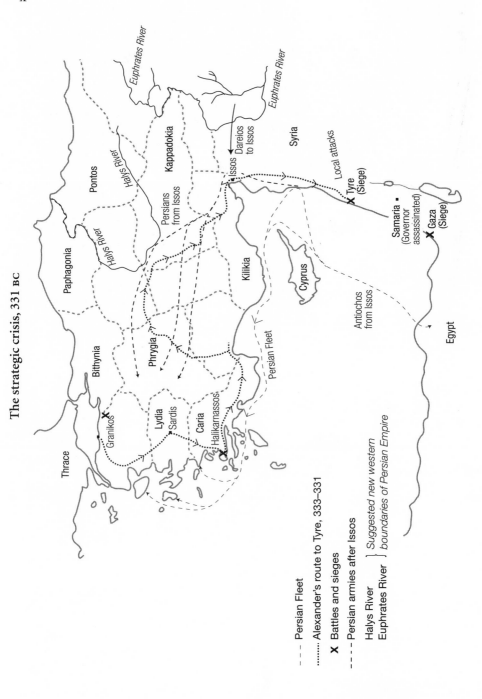

The strategic crisis, 331 BC

Euphrates River

Euphrates River

Euphrates River

Kappadokia

Dareios to Issos

Syria

Issos

Local attacks

Pontos

Halys River

Persians from Issos

Tyre (Siege)

Halys River

Paphagonia

Samaria ■ (Governor assassinated)

Gaza (Siege)

Kilikia

Cyprus

Bithynia

Antiochos from Issos

Phrygia

Persian Fleet

Egypt

Granikos

Lydia

Sardis

Caria

Halikarnassos

Thrace

— — —   Persian Fleet

....   Alexander's route to Tyre, 333–331

✗   Battles and sieges

– – – –   Persian armies after Issos

Halys River   }   *Suggested new western*
Euphrates River   }   *boundaries of Persian Empire*

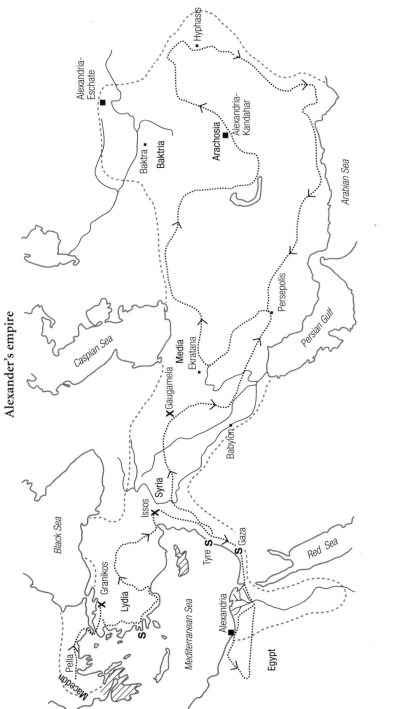

Alexander's empire

Black Sea

Caspian Sea

Pella
Macedon
Granikos
Lydia
S
Issos
X
Syria
Gaugamela
X
Media
Ekratana
Babylon
Tyre **S**
S Gaza
Alexandria
Egypt
Mediterranean Sea
Red Sea

Persepolis
Persian Gulf
Arabian Sea

Baktra
Baktria
Alexandria-
Eschate
Arachosia
Alexandria-
Kandahar
Hyphasis

...... Alexander's route
X Battles
S Sieges

■ Alexander's new cities
- - - Outer boundary
▧ Greek autonomous states

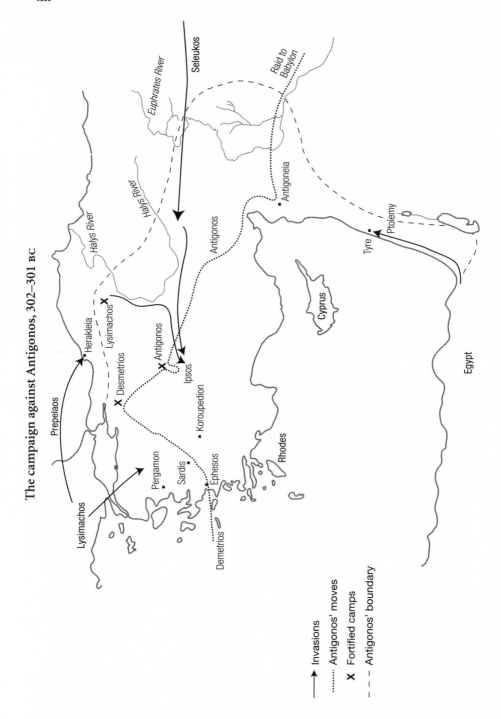

The campaign against Antigonos, 302–301 BC

Euphrates River

Seleukos

Raid to Babylon

Halys River

Halys River

Antigoneia

Antigonos

Ptolemy

Tyre

Prepelaos

Herakleia

Lysimachos

Cyprus

Demetrios

Antigonos

Ipsos

Koroupedion

Egypt

Lysimachos

Pergamon

Sardis   Ephesos

Rhodes

Demetrios

→ Invasions

····· Antigonos' moves

✗ Fortified camps

– – – Antigonos' boundary

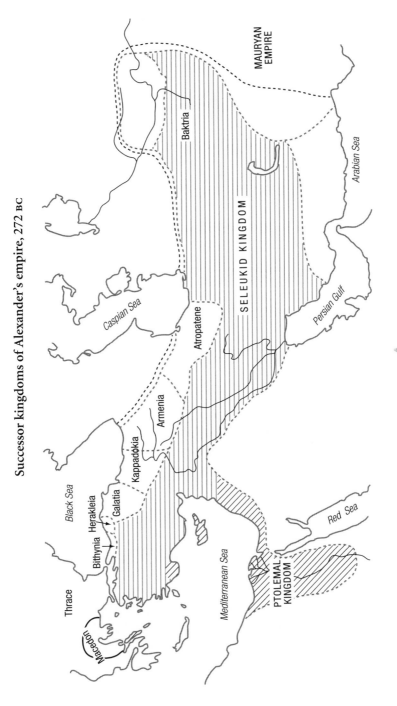

Successor kingdoms of Alexander's empire, 272 BC

- - - - - - Northern boundary of Akhaimenid Empire

THE ARGEAD KINGS OF MACEDON

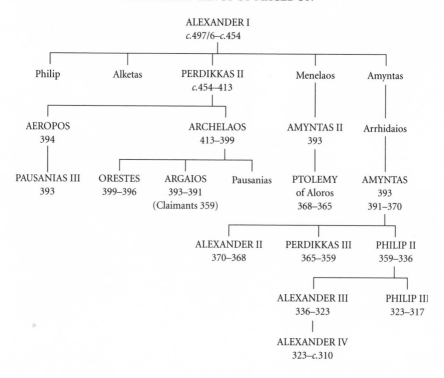

THE FAMILY OF ANTIPATER

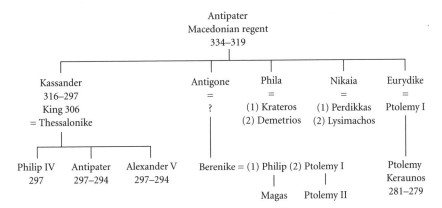

Dates are those of kings of Macedon.
Note that Antipater the regent had many other children.

THE HOUSE OF ANTIGONOS

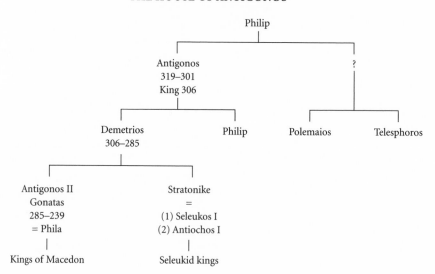

Introduction

For almost 100 years, between 360 and 270 BC, Macedon was one of the world's most dynamic states. Under the leadership of King Philip II its strength was exerted so as to dominate its Balkan and Greek neighbours. Under his son Alexander III that strength was projected eastwards as far as India. This is a fairly familiar story, especially that of Alexander, whose achievements are still astonishing over 2,000 years later. Though not intentionally so, the work of Philip was fundamental to that of Alexander; the two have to be considered together.

The number of biographies of Alexander is by now enormous, and new versions appear regularly.[1] This is due to the fascination the man's life evokes; it is also the result of the search for a new angle, a new apparent explanation for his life, or for his death; the search has extended itself at times into areas of nonsense.

Alexander's early death is all too often the point at which the story ends, by way of a variety of themes of conquering, drunkenness, disease, assassination and conspiracy. By virtue of the fact that five continuous accounts of his reign have survived, he is one of the few people of the ancient world for whom a biography can be written;[2] but it has always seemed to me that, while biographies of Alexander are invariably interesting and entertaining – the conquest of the world could hardly be otherwise – it is only part of the story. Rather as the *Iliad*, one of Alexander's standard references for behaviour, begins *in medias res* with regard to the Trojan War as a whole, and never reveals the result of that war, so a life of Alexander which skips over his father's work and pays no attention to the events which followed his own death neither accounts for his success in a proper way nor shows what he actually accomplished.

The fundamental facts of his life are that he was the son of Philip and was a Macedonian. It follows that these two elements need to be considered in some detail. The work of Philip in extending and developing the kingdom of the Macedonians was the foundation for Alexander's career of conquest, but Philip's work had its limitations, and Alexander was faced with similar limitations in the last year of his life. Alexander died in the midst of two projects: first, to establish a government for his empire, for which Philip's system of rule proved to be inadequate; and secondly, to go on conquering other places, for which Philip's army had proved to be more than sufficient. The effects of Alexander's early death therefore need to be considered in those contexts. A mere biography can never do that: it is necessary to look at where he came from, and what happened as a result of his extraordinary life.

So this book aims to discuss how Alexander's empire originated. This requires a consideration of the kingdom of Macedon, and Philip's work there. Then I aim to examine how it was that his empire failed. For it is this which is the most notable result of Alexander's life and work: for all his military prowess, he was one of the world's great failures – and that failure spelt misery and death for countless thousands of people. Not only that, but he brought that failure on himself. His arrogance was largely responsible for his own early death; and he was also responsible for the ultimate failure of his imperial enterprise; for he was king of a society where the king was absolutely central to the well-being of the society as a whole. When the king failed, the Macedonian kingdom imploded, something which had happened more or less every generation for two centuries before him, and happened when he died, and again afterwards. For the good of his people, Alexander needed an adult successor, and he both refused to provide one, and killed off any man who could be seen as one. This was irresponsibility of the most introverted sort, and the consequence was 50 years of warfare after his death, and the destruction of his empire. In the end it brought invasion and destruction also to his inherited kingdom.

This is what I try to explain here. The subject, then, is the construction and destruction of Alexander's empire. It is not a book in which a detailed examination of the source material is made, nor is it one in which a 'dialogue' is conducted with other historians' opinions. Both of these procedures are worth doing, and have been done frequently, but all too often they become ends in themselves, inconclusively, and obscuring the subject.

The book covers about a century of time. This period has been subdivided, not so much according to the deaths of kings but more as a way of emphasizing significant developments, particularly in the history of the empire. The deaths of both Philip and Alexander are therefore noted within chapters rather than as end points or punctuations.

A. J. Toynbee once wrote two amusing essays in which he imagined what would have happened if Philip or Alexander had lived on.[3] He brought out one fact which is too often ignored: Alexander's contemporaries – Ptolemy, Lysimachos, Seleukos – lived into their eighties, as did Philip's contemporaries, Antipater and Antigonos. Both kings, that is, died young and untimely. The century I am studying here therefore begins just before Alexander's birth, and ends only a few years after the deaths of his contemporaries. There were people who may have lived through the whole of that time; it is a period only a little longer than a single lifetime.

There was also a wider consequence. As the empire he had constructed

– consisting of Macedon, Greece, the Persian Empire and the Indus Valley – collapsed in on itself, so at the same time there grew in other countries other powers of an equal strength, partly as a result of the threat posed by Alexander's empire even in its disarray. In India, a new empire was built, supposedly in imitation of Alexander's; in Italy, the Roman Republic united Italy partly as a reaction to attacks from Greece. Both of these new states proved able to resist attacks by Alexander's successors. Further off, another empire, in China, was in course of construction, a development which is wholly independent of the events in the Middle East. It is not possible in the compass of a single volume to look at these contemporary developments in proper detail, but I have inserted three chapters at intervals to note them. Too often, the histories of these lands are taken in complete isolation from one another.

Macedon 370–359 BC: a failing state

In the decade between the death of King Amyntas III in 370 BC and that of Perdikkas III in 359, four men succeeded to the Macedonian kingship, three of whom soon died: so from 370 to 359 five separate kings reigned; and by 359, three other men were seen as possible kings and were fighting to seize the throne, while three foreign enemies were invading or preparing to invade the kingdom. That is to say, between 370 and 359 the Macedonian state collapsed and was in the process of being dismembered.

Any Macedonian who knew anything about the history of his country knew that they had been at this pass before. A quarter of a century earlier, in the 390s, a very similar situation had existed; half a century earlier the kingdom had been divided for two decades or more; in between there had been a convulsive crisis within the royal family. In all four of these crises – in 454–430, 413, 399–391 and 370–359 – the succession to the kingship had been disputed, and in each case many had died. The crisis of the 360s was thus a recurrence of an old pattern.

The kingdom of the Macedonians had existed since the seventh century. Its early history is known only through myth and the usual later genealogical self-aggrandizing of the ruling dynasty,[1] which claimed descent from a Greek family of Argos, which was ultimately descended from Temenos, a relative of Heracles; from these notions the royal family is called either Temenidai or Argeadai. This early 'history' is unproven and unlikely. It is only from the end of the sixth century that some relatively clear information can be discerned, thanks to external interest rather than to any internal records from the kingdom.

The crucial facts about Macedon are, first, that it was a kingdom, and that it remained so long after most Greek states discarded their kings; and, secondly, that the kingdom lay in a large, rich, well-watered plain surrounded by uplands inhabited by non-Macedonians. These were less numerous and affluent, or perhaps merely less well fed, than the plainsmen. These two elements went together and reinforced each other, so that Macedon was constantly threatened by invaders, and required a full-time war leader to be in command, a man who could organize and lead the military forces of the plains in defence of, or in retaliation against, raids from the surrounding hills. The kingship was the heart of the Macedonian state, and a crisis within the royal family was one which affected all Macedonians. The extensive plain also fostered the existence of a large landowning baronage, who fought on horseback, and who was kept in fighting trim by their constant need to ride out to defend the kingdom.

The heart of the kingdom lay in the plainlands north of Mount Olympos, and those around the Thermaic Gulf, Pieria, Emathia, Almopia, Bottiaia, an area about 100 or so kilometres from south to north and half that from east to west, a large country for Greece. It was watered by several rivers which flowed out of the hills on the west and north and converged to discharge into the Thermaic Gulf, where the alluvium they carried had been turning the head of the gulf into marsh. The valleys of these rivers in turn provided routes out of the plain into the hills – but they were also routes by which the hillmen could raid the plain.

Beyond the enclosing ranges of hills were a series of upland valleys, each the home of a people who were also near-Greek – Tymphaia, Elimaia, Orestis, Eordaia, Lynkos, Pelagonia, all with their own kings. This region is generally called Upper Macedon; as one moved further from the heart of Macedon so the languages spoken ceased to be Greek and became Illyrian and Thracian.[2]

The coasts of the kingdom were accessible to seamen, and several Greek colony-cities had been planted there – Dion, Methone and Pydna especially. Across the Thermaic Gulf numerous cities were founded in the peninsulas of the Chalkidike, so called because so many of the cities were founded from the city of Chalkis in Euboia. This area comprehended up to 30 cities, including Therme, which gave its name to the gulf. Most of these were small, but, besides Therme, there were notable cities at Potidaia and Olynthos. This was, therefore, a Greek land rather than Macedonian.[3]

These cities were organized as republics on the Greek pattern, choosing their magistrates annually, their male citizens mobilizable into a phalanx army at need. The Macedonians, by contrast, tended to be cavalry. This restricted the effective force the kings could muster to those who were wealthy, that is, the barons. The Macedonian infantry was untrained, and consisted of a *levée en masse* of the male population, mainly peasant farmers, poorly armed, lacking discipline and cohesion.[4] The urban centres in the kingdom were relatively small, local market centres rather than developed political entities, and were dominated politically by the baronage.

This difference in organization for war put the Greek cities in a strong position, at least defensively, since a hoplite phalanx bristling with long spears was not something cavalry could easily face, the untrained infantry was incapable of fighting it, and the walls of the cities were an effective deterrent. The hillmen of the inland states were organized like the Macedonians, but were less numerous; their lands were geographically smaller and could not produce large numbers of soldiers.[5] Macedon's wars with its inland neighbours were thus generally successful; those against Greeks usually not. The whole area was therefore in a constant flux of conflict, in which no power was capable of dominating the others for long, and in which momentary alliances based on briefly perceived identities of interest could be formed, and as quickly abandoned.

The theoretical advantage lay with the Macedonian kingdom, because of its sheer size and the numbers of its people; it was the largest state in the Balkans south of the Danube. The Greek cities were relatively small and were in control of the land around them for only a short distance – perhaps a day's walk away from the walls. The inland tribal states were each limited to a narrow valley enclosed by hills, a situation in which the population and resources were necessarily limited. Macedon's power remained no more than potential, partly because of economic underdevelopment and a social organization which limited its military power, but also because of the problems of the royal family.

The first king of whom much is known is Alexander I, who ruled in Macedon when the Persian Wars engulfed Greece and the Aegean. For 30 years it was a Persian sub-kingdom, and Alexander and his father were helped to expand their territories, particularly eastwards, but Alexander also established some sort of control over several of the hill states along his western border.[6] He was ambitious, slippery, devious and cunning, exactly the qualities required to survive and prosper in the dangerous times of the Persian Wars. He permitted the Persian forces to traverse his kingdom – he could hardly do otherwise – but he also made contact with the Greeks, operating so effectively that neither side took umbrage. As the Persian power ebbed after 478, he sidled up to the victorious Greeks. He had established his Hellenic credentials by proving to the judges at the Olympic Games that he was of Greek descent by citing the story of his Argive ancestors. The judges accepted his claim, though it is more than likely fictitious and mythical.[7] This did not apply to his people, though they spoke a Greek dialect: Alexander's claim was personal. As he conquered more lands, these new areas became Macedonian; Pelagonia and the rest had been thought of as Illyrian until the Macedonian conquest, when they became, and remained, Macedonian.[8]

Alexander's imperial expansion employed methods traditional to the Macedonian kings. In some areas he conquered and expelled the inhabitants, replacing them with Macedonians. This seems to have been the main method used in the early expansion of the kingdom. Just what this method involved, however, is not clear. To drive out a whole people was extremely difficult; more likely it was the ruling group which went, perhaps taking some of their followers with them, but leaving the bulk of the peasantry behind. So the Macedonian conquest was the imposition of a Macedonian ruling group upon the existing peasantry. The net result would be an increase in lands and wealth for the baronage, and an increase in their numbers as younger sons gained estates.[9]

The second method was imposing an overlordship. The royal houses of the western kingdoms in the hill states remained in place, despite the successes of Alexander I, and are noted by Thucydides in his account dated to the year 429.

They had presumably been defeated in battle; the peace agreement which followed will therefore have guaranteed the continuation of the royal house's rule, and marriage alliances were arranged with the Macedonian royal house – Thucydides calls these kingdoms, ambiguously but revealingly, 'allies and subjects'.[10] The subject kings were required to render armed assistance to the Macedonian king when he asked. Needless to say, the subordinate kingdoms tended to break away when they could.

Macedonian society was one in which the king was the leading member of a fairly widespread aristocracy which ruled over a submissive peasantry. The aristocracy was always keen to acquire new lands, hunting was their favourite pastime, and their mode of fighting was on horseback. Their support of the king was to an extent voluntary, solicited by his generosity with lands and gifts and feasts. Into such a polity, the subordinated kings of the hill kingdoms fitted without difficulty. Below the social level of the baronage was the peasantry, required to produce the food which supported the aristocratic superstructure, but also at times required to take up arms to see off an invader under the command of the barons and ultimately the king. In cultural terms the lords were to a degree Hellenized; the peasantry generally illiterate; economically all lived close to subsistence level.

Macedon in the fifth century was, therefore, a large state, loosely structured, fairly thinly populated and unstable. Its effectiveness depended to a large degree on the vigour and activity of the king. In internal relations the king had to keep the lords and barons on his side, and had constantly to conciliate or dominate the subordinate kings of his western border regions. The barons were liable to become disgruntled at almost any real or imagined slight; the hill kings would much rather have had their complete independence. The frontiers were indefinite and often the scene of skirmishing warfare. In both internal and external affairs, the kings required the deviousness and cunning which Alexander I showed so successfully.[11]

After the Persian War, the main power Alexander faced was Athens, first as the leader of the Delian League, and later as the *hegemon* of its empire. They came into conflict over control of the mouth and the lowest crossing of the Strymon River. The crossing was Macedon's gateway to further east; the river was Athens' entry into the continent from the sea. To add an extra edge to the situation, rich sources of gold and silver existed in Mount Pangaion, just east of the river. Almost simultaneously, in 477, Athens seized a Persian base, Eion, on the coast, and Alexander seized the crossing, Nine Ways, inland.[12] The local Greek colonial cities along the Macedonian coast and in the Chalkidike and on the Thracian coast were meanwhile recruited into the Delian League.[13]

The combination of menaces from outside and instability within was faced by every king of Macedon in the century after the Persian withdrawal. This is the basic explanation for the erratic fortunes of the kings and their kingdom in that time. Any continuity of policy was broken by the difficulties attendant on every royal succession. The only method of succession visible to us was designation by the previous king, though his choice was not always accepted by others.[14] Death of a king was therefore normally followed by a struggle for succession between those men who could be considered his heirs, a group which was restricted to the males of the Argead family. This inevitably encouraged interference from outside, attempts at independence by the subsidiary kings, and the possible division of the kingdom between heirs. It also rendered the life of any king somewhat precarious: assassination was the repeated resort of those who were disappointed in their ambitions.

Alexander I died about 454, leaving at least five living sons by at least two wives. He appears to have set up three of them as kings over various sections of his kingdom. This extended into the kingdom he ruled directly the system of suzerainty on the western borders. So Perdikkas II, the eldest or most vigorous son, was regarded as the king; Philip ruled lands along the eastern border, perhaps Amphaxitis, the land between the Axios River and the hills to the east; Alketas ruled somewhere else, it is not known where. Two other brothers, Menelaos and Amyntas, had no principalities of their own, but certainly survived and will have had landed estates for their livelihood. The whole situation is unclear and subject to controversy.[15]

Such a division had been Alexander's responsibility, but it could also be an arrangement made between the brothers. It may have been subject to acceptance by the Assembly of the Macedonians – or perhaps it was only the person of the king who was so subject. The Assembly is a vague entity in the sources, but it would seem to be composed of wealthy landowners, the barons, but was also attended by non-noble freemen. The Assembly, if it followed the pattern visible in other Greek tribal states, met every spring and autumn (at the equinoxes), probably at Dion in Pieria, and at Aigai. When the king died, his successor presented himself to the Assembly for acceptance by acclamation. There is, in fact, no record of a king ever being rejected. Special meetings could be called, no doubt by the king, and any sizeable group of Macedonians could be regarded as an Assembly.[16]

It follows that the determinant of the royal succession was first of all the previous king, but his decisions could be altered. Succession was confined to members of the royal family, the Argeads, but this was a fairly large group. Kings were liable to marry more than once, either serially or polygamously; this all imported a good deal of uncertainty into the process. Assassination, murder and civil war were part of that process.

Alexander I's division of the kingdom led to a generation of trouble. Philip disputed Perdikkas II's authority as king, but was eventually driven out and probably killed. When Perdikkas himself died, about 413, Alketas claimed the kingship, perhaps having been emplaced as successor by the dead king; this was disputed by Perdikkas' own son Archelaos, and it was the latter who emerged as king. Whether this was due to a belief among the Macedonians that it was his due as the son of the last king, or simply because Alketas and his sons died in the fighting, is unknown.[17] The time of division was also one of weakness, and two areas at least, Bisaltia, east of the Axios, and the Edones, even further east, became independent under their own kings. The western regions of Upper Macedon became even more loosely attached than before. During this period also Athens managed to found its colony at Amphipolis at the former Nine Ways, with the aim of controlling the trade route along the Strymon Valley, and the mineral sources of Mount Pangaion.[18]

Archelaos made attempts to develop his kingdom's power but results came only slowly. He reopened a profitable silver mine in Bisaltia, let Athens build ships in a Macedonian dockyard, selling the city the timber for the work, and developed a more effective army. After the defeat of Athens in the Peloponnesian War he meekly did as Sparta told him. Macedon did not have enough strength to cut a large figure in international affairs in the face of either Athens or Sparta.[19]

Archelaos, however, made progress at home. He subordinated Elimaia and Orestis on the west. With Athenian help he conquered the Greek city of Pydna on the coast and moved its population inland 3 or 4 km. He pushed his control eastwards to the eastern side of the Chalkidike. He pushed north along the Axios River to gain control of the crucial Demir Kapu Pass by planting a Macedonian settlement a little way beyond it, blocking access to it from that direction.[20] This involved a decade of effort and warfare, and had required the enlargement of his military forces.

He also moved his royal seat from Aigai on the Haliakmon to Pella on the northern shores of the Thermaic Gulf. This marked a partial break with the past, though the kings continued to be buried at Aigai, and the Assembly still took place at Aigai. A greater openness to the outside world would result from the move, for Aigai was awkwardly inland while Pella was a seaport, more central to the kingdom, and residence there brought the king closer to the problem frontiers of the north-west and the east.[21]

Archelaos was killed in 399, either in a hunting accident or as a result of a conspiracy in the royal court.[22] Between his death and the final accession of his cousin Amyntas III in 391, four other men were kings: Orestes, Archelaos' child, who died or was killed; Aeropos, Archelaos' half-brother who was regent for Orestes, and whom he succeeded as king, dying after a reign of only two or three years; Amyntas II 'the Little', a son of King Perdikkas' brother Menelaos, who was killed by one of the courtiers called Derdas, whom he had humiliated; and then Pausanias, the son of King Aeropos, who died, possibly murdered, after only a short reign. Amyntas III became king in 393. He was a great-nephew of Archelaos and grandson of the fifth son of Alexander I, and so of a line hitherto nowhere near the kingship. The succession had moved steadily further away from the direct line; the only qualifications for being king were a connection, however distant, to the royal line, and the ability to survive. There is no indication that the Assembly had any influence in all this, but it had presumably ratified each new king.[23] (See Genealogies, p. xiv).

The inevitable result of the long succession crisis was a weakening of the state once more. The struggle was wholly within the royal family, and no outsiders had much influence on the outcome, except as murderers. Amyntas III's authority as king was seriously diminished, and his kingdom was almost at once invaded by Illyrians from across the north-western border. His predecessors had lost control of the border kingdom of Lynkos, and Amyntas was driven out by the invaders, who put up a man called Argaios as king; he is said to have maintained himself for two years before Amyntas managed to return.[24] So by 391, when Amyntas returned, the kingdom had had eight kings in nine years, including Amyntas for the second time.

Argaios is not certainly identifiable, but was probably a brother or half-brother of Orestes, and so a son of King Archelaos. Orestes had been a child king; perhaps Argaios was even younger, in his teens by the late 390s. It was always a temptation for a defeated or ignored royal candidate to look for support outside the kingdom during a period of confusion in the royal house, and neighbours would hope to influence a puppet ruler. It did not usually work for the candidate in the long term, since by definition he was lacking in supporters within the kingdom, but the invaders usually found it profitable. The Illyrians, the Thracians, Athens, and later the Epirotes, all tried to influence affairs in Macedon and ultimately failed. Their interventions, however, generally ensured that the kingdom continued in a weakened condition, which was probably a secondary aim.

Amyntas had considerable internal support and recruited help from Thessaly; he also made some arrangement with the city of Olynthos in the Chalkidike by which he handed over land near that city as a gift in exchange for armed help. The Thessalians succeeded in returning Amyntas to his kingship[25] and then were thanked and went home. (This is a fairly tentative reconstruction, and a different version is possible.)[26] Macedon at this time was clearly much weakened as a result of the uncertainty at the top. A new king required some time – up to a decade perhaps – to establish himself and after his death his achievements, if there were any, were swiftly dissipated by the struggle for the succession. After ten years of confusion, Amyntas required longer than most to secure his position and develop his power.

Macedon's weakness coincided with the growth of a new league of Chalkidian cities led by Olynthos, and during the 380s the league took in the nearby

Macedonian towns, including even Pella,[27] so depriving Amyntas of his royal seat. During the fifth century, under the impulse of expanding trade and the example of the Greek colonial cities nearby, and along the kingdom's coast, the urban centres in Macedon had multiplied and grown.[28] Few were really large as yet, and most were still basically rural, but they constituted markets for rural produce, and were places where imported manufactured goods were available, and the skills of local craftsmen could be marketed. Their populations were also alternative power bases for the kings, whose dependence on the rural barons and the peasantry was thus lessened. They were reinforced by immigrants from Greece, such as the people of Mycenae who were forced out of their city by the Argives in 464 and given refuge by Alexander I.[29] Perdikkas repeated the gesture for the Hestiaians from Euboia, forced out by the Athenians in 446.[30] In particular it was such men as these, and those from the towns, trained as hoplite infantry, who were able to give the kings the ability to fight Greek invaders, as compared with the Illyrians and Thracians, who could normally be dealt with by the barons' cavalry and the peasants.

Loss of control over several of these urban centres to the Chalkidian League meant that the kings lost access to their financial resources, the use of their hoplite soldiers, and control of their lands. Amyntas III was reduced to dependence on the rural areas, on the support of the barons, and on the peasant soldiers who were useless against cavalry or hoplite infantry. The advance of the Chalkidian League into the urban centres of Macedon bade fair to destroy the kingdom.

Amyntas may have been driven from his kingdom for a second time by another Illyrian invasion in 383, though if so he quickly recovered, and indeed it is not clear that he was facing more than another momentary Illyrian raid.[31] By this time, however, he had become so concerned at Chalkidian power that he turned to the predominant power in Greece, Sparta, appealing for help. Complaints also reached Sparta at about the same time from a couple of Chalkidian cities not members of the League. At last appreciating the potential of the League for power and future expansion, the Spartans intervened.[32]

This was the time when Sparta's imperial reach was at its greatest. The Chalkidian League was seen by the Spartans, once the case was pointed out to them, as a major threat to its neighbours and to the Spartan hegemony of Greece. A force of Spartan soldiers came north and, in alliance with Amyntas, laid siege to Olynthos. The siege lasted three years, demonstrating to the Spartans just how formidable a force the league already was. No doubt congratulations were handed round at Sparta when the eventual peace treaty broke up the League, but the major beneficiary was Amyntas, who regained his lost lands and his towns and cities.[33]

Amyntas III was almost as slippery in his international relations as his great-grandfather Alexander I, and with as much justification and necessity. He allied himself at various times with Thessalians, Athens, the Chalkidian League, Illyrians and Sparta, all with the purpose of gaining, regaining or reviving his kingdom. The destruction of the Chalkidian League at Sparta's hands did not induce him to remain friendly with that city for very long, and soon afterwards he was allied once more with Athens, which had recovered sufficiently from its defeat to form a new league of its own.[34] This was a balance to Sparta, and the whole Spartan hegemony loosened in the 370s. In the end it was the Thebans who brought it down, first by defeating a Spartan detachment at Leuktra in 371 and then by carrying the war into the Peloponnese under the leadership of Epameinondas and Pelopidas. It was, however, only beginning to make progress in this when Amyntas died, in 370, of natural causes.

Macedon was for the moment a relatively stable state, but it was still ringed by enemies, and its internal structure remained extremely volatile. Below the level of the royal court, the state's infrastructure was no more than rudimentary. The king's income was based largely on his ability to control and dispose of the natural resources of the kingdom: these consisted particularly of precious metals and timber; so when the king lost control of the mines, as Perdikkas II had lost control of the Bisaltian silver mine, the minting of coins ceased. Sales of timber were in part an index of the kingdom's foreign policy: the alignment with Athens was linked with that city's constant demand for shipbuilding timber for its fleet.[35]

The kingdom's military power still lay with the horse-riding baronage. The peasant infantry was probably unwilling to turn out without compulsion being applied, or the inducement of either pay or the likelihood of loot – and the kings were not rich enough to pay wages. And so only a king with good control over the kingdom – meaning the ability to control the baronage – could cut a major figure in foreign affairs. All too often it was relatively easy for one of his enemies to knock Macedon out of the game by inducing an invasion by one enemy or another, or by persuading a pretender to the throne to raise a rebellion.

The absence of a governing infrastructure meant that there was no kingdom-wide bureaucracy to provide a continuing administrative spine to the country, no professional military force to control internal dissent, discipline unruly barons, or stand guard to deter invaders. The Chalkidian League could dispose of fewer than 10,000 soldiers in 383, and yet it was able, with no real difficulty, to mop up the nearby Macedonian towns; and Amyntas had been unable to prevent it.[36] Therefore, as a state, Macedon was still a primitive political entity, overly reliant on the strength and wealth and personal charisma of individual kings. Hence the repeated instability whenever a king died.

A clear pattern can be seen during the century and a half before Amyntas died. It can even be tabulated without too great a distortion of reality, as alternating periods of collapse and royal stability:

1. 497–454: Alexander I's rule;
    2. 454–430: the kingdom breaks up;
3. 430–413: Perdikkas II's sole rule;
    4. 413: a royal bloodbath;
5. 413–399: Archelaos' rule;
    6. 399–391: royal succession dispute; and
7. 391–370: Amyntas III's rule.

The alternation of chaos in the royal household and the subsequent revival of royal rule under the winning candidate was itself thoroughly unsettling. The presumption had to be that no king would be able to pass on his power to his successor, who was likely to be weaker for an ever-longer period. The turbulence of Amyntas III's reign is one result – he was clearly a less effective king than his predecessors.

The kings understood what needed to be done. Archelaos' rule may be taken as example: he cut roads through the forests; he organized a professional army, though it was never large; he gained control of the Greek cities on his coastline; he moved the royal centre from traditional Aigai to coastal Pella.[37] This he did in his decade and a half of rule, but he was able to do it because he took over a kingdom which was more or less intact. His predecessor Perdikkas had had to spend over 20 years recovering lost territories, and the succession dispute in 413, though lethal to several members of the royal family, had been brief, and had affected the royal house rather than the rest of the kingdom; the fact that the Greek powers were locked into their Great War also helped to insulate the dispute from outside interference. But the larger succession dispute of the 390s rapidly wasted Archelaos' achievements, and the continuing troubles of Amyntas III's reign did not allow a full recovery.

It was only by the 370s that Amyntas III recovered some of his predecessors' powers, but by then he was an old man, and when he died the whole structure fell apart again. But by now simply regaining control in the traditional manner was not enough; a more robust governmental structure was clearly needed. Macedon in the 370s was a weaker state, internally and in its foreign relations, than at any time since the Persian invasions.

In this situation it did not help that Amyntas had fathered no fewer than six sons, by two different wives. The order of their birth is unclear, and it is possible that Amyntas' marriages were bigamous (not a matter for condemnation in Macedon). The senior wife was Eurydike, a princess of the Lynkestian royal family; the second wife was Gygaia, whose origin is not known; both wives gave birth to three sons. A son of Eurydike, Alexander, appears to have been recognized as Amyntas' heir during his lifetime, for he is named directly after his father in a treaty with Athens;[38] he was probably the eldest son. There was also a daughter, Eurynoe.

Alexander II was about 20 years of age when his father died. His accession was peaceful and undisputed, as far as we can tell. He quickly made an agreement with the Illyrians to pay them tribute to prevent an invasion,[39] and he was confident enough of his power to intervene the next year in Thessaly, to assist the rulers of the city of Larissa, his father's old ally, against a local tyrant, but his confidence was misplaced. By intervening in Thessaly he had attracted the attention of the current Greek hegemonic power, Thebes. He occupied the cities of Larissa and Krannon, and promised to leave them independent once the crisis had passed; but then he changed his mind; his liberation of his ally became an occupation.[40]

In his absence a rebellion began in Macedon, headed by Ptolemy of Aloros, probably a son of Amyntas II 'the Little' (king briefly in 393), and married to Eurynoe, Alexander's sister. Ptolemy does not appear to have claimed the throne, yet, but he had been a prominent counsellor of Amyntas III in the 370s, he was experienced in affairs, and he was one of the men who could be counted as a candidate for the kingship. In Thessaly the Theban general Pelopidas bundled the Macedonian troops out of the cities they were occupying and then marched on into Macedon, where he arbitrated the internal dispute. Ptolemy was reconciled to the king, and Alexander became an ally of Thebes. But Alexander had to provide hostages to Thebes as an earnest of his good behaviour; and Ptolemy was still around. Alexander had been humiliated with depressing ease. Pelopidas' 'settlement' guaranteed continuing trouble.[41]

Given the previous history of the kingdom, the events which followed are not a surprise. Having been pushed out of Thessaly, Alexander was seen to be in a weak position and was humiliated by the ease with which Pelopidas had swatted him down. Ptolemy of Aloros had the support of Amyntas' widow Eurydike, in a relationship distant observers assumed was sexual. In the spring of 367 Ptolemy organized the assassination of King Alexander, his brother-in-law.[42] This had clearly been likely from the time he had become 'reconciled' to Alexander after his rebellion the year before, yet allowed to live on in the kingdom. Ptolemy now seized power, supported by Eurydike. The Thebans, who had been allied with Alexander and had brought about the arbitration and the reconciliation, did nothing.

Ptolemy's technical position was that he was the guardian of the next son of Amyntas, Perdikkas III, and it was in Perdikkas' name that the coins were minted for the next three years.[43] Ptolemy was the man to whom foreigners went for decisions, though we are not informed of the extent of his authority over his fellow barons – it was probably even less than that of Amyntas and Alexander. Perdikkas was probably only a year or so younger than his dead brother; the youngest of the three sons of Amyntas and Eurydike, Philip, was 13 or 14 in 368, when he was sent to the Thebans as one of Pelopidas' hostages, so Perdikkas was about 16 in 367. Alexander's youth had shown that an older head was required.

Ptolemy clearly believed, as did Eurydike, that he was the right man for the post. The temptation to rid himself of Perdikkas and take the kingship for himself must have been strong.

If Ptolemy could hoist himself to power by the aid of some local adherents and a foreign power, so could others. A pretender called Pausanias, probably a younger son of King Archelaos and brother of the former king Argaios, approached from Chalkidike, presumably gaining assistance from the quiescent Chalkidian League. He recruited a force of Greek mercenaries and gained control of the Anthemos district in the north-west part of Chalkidike, and of some small cities close by. This gave him a useful base, perhaps centred on his own estate (as Ptolemy's original base was his estate at Aloros). Ptolemy was not strong enough to combat this threat himself. The Greek soldiers employed by Pausanias, and those of the towns and cities under his control, obviously gave him the edge. Instead Ptolemy contacted the Athenian general Iphikrates who was in nearby waters with a small fleet, attempting to gain control of Athens' long lost colony city of Amphipolis. Iphikrates was able to drive Pausanias out with ease, thus once again demonstrating Ptolemy's weakness.[44]

After some time Pelopidas of Thebes led a force north, having been asked to do so by some Macedonians who were adherents of Alexander. But they were disappointed in the outcome: Ptolemy was confirmed in his position, a humiliation, but it certainly stopped his competitors from rebelling; Pelopidas left with another set of hostages, including Ptolemy's own son Philoxenos. The Theban purpose was clearly to ensure that internal disputes in Macedon would continue.[45]

Ptolemy's authority was reduced to the original Macedonian kingdom, from the north slopes of Olympos to Almopia, and east to the Axios valley. The eastern area beyond the Axios had gone, much of Chalkidike was hostile, as Pausanias' career showed, and the western hill-kingdoms had all slipped away into independence or the Illyrian orbit. Amyntas III had not been able to recover control over these kingdoms, and Lynkos (Eurydike's homeland) had become subject to King Bardylis of the Illyrians. This brought the enemy boundary to within 50 km of Pella and Aigai. Elimaia, the southernmost of the hill states, was in dispute with its southern neighbour and Amyntas had arbitrated the disagreement, which he could only have done had both been independent of his authority.[46] Between Elimaia and Lynkos, Orestis was thus also no doubt out of Amyntas' reach, though King Derdas had been Amyntas' ally in the Chalkidian war. The whole of the west was dominated by the extensive kingdom developed by Bardylis over the previous generation.

The humiliations heaped on Ptolemy brought his assassination in 365, just as had those of Alexander II. His killer was his own ward, Perdikkas III, who was thus making it clear that he had come of age.[47] Perdikkas was the fourth ruler in five years. The problems of the kingdom – murders in the royal family, intervention by outsiders, internal rebellions – had again emphasized its weakness. The basic problem was still the structural weakness of the kingdom, which left the person of the king vulnerable, and the kingdom's military strength always minimal. Perdikkas, almost as young as his brother Alexander had been when he succeeded to power, was less impetuous, but then he had witnessed the troubles of the last five years at close range, which would make anyone cautious. His organization of the killing of Ptolemy at least suggested a personal decisiveness.

In the developing conflict between Thebes and Athens, Perdikkas opted to ally with Thebes, and some of the hostages – who had been taken originally to control Ptolemy – were returned, including Perdikkas' younger brother Philip, who was about 16 or 17 at the time. The Theban alliance with Macedon was part of the Theban programme of developing a naval strength, to challenge Athens, but for the moment this was not yet effective.[48]

The Athenian general Timotheos came north with a major fleet to counter this threat. He seized control of the cities of Pydna and Methone on the Macedonian coast, and of Potidaea in the Chalkidike, thereby establishing control over much of Macedon's seaward aspect; thus preventing ships being built for Thebes. He made diplomatic contact with the Thracians and the ruler of Pelagonia to the east and north of Macedon.[49] Perdikkas' kingdom was thus virtually surrounded by Athenian power and allies, while the death of Pelopidas in 364 removed the one Theban politician who was seriously interested in the north. Having thus neutralized Macedon, Timotheos then set about his real work, which was to besiege the city of Amphipolis. This all convinced Perdikkas to bend with the political wind, and he joined in Timotheos' siege:[50] a policy shift which was soon reversed.

Perdikkas was showing himself to be just as slippery and devious as any of his royal ancestors. The war in Greece came to a climax in 362, when the allies Athens and Sparta fought Thebes at the battle of Mantineia. The Thebans won but their leader Epameinondas was killed, and Thebes proved to be less than resolute afterwards. Perdikkas' war with Athens included a most unpleasant defeat in battle, but he also made quieter advances, and at some point he managed to insert a Macedonian garrison into Amphipolis, which implies that he had gained control over the approach road and so of the Bisaltia area. Timotheos had to give up the siege of the city in 360; whether this was before or after the introduction of the Macedonian soldiers is not clear.[51] Perdikkas' manoeuvring had clearly aligned his kingdom against Athens, just at the time that, despite the defeat at Amphipolis, Athenian power in the Aegean was again unchallenged.

These events suggest that Perdikkas had a fairly efficient military force at his disposal. It was partly cavalry, the traditional arm of Macedonian power, but he must also have had a force of hoplite infantry, probably fairly small in size, to be able to put an effective garrison into Amphipolis. Amyntas III had had some troops of this type, and Alexander II will have inherited them, and it was presumably this force which he had used in Thessaly. The indications, therefore, are that they were used as garrison troops. Perdikkas, of course, had to maintain a large cavalry force, since this was the arm his northern and western enemies would use, and this was the Macedonian baronage's preferred method of fighting, for reasons of prestige if nothing else. His infantry will have come in part from the Greek cities within his borders, and from the several parties of Greek settlers imported and settled in the kingdom in the past, but it is probable that the troops posted to Amphipolis were mercenaries, since the posting was clearly expected to last some time.

Perdikkas ruled for about five years. He showed suppleness in his diplomacy, combined with an insistence on resisting Athens. He employed at least one Greek expert, Kallistratos, an exiled Athenian politician, to reform his financial system, which brought him an increase in the customs duties he collected – or rather brought him a higher fee from those who bid for the farm of those duties.[52] Yet the undeveloped nature of the kingdom is suggested by the results of that very reform, for the king's income from the customs farm rose from 20 to 40 talents a year, a derisory sum for a state the size of Macedon: in fact, it shows that there was very little trade to tax.

The basic weaknesses of the kingdom remained firmly in place, therefore, and such reforms and developments as Perdikkas was able to begin were long-term affairs. Only when he had wealth could he develop an army, but maybe it was because he was making progress that the Illyrians attacked him. Bardylis was always aggressive, and he had attacked Perdikkas' kingdom very early in his reign, perhaps in 365 or 364.[53] In 360 he sent a great raid into Epiros, which was only partly successful.[54] This would require the next raid to be more productive, and Macedon was the new target. Perdikkas, faced by the biggest attack from that quarter for a generation, took the whole of the Macedonian armed forces to meet it. He was beaten, 4,000 of his soldiers lost their lives, and Perdikkas himself was killed as well.[55]

A new king had to be installed quickly. Perdikkas' (and Alexander's) younger brother Philip was present, and had survived the disaster. He had been a loyal supporter to Perdikkas during his reign, being granted, it seems, a section of the kingdom to rule, and he was no doubt known to many of the Macedonians who were present at the meeting of the Assembly, which was, in effect, the survivors of Perdikkas' army. He controlled whatever there was of government in Macedon, which meant the royal court and the army. He was the man on the spot, adult, experienced, clearly able and intelligent. Given that Bardylis' victorious army was invading, and other threats would obviously soon emerge, Philip's assumption of the kingship and acclamation of the Assembly were obvious and immediate steps to take. He was clearly accepted as king very quickly.

There had been alternative candidates. One was Perdikkas' son, Amyntas, but he was only a child. The two men who had already attempted to seize the kingship reappeared: Pausanias, Ptolemy's opponent in 367, was supported by the Thracian king Kotys; Argaios, the rival of Amyntas III in the 390s, had Athenian support. These two were probably brothers, so their attacks may have been coordinated, though it is more likely they were rivals. Then there were the three half-brothers of Philip himself, the sons of Amyntas III and his secondary wife Gygaia: Archelaos, Arrhidaios and Menelaos. Archelaos at least made some sort of a bid for the kingship in 359, but they were effectively ruled out because of their external sponsors; Philip arranged the death of Archelaos, and the other two half-brothers fled.[56] Furthermore, apart from the invasion of the victorious Illyrians under Bardylis, the Paionians, who lived to the north, beyond the Demir Kapu Pass, were gathering to join in.[57]

There is a possibility that Amyntas was accepted as king, with Philip installed as his guardian and regent, on the pattern of Aeropos/Orestes and Ptolemy/Perdikkas. The evidence for this arrangement is, however, late, poor and unconvincing: a passage in Justin, who was epitomizing Trogus, whose work was based on other sources, and an inscription from Lebadeia in Boiotia, now lost;[58] this is all very distant from Macedon in 359. The only reason to assume that there was a regency is if one assumes also that there was a rigid rule of succession of father to eldest son. It was certainly the usual practice, though in crises other factors clearly operated, particularly the preferences of the deceased king. Perdikkas had presumably been unable to indicate any such preference. Philip was ruthless about eliminating internal competition and killing off pretenders whenever they appeared, but Amyntas lived on in the palace unmolested.[59] It follows that Amyntas was not seen as a threat to Philip's kingship. We must conclude, therefore, that Philip became king directly after Perdikkas' death, and was accepted as such by the court and the Assembly.

There were surely doubts about him and about his accession. He was not much older than his brothers when they had succeeded, and both had failed; nor had his father been wildly successful as king. Yet the only other adult claimants were those with foreign support and the only internal claimants were even younger than Philip. So another reason he became king was the lack of any real alternative.

He took over a kingdom which had failed for the second time in 40 years. Each failure had lasted a decade (399–391, 370–359). It would be reasonable to assume that Macedon as a political entity was unviable. If Philip failed as his brothers had, the reviving Chalkidian League was likely to move in. The cities of the coast had been lost, the hill kingdoms were independent or subject to Bardylis. If Philip had been killed in the great battle, it is unlikely that Macedon would have survived as anything more than the name of a region. This was precisely the sort of situation in which it was necessary for new policies to be attempted. Philip survived, and he had ideas.

World view I: 360 BC

The previous chapter concentrated single-mindedly on Macedon, an unimportant minor state until the accession of Philip II in 359. Few people paid much attention to it at any time, and other powers rarely had any difficulty in walking all over it when they chose. Philip II changed all that, and from soon after his accession Macedon became an important power, and then a great power. This will be the story pursued in the following chapters. Meanwhile it will be well to take a wider look at the surrounding world, which was to be the political environment in which Philip, and then Alexander, had to operate.

When Philip II became king, he already had, unlike most of his royal pre-decessors, some experience of the world outside his kingdom, and he was also the first Macedonian ruler to make a serious mark on that world. The collapse of the kingdom he had inherited was surely no surprise to outsiders. So Philip's and Macedon's impact in the next generation was therefore unexpected and unexpectedly powerful. One reason for this was Philip's abilities; and another was the condition of the world outside his kingdom.

The Greek city states to the south, after another inconclusive war, had met and concluded a Common Peace in 360, mainly because of mutual exhaustion. The peace agreement did not make any serious attempt to sort out the various quarrels between the cities, but it did include a clause by which each city should keep what it had. This allowed all involved to sink back into a period of recuperation; though it scarcely ensured a durable peace.[1]

Sparta refused to be involved; but then Sparta had been the main loser in the war, having been deprived of its ancient conquests in Arkadia and Messenia, and of its hegemony over the rest of Greece. The condition of Greece at the peace was thus one in which the old powers were diminished, but in which new powers had not yet emerged. Sparta's loss of empire was mirrored by Athens' difficulties in holding members to its new league, which they perceived as scarcely needed now that Sparta had been reduced. Thebes proved to be less of a threat to everyone else now that its two political leaders, Epameinondas and Pelopidas, had died. A brief period of Thessalian unity under Jason of Pherai in the 370s had been ended by the Thebans. The Common Peace might have inaugurated a time of balance, since experience suggested that a new imperial power could be blocked by a timely combination of those who felt threatened, but it did not promise to last long, for the balance was always liable to be upset fairly easily, and the only way to re-balance affairs was by another war.

Beyond Greece other events took priority. The Greek cities of Sicily and southern Italy had solved the problem of internecine fighting by the very opposite of a balance of power. The greatest of them, Syracuse, had succeeded in reducing all the rest to provincial status three decades earlier. The dire threat of being conquered by Carthage, the wealthy African city which controlled the western end of Sicily and the opposite North African coast, had been the stimulus. Under the leadership of Dionysios, the Syracusans had driven Carthage back to its last Sicilian foothold, and the rest of the island had been united under Dionysios as a consequence; he had then extended his control into southern Italy.

The price was that Dionysios could not be removed, and he managed to so institutionalize his power that he could bequeath it to his son, Dionysios II, in 367. The only Greek political term which seemed to fit this situation was 'tyrant', but in effect it was a monarchy. For the past 40 years Greek Sicily had formed a powerful kingdom dominating the central Mediterranean. The result was a Common Peace of a different sort.[2]

Carthage in the end accepted the situation and turned to concentrate on trading with the rest of the Mediterranean and developing its own African hinterland. It maintained a strong defence of its Sicilian outpost in the western end of the island, and had other outposts in Sardinia, the Balearic Islands, along the North African coast, and on the south and east coasts of Spain; it dominated the whole of the western Mediterranean.[3]

The northern Mediterranean coast was lined with Greek cities from northern Italy to the north-eastern corner of Spain. Massalia (modern Marseilles) was the main power here, but was only of the second or even third rate compared with Carthage and Syracuse. Its citizens tapped the trade of inland Gaul along the Rhône Valley and the Atlantic route by way of Tolosa.[4] Most of Italy, away from the southern peninsulas, was in the process of developing in its own indigenous way. Both Carthage and Syracuse were watching the situation in central Italy with some interest, not to say anxiety, for a new power centre was busily emerging.

There were cities throughout the Italian peninsula from the Po valley southwards, except in the mountainous spine, and the whole land was organized as a set of clearly defined states, cities or tribes. Greek cities dominated Campania and the southern coasts, Latin cities to the north of that, and Etruscan cities between the Tiber and the Arno. The Etruscans had expanded both to the south and to the north-east, so that other Etruscan cities were founded in the Po valley and in Campania; native Italian communities were developing as cities elsewhere: the competition for land and wealth was stimulating fortification and urbanization. The whole process was volatile and extremely disturbing, made more violent by the intrusion of bands of fierce Gallic warriors, who had conquered the Po valley about 30 years before, and raided into the central and southern parts of the peninsula frequently ever since.[5]

By 360 BC one city, Rome, had begun to emerge from the pack as being bigger, more populous, better organized, and with a more intelligent programme of imperialism, than any others. It had developed under both Etruscan and Greek influences, though using the Latin language, and now dominated a group of smaller Latin cities which had long formed a religious and defensive league. Rome had recently sorted out its internal affairs, by the Licinian-Sextian laws of 367, and took the lead in combating the Gallic raids.[6] Carthage had been sufficiently impressed by all this to make a new treaty with Rome which recognized Rome's political supremacy in central Italy.[7] Syracuse had also reacted, by sending ships to raid the Latin coast.[8] The word had reached Greece, where those who noticed such things were impressed enough to decide that such a notable city must be Greek.[9]

How much of all this Philip II knew when he became king is not certain, but he was clearly familiar from his years in Thebes with the condition of Greece. Living in the house of Pammenes, a prominent Theban politician, in the 360s, will have been an education in power politics and political manipulation few contemporary places could match. The power of Syracuse was a familiar thing, and Dionysios had certainly extended his influence to the mainland, proudly displaying his wealth at the Olympic Games, just as Philip's ancestor, Alexander I, had argued his way into the competition a century before, and just as Philip himself was to do later. At Corinth, Syracuse's mother city, Dion, the uncle of Dionysios II, lived in exile, learning and teaching philosophy, and harbouring his own ambitions. The Italian and Carthaginian situations were more distant, but certainly Carthage and its power, if only because of the conflict with Syracuse, was a known political factor.

To their north, the Macedonians knew the Illyrians all too well. King Bardylis had been a constant threat for a generation; the Thracians to the east had kings who had much the same problems of control as those of Macedon. Beyond these peoples it seems likely that some knowledge may have reached them of the expansion of the Celts, one branch of whom were in Gaul, a second in north Italy, and a third had recently reached the lower Danube Valley. This is likely to have been the limit of Macedonian knowledge, partly because the arrival of the Celts was quite recent, and their presence had been thoroughly disturbing to all the local peoples.

These Balkan peoples were only part of the social mixture of inland Europe, referred to by both Greeks and Italians as barbarian. There were few cities in those areas, but apart from that the people lived at much the same economic level as those round the Mediterranean. They were mainly farmers, living in villages, but there were also miners, traders and seamen, and there were kingdoms and tribes, competing, trading and intermarrying with each other. The difference between the communities of the Mediterranean shores and those of inland Europe were thus primarily differences of political organization and literacy, not of economic development. Macedon partook of both types: the general population lived as did the barbarians of Europe, but the culture of the elite more resembled that of the Greek cities, if with a distinctive Macedonian tinge. The Macedonian kings resembled those of the Illyrians, and the Thracians, but at the same time they were strongly attracted to Greek culture: King Archelaos had welcomed Euripides to his court, and King Perdikkas allowed the Greek philosopher Euphraios to organize his court. These differing elements could create dangerous tensions – some of the Macedonian barons detested Euphraios – but the combination of Greek culture and administrative expertise with the aggressiveness and vigour of the Macedonian elite was to have extraordinary effects.

East of Greece were series of societies and political entities that were wholly different from those of Greece and Italy, and from those of inland Europe. These lands were the old, long civilized, imperial territories, and in 360 BC they were included within the greatest of the empires, that of the Persians ruled by the Akhaimenid royal family.[10] For two centuries this enormous empire had dominated the whole world from India westwards to Greece. In many ways, it was even more of an antithesis to the Greek cities than were the barbarian tribes and kingdoms, but it was far more flexible and adaptable than either of them, and included within its boundaries ancient kingdoms, Greeks in their cities, barbarian tribes, merchant cities and nomad tribes.

The Persian Empire was the basic geopolitical fact of life for every person and state in the world between eastern India and the Strait of Gibraltar. Its sheer size meant that it had no choice but to be tolerant of the varied groups of people and societies it had conquered, though some remained determinedly discontented. Egypt had successfully shaken itself free of Persian rule, and in 360 had been independent for four decades, and Persian rule had receded from the Indus Valley.[11] The Greek cities of Asia Minor, however, had been reclaimed at the King's Peace in 387, and had accepted their situation of subordination with little demur.[12] The rule of the Great King and his governors, the satraps, lay fairly lightly on their subjects.

This did not make Persian rule any more attractive to outsiders than to the Egyptians. For Macedon, the empire was a former suzerain and a near neighbour, its western provinces only a day's sail eastwards across the Aegean Sea. From the Black Sea to the borders of Egypt the empire controlled the whole Mediterranean coastline, and to the Greeks it stretched away eastwards, through Anatolia and Syria to Babylon and Iran and beyond, apparently to infinity; no Greek shows any knowledge of land beyond Susa.[13]

The empire in 360 was in less than robust health. Attempts for years by the Great King Artaxerxes II to recover control of Egypt had been ignominious failures, and in the late 360s a widespread rebellion broke out among the satraps of several of the western regions. This had fizzled out by 360, but not before giving a vivid indication of the empire's fragility. The suppression of the revolt, however, was also a sign of the empire's resilience.[14] The concept of 'decline' of this empire is not very helpful, being a projection back from its defeat by Alexander; the surmounting of imperial difficulties in the 360s and 350s implies strength, not decline.

There is no sign of similar trouble in any part of the empire east of Syria. Babylonia, Iran and Baktria were all calm and loyal, and Artaxerxes II, king since 405, was able to concentrate on his western problems without being interrupted or disturbed. He was tough and persistent, but constantly suspicious. Repeatedly he recalled his generals when they were on the verge of victory, perhaps because he could not trust them to be loyal if they were victorious – he had, after all, been attacked by his own brother as soon as he had inherited the throne. He died in 359, the year Philip became king in Macedon, and was succeeded by his son Artaxerxes III Ochos, a more ruthless and determined ruler.

Beyond the uncertain Persian eastern boundary, India was as complex a mixture of kingdoms, tribes, cities and republics as Greece and Italy, though one state had been growing in the Ganges Valley for some decades. This was Magadha, centred at the city of Pataliputra, and ruled by a ruthless dynasty, the Nandas. Their power was growing, but so was the dislike other Indians felt for them. The violence and volatility of Indian political life had provoked the development of a new religion in the previous century or so, and as Buddhism it was to increase steadily in importance.[15]

China was separated from all the rest of the civilized world by formidable mountains and by the nomad-inhabited Steppes of Mongolia and Central Asia. It was, like India and the west, divided and violent, consisting of a collection of states spread along the valley of the Yellow River, constantly fighting each other with diplomatic intrigue and warlike weapons.[16]

It is useful to see Persepolis as the political centre of the world, with the Akhaimenid empire the stable and rich element around which other political societies were grouped – China, the nomads, India, Greece, Italy, Sicily. But it is also notable that by 360 or so all these peripheral groupings were undergoing major changes. In Italy, Rome was emerging; in Greece, mutual exhaustion among the cities was about to open the way for Philip of Macedon; in India, the power of Magadha threatened all other states; in China, the many competing states were being steadily reduced in number. And all of them were faced with the problem which only the Akhaimenids had so far solved: how to rule an empire without exerting continuous and repressive force on its inhabitants.

The problems of the Macedonian kingdom were not dissimilar in many ways to those of its contemporaries. Holding a state together was as difficult in the Akhaimenid empire and in the Peloponnese as in Macedon; building a state was equally difficult in Italy or India, or China, or the Athenian Aegean. Even states whose longevity seemed to show that they had solved the stability problem proved to be controlled by aristocracies that were liable to be dispensed with as and when they became oppressive and inefficient. But the methods of state building were known, and had been seen to be successful, in Persia, in the Greek cities, in Sicily, in Egypt. The necessary tools, honest governors, efficient bureaucrats, professional armies, were available for the constitution of a stable state in Macedon. Several of its kings had made tentative attempts to use them; it was Philip who succeeded, for a time.

2

The security of Macedon, 359–354 BC

Philip II developed into the master-statesman of his time, a creative politician whose work made Macedon a world power for three decades and a great power for a century after that. This aspect of his achievement took some years to emerge, however, since for the first period of his reign he was preoccupied with securing his own position, and with providing security for his kingdom. These were, of course, much the same problem.

Philip had to use a combination of qualities: a wily and cunning diplomacy, military leadership which brought victories, and a keen eye for developing the resources of his kingdom. He had precedents in the activity of previous Macedonian kings, but not every new king in his early twenties would have deployed them. It is part of Philip's genius that he was able to utilize all these actions and qualities successfully at the same time.

Philip was about 23 years old when he became king, a few years older than his brothers at their accessions, with a life experience somewhat different from theirs. He grew up at the court of his father, Amyntas III, in a time when Macedon was more or less at peace, having been born in the year following Amyntas' recovery of his kingdom in 383/382. He saw the efforts his father had made to develop his kingdom, but he had also witnessed the threats the outside world forced upon him. In his family he was one of the middle children, with older brothers, an older sister and their younger half-brothers. Getting attention cannot have been easy.[1]

At the age of 12 he was sent as a hostage to the Illyrians – presumably to King Bardylis – along with tribute which Alexander II paid to avoid an invasion.[2] Soon after, at 14 or so, he was sent to Thebes, again as a hostage. This was not a situation of danger or discomfort. A hostage, especially a child, was taken into the household of a prominent man, treated as a member of the family and given an education. At Thebes Philip lived in the house of Pammenes, an important politician,[3] in the years when Thebes was the greatest power in the Greek peninsula. He missed the killings in Macedon of his brother Alexander and of Ptolemy of Aloros, returning home when his other brother Perdikkas emerged as king in his own right in 365. For the next five or six years he was completely loyal to Perdikkas, and was entrusted, perhaps after some years, with lands of his own, on which he is said to have maintained an armed force, possibly little more than a bodyguard.[4]

His conduct in his first year as king suggests that he had given thought to what was required. In what he accomplished in his first years, Philip was clearly helped by two important factors: the crisis in Macedon was so bad that he had a free hand in dealing with it; and the Greek powers ignored what was going on in Macedon, reasonably assuming that the continuing political collapse of the kingdom was yet another example of its fragility and instability. They were rather slow to intervene, and then only minimally. Despite the Common Peace of 360, further international crises developed, notably at Athens, whose league began to crumble in 357; then the 'Sacred' war embroiled all central Greece for the next ten years. Philip had a breathing space in which Macedon's main enemies were either uninterested or preoccupied elsewhere. In this time he laid the basis for his later more extensive achievements.

The first priority was to attend to the internal condition of the kingdom. Philip had his half-brother Archelaos killed; this secured him the throne, for Archelaos was the next member of his family. The invading pretenders were next. Pausanias came with Thracian backing, originally that of King Kotys, and then his successor Berisades. Perhaps because Berisades was also newly in power he was persuaded to accept a bribe to leave. Philip's persuasiveness was at work here: Berisades was joint heir to Kotys with his two brothers, who now fought each other; Thrace could thus now been ignored for a time.[5]

Argaios' support from Athens was as uncertain as that of Pausanias from Thrace. A force of 3,000 Athenian hoplites landed with him at Methone, but Argaios was then expected to make his own way to the throne. This was reasonable, since a pretender needed to show he had local support, and without it no backer would bother with him. Athens' main ambition in the north was to gain control of Amphipolis, now an independent city, with a Macedonian garrison. Philip withdrew these troops. No doubt he was glad to have them available for more active uses, but the act of withdrawal was also directed at influencing Athens. Supposedly it signalled Amphipolis' new vulnerability, and by implication Philip's political acquiescence in an Athenian takeover. Argaios' Athenian troops stayed in Methone, and Argaios went on to Aigai with only his own small force of mercenaries and the few Macedonian exiles and Athenians who supported his enterprise.

He marched the 20 km to Aigai, but gained no support from the locals, either on the march or in the city. He turned back to return to Methone, perhaps hoping to persuade the Athenians there to be more active in his cause, but was intercepted by Philip on his march. Philip easily beat Argaios' troops: many of the mercenaries were killed; the Macedonian exiles, many of them related to loyal Macedonians, were taken prisoner; the Athenians were released with gifts. Philip had no wish to set up a situation where Athens might seek revenge; the Athenian force in Methone then sailed home, taking the released men away as well. At Athens, the prospect of regaining Amphipolis, combined with the failure of the intervention in Macedon, persuaded the Assembly towards peace. Argaios vanished, no doubt executed, if he had survived the fight. What happened to the exiles is not known, but Philip is as likely to have held them as hostages for the good behaviour of their relatives as to have had them executed as traitors.[6]

The landward invaders of the kingdom were tackled with a similar mixture of force and diplomacy. Bardylis did not follow up his successful invasion, either because of the casualties his own forces had suffered in the battle, or because Philip had arranged a truce with him.[7] Philip certainly bought off the threatened Paeonian invasion from the north by gifts to the Paeonian king.[8] Neither of these measures could be decisive in the long term: gifts would only whet the Paeonian appetite, and Bardylis' victory could only encourage him to mount another invasion.

The precise sequence of all these invasions, diplomacies and manoeuvres is uncertain, but they certainly all took place during 359, very early in Philip's reign; indeed, most of the manoeuvres and diplomacy probably took only a fairly short time, probably more or less simultaneously. Their success will have consolidated his local support among the Macedonians. The unwillingness of the people of Aigai to join Argaios is a sign of this.

Philip had to attend to internal governmental matters. Even in his first year he had no difficulty in finding gifts rich enough to buy off the Paeonian and Thracian kings, and to give presents to the Athenians in Argaios' force – nor to forgo the ransoming or selling of those captives – though where he found the money is unclear.[9] Kallistratos' customs reforms may have helped, but not by much. But the main internal problem he faced was the development of an effective army.

In 358, after a year as king, Philip was able to muster a force of 10,000 infantry and 600 cavalry for a campaign in which he needed his full strength.[10] Perdikkas' defeat had cost 4,000 Macedonian lives. By adding these figures together it seems that the maximum force available to the Macedonian kings before Philip was about 15,000 men, of which the effective element, the cavalry, numbered 1,000 at most. This was a fairly small force for such a large kingdom – Athens could produce forces double that. Yet even with that smaller force, Philip won battles against larger armies. This was due to his intelligent generalship in part, but he also instituted better training for the men, in particular the infantry. He had seen, during his earlier life in Thebes and Macedon, that infantry needed to be properly trained, drilled and equipped for them to be effective; he only needed to compare the old ineffective Macedonian foot soldiers with the all-conquering Theban phalanx. He was up-to-date with the military developments which had taken place in recent years in Greece, including the use of light infantry, peltasts, developed by Athenian commanders. And he added something particularly Macedonian, the use of a shock force of heavy cavalry.

It will not do to emphasize the innovations Philip made at the expense of the continuities. The kings had always had a bodyguard of cavalrymen, called Companions (*hetairoi*). The very name shows that they were of high status, socially almost the equals to the king by birth, being noble landowners and their sons. They numbered only 600 in Philip's army of 358, no doubt the survivors of Perdikkas' disaster, and probably others were available who did not turn out for the new king. Their numbers increased in the next generation as Macedonians and Greeks were awarded lands in conquered territory: by 334 the cavalry numbered 3,500.[11] As the numbers grew, Philip implanted change. One group was singled out as the Royal Squadron, 300 strong, and the rest were organized as squadrons (*ilai*), recruited from the several regions of Macedonia. They rode bareback, wore a metal breastplate and helmet and were armed with a longish spear. They were 'heavy' only in a relative sense, owing their shock value to their ability to charge in formation, particularly in a 'wedge formation', in which the narrower front allowed a widening penetration of the enemy formation and the maintenance of good control.

This is the most remarkable of Philip's military innovations. By the end of his reign it is clear the cavalry had been induced to put aside their innate individualism and submit to discipline, just like hoplites. This involved a major change in behaviour by the baronage, whose preferred method of fighting was in loose formation, leaving room for individual display and activity. This would seem to have been one of the lessons Philip had brought from Greece. The Balkan tribes fought in the 'old' manner, loosely, and the Persians in Alexander's battles were almost as undisciplined. The carefully controlled cavalry Philip developed was capable of defeating any number of their undisciplined enemies – just as hoplites could beat their less controlled light infantry enemies.[12]

The infantry were little more than a mob in earlier battles, more notable for their speed of retreat than their constancy in the fight. There had been an earlier elite group, called the Foot-Companions (*pezhetairoi*), which may have fallen out of use; Philip re-formed it.[13] They were the equivalent of the *hetairoi* of the cavalry: well equipped, polished, proud, and capable of standing guard over the king and the palace. The rest of the infantry was levied, like the cavalry, by regions. This was not a new system, but Philip did insist on improvements: drill, discipline, uniform armament and, above all, obedience to orders. It seems likely that the improvement was mainly due to the fact that the infantry had earlier been simply the followers of the nobles, brought along when the army was called out. Philip's innovation was thus to separate them from their landlords to organize them into disciplined formations. Both cavalry and infantry became better drilled and more competently employed. He spent a good deal of time in the first year of his reign meeting his forces, consulting them in assemblies, speaking to them, drilling them, getting to know them, and them to know him.[14]

The infantry were trained to move and march as units; instead of a mob they became a phalanx.

It is in this organization of the troops that Philip's real contribution to Macedon's military power lies, but he is also credited with the introduction of a longer infantry spear, the sarissa. Its effect in battle was to keep the enemy at a greater, and so safer, distance.[15] The heavier weapon also required a reduction in defensive armament, so the troops used a smaller shield, and wore no breastplate. The net effect was to make the infantry much more mobile and aggressive, and yet also more vulnerable. Philip had taken in the power of the heavier Theban phalanx, and the Athenian innovation of the use of peltasts and the overall value of drill, discipline and careful preparation, and had added in his own longer spear.

He was able to do much of this reorganization in his first year, which suggests that he had worked out what needed to be done during his years as his brother's subordinate, based in part on his experience at Thebes. But to think it all out and to apply his ideas were two different things; and to put into practice what he was preaching required him to win battles. The Paeonians and the Illyrians of Bardylis were to be his testing ground. No doubt the disaster suffered by Perdikkas' army had predisposed Macedonians to accept, or at least to try out, new methods, but only victory would be convincing.[16]

Most of what Philip imposed on the Macedonians was not new. The sarissa, possibly, but the Macedonian barons were used to wielding long spears in hunting. Infantry in phalanxes, cavalry under discipline, uniform equipment, drill, obedience to shouted orders, pride after victory, were all part and parcel of Greek warfare. He adopted the use of siege weapons developed particularly in Dionysian Sicily, and had them available for use by 357.[17] This basic unoriginality may be an aspect of the changes which led to their acceptance: Greek warfare was something familiar to the Macedonians, who had been easily beaten in the past by smaller Greek forces. Earlier kings back to Alexander I had tried to implement many of these innovations, but Philip would seem to have been the first to try them all out at once on a receptive population at the beginning of his reign. There was also Philip's generalship, a quality enhanced in his son, which was even more important than all his innovations.

That he was able to do all this so early in his reign is what makes Philip so important in Macedonian history. Earlier kings had established themselves in power first and then introduced changes, generally on a fairly small scale. Given that the average reign of a successful Macedonian king was only two decades, the reforms had only started to have effect when the king died, and were then lost in the subsequent succession crisis. Philip, compelled by the all-enveloping crisis at his accession, had a relatively free hand as well as a compelling necessity to innovate. It was essentially a succession crisis followed by a military crisis; the first was dealt with diplomatically and by assassination, so it was in the military area that he introduced his changes. Other governmental deficiencies were ignored or tackled later. The emphasis on the current crises coloured the future indelibly with a military hue; once Philip had survived, any other innovations could be introduced in the old manner, slowly and cautiously, if at all.

The several pretenders had not, thanks to Philip's diplomacy, presented a real threat. The Macedonians' northern and western neighbours were more dangerous. The Paeonian king died soon after the agreement with Philip, and the agreement became void. Philip had made progress with his new army, and in the spring of 358 he invaded Paeonia, won a victory, and imposed a treaty on the new king, making him a subordinate ally of the type well understood in the region.[18] This was an easy victory; Philip was able to choose his victim, so giving his new army confidence, something the army surely needed after Perdikkas' disaster.

The Illyrians were next. Bardylis, perhaps prompted by a peace offer from Philip, demanded that Philip accept that Bardylis should keep those parts of Upper Macedon he had occupied,[19] regions such as Orestis and Lynkos. These Illyrian demands, when publicized, demonstrated to the Macedonians that the Illyrian threat remained, so an Illyrian war could be justified, both as revenge for their dead comrades and Philip's dead brother, and as a preventive against future Illyrian attacks. Philip inevitably refused Bardylis' demands, and marched his new army into Illyrian-occupied Lynkos.

Of all the enemies besetting Macedon in 359, Bardylis was the most formidable, and it was no doubt for this reason that Philip had left him to the last. Philip had agreed to an armistice – perhaps he even requested one – as soon as he became king, though this left Bardylis in possession of the conquered lands. Philip had, it seems, accepted an Illyrian princess, Audata, as his wife. Philip was always willing to marry, but if Bardylis imagined that Philip was now his ally, or even his subordinate, he discovered otherwise when he presented his peace terms. Between Perdikkas' death and the spring of 358, Philip had survived, seen off many enemies and invaders, and trained up his new army. He had been king for a year, and had done very little actual fighting, for the victories over Argaios and the Paeonians were fairly minor affairs. Bardylis had good cause to be confident that he could again win a battle.

The two armies were approximately equal in numbers, each with 10,000 infantry, and Bardylis with 500 and Philip 600 cavalry. Bardylis formed his men into a square, which is an interesting action, suggesting that he was well aware of the new Macedonian tactics. Philip commanded the *pezhetairoi*, his newly trained Foot Companions (described by Diodoros as 'the best of the Macedonians') personally. They were armed with the new long sarissa, and were used to break into the square, no doubt at a corner. When the square broke he sent the cavalry on a ferocious pursuit. Bardylis' army was destroyed, losing 7,000 men killed, and he at once made peace. The terms were the return of the Upper Macedonian kingdoms to Macedonian suzerainty.[20]

The battle, described fully enough by Diodoros for us to appreciate the tactics involved, demonstrated to any who cared to notice that a military commander of genius had arrived. Philip coordinated the actions of his soldiers and operated on his opponent's weakest point. He cannot have faced an infantry square before, nor can he have expected to face one now, but he took command personally at the decisive point, and understood that the battle was only won after the pursuit was finished. He was able to inspire his soldiers to fight, and to fight as he wished.

On top of this newly revealed military expertise, Philip showed in his dealings with his enemies that he was a most cunning and accomplished diplomatist, using negotiations to hold off dangerous enemies (Bardylis, the Paeonians, Athens) until he was ready to confront them, to deal with his enemies one at a time, and to choose the time to strike. This combination of military genius and diplomatic finesse was the key to the history of Greece for the next quarter-century.

If Audata was not given to Philip at the armistice in 359, she was now, in the peace terms. One of Philip's diplomatic innovations is here on view: instead of offering daughters and sisters to neighbouring kings as wives and daughters-in-law, he used himself, collecting daughters of other kings. These marriages performed differing diplomatic purposes: Audata symbolized peace and the subordination of an enemy, whereas his second marriage, to Phila, daughter of Derdas of Orestis, bound the important Elimaian region to Macedon. A year later he married Olympias, the niece of the king of the Molossi, whose lands had also been subjected to Illyrian raids just as had the Macedonians'.[21] These marriages linked these areas together politically, but the destruction of Bardylis' army had been the key to the whole system. This diplomatic structure was designed, presumably, to block Illyrian expansion southwards. By these military and diplomatic victories Philip revived Macedonian power and added an association with the Molossi to a serious restriction on the power of Bardylis.

There was little reason for others to take much note of what was going on. To southern Greeks, the battle in Lynkos was one between barbarian kings, of no real interest. Dangers still lurked to the south, in Thessaly, and to the east, at Amphipolis, areas that were possible sources of hostility to Macedon. Athens' enmity was not something to be conjured away by eliminating a pretender, and the possibility of it recovering control of Amphipolis was ominous. Thessaly had been troublesome for Macedonia repeatedly for the past 20 years, either in the persons of Thessalians, or from Thebes by way of Thessaly.

There were even closer potential Trojan horses: the Greek cities which lay along the two sides of the Thermaic Gulf, Pydna and Methone (Athens' base with Argaios), and the reviving league of Chalkidian cities, an old intermittent enemy. The league once more was interested in expanding, and this inevitably would be at Macedon's expense.

The victory over Bardylis and the settlement of the western borders did not necessarily make these polities apprehensive. For Macedon the major problem was Thessaly, which was a close neighbour, and was potentially powerful if it was united; Philip had to ensure that it remained divided, and in 358 he helped Larissa defend itself against an attack by Alexander of Pherai, who aimed to reconstruct the quasi-kingdom of his father Jason. Alexander was thwarted, and Philip came away with an alliance with Larissa, and another wife, Philinna.[22] Not long after, Alexander was killed by Thessalian assassins; more than Philip's intervention, this ensured Thessaly's continued division.

Philip turned to Amphipolis. A dispute developed which led to Philip laying siege to the city. He cannot have been trusted by the citizens since he appeased Athens by withdrawing Perdikkas' garrison. The city asked for help from the Chalkidians, and two Amphipolitans even went to Athens, suggesting that an expedition be sent to 'take over' the city. Athens, preoccupied by the 'revolt' of its allies, did not respond. It is doubtful that the two Amphipolitans spoke for more than a small group in the city, but it seems that some of the citizens were so desperate to stay out of Philip's control that they contemplated Athenian rule instead.[23]

Philip deflected Athens with negotiations, implying that once he had taken the city he would hand it over to Athens: the negotiations were on how this would be accomplished, or so the Athenians believed. The Chalkidians wanted an alliance with Athens before tackling Philip, but the 'offer' of Amphipolis persuaded Athens to reject this request. When he took Amphipolis by assault after a siege Athens hinted at a swap, Pydna for Amphipolis. Pydna was therefore not a city Athens would fight for, so Philip took it for himself, and Athens found itself with neither city. Angrily the city declared war, but several of its island allies now broke away, leaving Athens fighting its old allies rather than its new enemy. Yet the condition of war remained.[24]

The Chalkidian League, led by the Olynthians, began to grow again. It was at enmity with both Macedon and Athens, though Athens' preoccupation with the break-up of its league relieved the pressure. The Chalkidians allied with the Illyrian King Grabos whose territory lay to the north of Macedon, and in one of his diplomatic feats in his accession year, Philip had neutralized the league by handing it Anthemous, the rich valley disputed between the two in the past.[25] Then he helped the league to capture Potidaia, a lapsed member which was also an Athenian ally. Potidaia had been reinforced by a band of Athenian cleruchs (settlers), and the siege of the city, in which Philip deployed an effective siege train, took up much of 356. It was conducted jointly with the Chalkidians. During the siege Philip received an appeal for help from Krenides, a mining town about 50 km east of Amphipolis which was threatened by the Thracian king Kersobleptes. Philip took part of his army there and seized the town, probably without a fight, before Kersobleptes could take it.[26]

Leaving a garrison at Krenides, he returned to finish the siege of Potidaia. When he took the city – and it was Philip's achievement, no matter the Chalkidikian involvement – he destroyed it, handed over the site to the league, released the Athenian cleruchs, and sold the rest of the inhabitants into slavery:[27] he thus conciliated an enemy, bribed a new friend, enriched his treasury and pleased his army, all at once.

The capture of Krenides took Macedonian power much farther east than ever before. This and the Chalkidian alliance with Grabos the Illyrian roused two powers, Grabos and another Thracian king, Ketriporis, and they were joined by the Paeonian king Lyppeios, whom Philip had defeated in 359. Athens joined in, but could do nothing concrete to help. The coalition was not much of a danger to Macedon; Philip could deal with the members, one at a time. Philip sent his general Parmenion to cope; he defeated Grabos, who had to fight alone.[28] We know nothing of what happened to the others, but presumably the alliance broke up after Grabos' defeat.[29] The threat cannot have been too serious, for most of Philip's army was involved at Krenides and Potidaia at the time. Lyppeios probably reverted to his earlier vassalage; Ketriporis, a neighbour of Krenides, was intimidated into a subject alliance.[30]

Philip finished off this sequence of victories by the siege of Methone; the ease with which Argaios had reached Aigai from there was ominous, and the city was an Athenian ally, so at war with Philip. It was a small city but well fortified, and its people defended the city stoutly. Philip was severely wounded by an arrow in the process, but went on to force surrender, the terms being that the people could leave with what they could carry. Athens had yet again failed to assist an ally, even though by the end of the siege she was free from the war against her other erstwhile allies.[31]

The fighting in the past three years had dealt with Macedon's closest enemies. Bardylis, the Chalkidian League, Ketriporis, Lyppeios, the Athenian bases at Pydna, Methone and Potidaia were all reduced to the status of subjects or allies, often after smashing military defeats. Beyond the gains in territory and security, however, the problems of Thessaly and, above all, Athens, still existed. Philip may have had to help Larissa again in 355 or 354, more or less at the same time as he was besieging Methone. The issue was still the independence of Larissa in the face of the ambitions of the rulers of Pherai to control all Thessaly, ambitions not quenched by the failures of Jason and Alexander. A loan of troops seems to have been enough, just as Perdikkas' loan of troops to Amphipolis had warded off Athens a decade or so earlier.[32]

The acquisition of Krenides had opened up a new set of problems. The city was founded a few years earlier by the Thasians on the suggestion of Kallistratos, who had assisted Perdikkas over his finances. No doubt one reason for the city's needing help had been its very newness. It was founded to provide access to the rich metal resources of Mount Pangaios nearby, hence its attraction for all its neighbours. Philip followed up his acquisition by reinforcing it with Macedonian settlers, fortifying it, and renaming it Philippi. He also gathered into it the people of several nearby villages and towns. His capture of Amphipolis – also partly colonized by Macedonians at this time – and the settlement of Philippi meant that the whole area became firmly Macedonian, loyal to him personally, and a producer of great wealth for his kingdom.[33]

Philippi was close to an Athenian ally, the port city of Neapolis, and between Neapolis and Amphipolis there were three small coastal cities, Apollonia, Galepsos and Oisyme. These were later either inhabited by Macedonians or desolate;[34] it may well be that this was another result of Philip's Krenides operation. Neapolis was worried, and two of its citizens visited Athens about the time Philip was operating there; their precise message is not known, but can hardly have been anything other than a warning of what Philip was doing, and an appeal for Athenian help.[35] Nothing was provided, at least immediately, perhaps because Philip was not actively threatening the place.

The colonization of Amphipolis and Philippi established a firm and powerful anchor on the east of the kingdom, which could be used either as a defence against attacks or as a base for further advances; the removal of Athens from Pydna and Methone eliminated a standing threat to the heart of the kingdom; the Illyrians and Paeonians had been beaten and pushed out on the north and north-east. Philip by 354 could claim that the kingdom was secure from any immediate danger. The old enemies had been beaten, Thessaly had been neutralized. He must also have realized that in dealing with all these close-by enemies he had failed to attend seriously to the most important enemy of all, Athens.

3

The defence of the kingdom, 354–346 BC

By 354 Philip had enlarged the kingdom he had inherited to the greatest extent of earlier reigns and further to include Amphipolis and Philippi, and its military power was greater and more efficient. Internally, Philip used the existing local institutions while tightening his overall control. Most local communities were self-governing through local assemblies. A development of Philip's reign was the growth of towns and cities, by natural expansion, thanks to peace and increasing prosperity, or new foundations by the king. The whole kingdom was a complex mixture of jurisdictions, not all of which had the same powers. From a Machiavellian point of view one might see this as a deliberate process of ruling by division; in fact it has more the marks of a natural intermittent growth; Philip does not seem to have attempted to impose uniformity.

The kingships of the Upper Macedonian states – Elimaia, Lynkos, Orestis, and so on – were abolished, and the local barons incorporated into his court, the royal families becoming courtiers and Companions. The districts were left to run their own affairs through local assemblies and aristocracies with no attempt to create uniformity; they contributed men to the forces and money to the treasury. They were, that is, reduced from a precarious independence to a secure provincial status.[1]

In some areas of particular sensitivity, notably newly conquered and frontier areas, Philip appointed governors. Border areas such as Philippi and Amphipolis and the area around Damastion in the north-west were sensitive because they could be objects of an enemy attack. Macedonian garrisons were presumably installed in these places, for both defence and control. The title of a governor might be *strategos*, which would imply a military function, or *epistates*, certainly attested at Amphipolis in the 350s. It is a title whose duties varied with time and place, but usually implied appointment by the king as his representative at a particular place.[2] Both Amphipolis and Damastion had mineral resources, which belonged to the king; no doubt one responsibility of these officials was to ensure that the king's share of the product of the mine reached him.

Large parts of the kingdom belonged directly to the king; *epimeletai* managed groups of his estates. Forests were royal preserves; managers of these forests were surely required, particularly since the sale of timber had long been one of the prime sources of royal revenue.[3] Taxes and customs duties collected at cities and ports were farmed out: financial officials were clearly required to supervise the process.[4]

None of this was unusual or innovative: essentially the same system can be seen in the Roman and Akhaimenid empires. Philip was simply applying the normal systems of the ancient world, but the expansion of his kingdom required the administrative system also to expand, hence governors for certain areas. The usual variations in efficiency, and the usual instances of corruption and oppression of any bureaucracy, surely existed; one of Philip's duties as king was to rein in managers when such problems became too visible. The bureaucracy remained fairly undeveloped, though the *epimeletai* were assigned to duties other than supervising the royal estates. This was a start, but it was not Philip's priority once he had survived the early crises by means of the development of his new army. For the general population, Philip's primary responsibility, apart from security, was administration of justice. Philip was the chief judge and final court of appeal of the kingdom, but day-to-day justice was administered by magistrates in the towns and cities, or by judges appointed by the king.[5]

Judges and *epimeletai* were appointed from among the king's Companions, men who lived at court, accompanied him, acted as his bodyguard, fought with him, drank and ate at his table. These were barons from rural areas, former royals from the hill states, Greeks from the cities or from abroad, all known to Philip personally, men whose capacities he judged with a shrewd eye. They might be appointed to any or all of the tasks Philip required of them: guards, judges, diplomats, admirals, administrators, governors, *epimeletai*. He also collected together the younger sons of barons, making them Royal Pages, another existing institution Philip enlarged and increased in importance: it was from the pages that the later Companions were recruited. The kings of the kingdoms after Alexander were all pages as youths.

For all the enlargement and innovation, this was still a personal government, in which the king was involved at all levels. The numbers of Companions available for these administrative and command duties was only a few hundred. Administration was largely informal, with little in the way of detailed record keeping: the number of inscriptions on stone for the period is few, for instance. Athens with a smaller population used more bureaucrats than all Philip's Macedon; it is one reason Athens and Thebes were as powerful as the much larger kingdom. Macedon had, that is, no institutionalized government system above the local level. Philip, whose energy was prodigious, ran the whole show. One result of this under-development is that when Alexander needed to organize an imperial governing system, he failed.

The frontiers were strengthened with colonies of Macedonians planted at strategic points: Krenides/Philippi and Amphipolis were two examples, Damastion another; the people of Balla in Pieria were moved to a site called

Pytheion in part of Perrhaebia.[6] In Lynkos, Herakleia controlled the upper valley of the Erigon River and the route used by invading Illyrians.[7] Philippopolis was placed to overlook the middle Strymon Valley.[8] At the centre, Pella was enlarged, becoming wealthier and more frequented as a result of Philip's work.[9] Philip moved 'peoples and cities … even as shepherds move their flocks', so that 'from many tribes and races he formed one kingdom and one people'.[10]

By these colonies and urban developments Philip was, perhaps unintentionally, developing a new type of city. The normal Greek city was independent, or subordinate by some sort of agreement to another. The Macedonian version was never potentially independent, though it did have the usual institutions of self-government, magistrates, priesthoods, assemblies, and so on.[11] These cities were directly subject to the king, and often answerable to a governor appointed by him. This pattern became the usual method applied in the later kingdoms to the huge number of new cities founded and developed there.

The central factor in Philip's actions between 354 and 346 was his war with Athens. Neither power could seriously attack the other directly, but only through associates. Athens, now without the major allies of her second league, did not have the military strength to tackle the newly potent Macedonian army; Philip, supreme on land in the north, was never willing to build ships to challenge Athens by sea. So Athens' policy was to threaten Philip through alliances, in Thrace or the Chalkidike, while Philip developed his diplomatic contacts in Greece so as to threaten Athens. Each side accused the other of underhand tricks, and both used them. Athens was generally able to keep Philip at a distance, but Philip gradually eliminated the allies of Athens who were close to his kingdom. Direct hostilities were few, at least until nearly the end.

The contest was complicated by a simultaneous war in central Greece. Originating in a quarrel between Thebes, which claimed to control Boiotia, and Phokis, its next-but-one neighbour to the north, this war became internationalized when the Phokians seized control of Delphi and used the treasures there to hire an army of mercenaries. The Delphic Amphiktyony, the committee of local communities which governed the sanctuary, appealed for help to recover its lost riches and to punish the sacrilegious perpetrator, and this involved all Greece, in the 'Sacred' war. Operating along the political fault lines of Greek affairs, the war allied Athens and Sparta unenthusiastically with Phokis, and Thebes found itself struggling. In Thessaly the tyrants of Pherai were keen to use the crisis to extend their control over other parts of Thessaly. The Pheraians allied with Phokis; threatened Thessalian cities appealed to Philip for help.[12] Only four years after the Common Peace of 360, all Greece was involved in war again.

Macedonian kings had intervened in Thessaly several times, always in the interest of blocking the growth of Pheraian power. It was not in Macedon's interest to see Thessaly under one ruler, for that would constitute a major threat;

and Pherai was aligned, through Phokis, with Athens, with which Philip was already at war. Macedon was thus aligned with Thebes, and early in 353, after a Theban victory, a Theban army marched through Macedon to assist the Persian satrap of Hellespontine Phrygia, Artabazos, who was in revolt. The commander of the Thebans was Pammenes, Philip's old host, and Philip brought up a Macedonian force to escort the Thebans through Thrace.[13]

Philip used this expedition to assert his power in Thrace, though the result was to alert the Thracian kings to the threat he posed. He had clashed already with several kings, Ketriporis, Kersobleptes, even Amadokos in the east. Now they began diplomatic explorations. Philip had negotiated with them to ensure a safe passage to the Hellespont for Pammenes and his troops, in the process apparently agreeing to fight Amadokos in alliance with Kersobleptes. Philip's army also ravaged the territories of two Athenian allies, Abdera and Maroneia, but neither city was seriously assaulted.

Philip was accompanied by a fleet of supply ships, convoyed by ships of the small Macedonian navy. On his return his ships were threatened by an Athenian force commanded by Chares. Athens was now willing to pay attention to the problems of its northern allies. Amphipolis, Methone, Pydna and the small cities west of Neapolis had been lost to Macedon, and those left became the more valuable. Since the joint Theban-Macedonian march took place in the spring, Chares would seem to have been sent north to intercept Philip's fleet, and perhaps to help defend Neapolis, Abdera and Maroneia. Philip detected the waiting Athenian ships, sent four of his fastest warships to distract them, and then got his cargo ships past Neapolis in safety.[14]

This Thracian march, as with many of Philip's actions, had several aspects: the war with Athens, the immediate position in Thrace, relations with Thebes and the Sacred War. Pammenes' march shows Thebes and Macedon in active alliance; later in the year this would affect Philip's actions in Thessaly.

It is also the first sign of Philip's interest in Persian affairs. The Great King could note that both Thebes and Macedon were assisting the rebel satrap; a year or so later, when Artabazos was finally defeated, he escaped to take refuge at Pella with Philip, bringing with him a number of associates, including his brother-in-law, the mercenary captain Memnon of Rhodes. Thus Persia came to Philip's attention and Macedon to Artaxerxes'. The refugees' presence at Philip's court was a constant reminder of the possibilities available in Asia. But it would take more than Pammenes and his 5,000 men to make an effect.

Philip went to Thessaly to help his friends there. The Phokian general, Onomarchos, collected a new army, and this revived the hopes of the Pheraian tyrants. Philip took only a part of the Macedonian army with him, intending only to tip the balance in a conflict in which the two sides were roughly equal. In reply Lykophron, the joint-tyrant of Pherai, appealed to Onomarchos, who sent a Phokian force north under his brother Phayllos. This was defeated in battle by Philip.[15] Escalation continued: Onomarchos brought the main Phokian army north; and Philip his own main force south. Philip was outnumbered to some degree and was defeated in two major battles. Philip retired to Macedon, leaving garrisons in some cities, and Onomarchos set about besieging and capturing them. Philip was determined to return the following year.[16]

Philip's defeat was the first he had suffered in six years of fighting and campaigning. It was his new army's first encounter with a large and well-commanded Greek hoplite army; until then, the enemies had been less well organized and less disciplined and, in many cases, less numerous. Some of the Macedonians deserted, blaming Philip, and considerable numbers had died. Philip's comment, that he withdrew to butt the harder, argued his own determination, but the army may well have been apprehensive at further fighting on this scale. One must assume that Philip spent the winter working hard to convince his men that they could win.

Thessaly was a complication inherited from his predecessors. It was a country similar to Macedon in many ways, ruled by an elite baronage but including a substantial urban element, rich in resources, about the same size as the old Macedon without the hill kingdoms. Under the rule of one man it was potentially dangerous to all its neighbours, and the intervention of Onomarchos established an alliance between Phokis, enriched by the Delphic treasure, and Pherai and its tyrants. This enemy alliance was far too much of a threat to be ignored. For the sake of his army Philip had to fight again; for the sake of his kingdom he had to break the enemy alliance.

Philip's allies in Thessaly were the cities of the Thessalian League threatened by Pherai's ambition. Being more or less equal in strength, the two Thessalian groups were each able to field a substantial army, and Thessaly was good cavalry country. In 352 Philip returned south, with his full army, collected the forces of his allies, and set about taking back the cities which Onomarchos had captured the year before: in particular he attacked Pagasai, only 10 km south of Pherai. An Athenian fleet under Chares had also been directed there as naval support for Lykophron and Pherai.

Onomarchos came north in full strength. The subsequent fighting took place in the south of Thessaly, so Onomarchos had few Thessalian forces with him. The battle at the Crocus Fields, near the southern border of Thessaly, was thus fought on Philip's terms. His cavalry, outnumbering that of Onomarchos by six to one, was overwhelmingly effective, and when the Phokian army broke in defeat, 6,000 died and 3,000 became prisoners. Onomarchos either died in the rout or by execution; the prisoners were drowned, this being the punishment for temple robbers.[17]

Philip stayed in Thessaly for some time. Lykophron and his brother Peitholaos gave up the tyranny of Pherai in exchange for safe conduct out of Thessaly for them and their supporters; the other cities they had controlled fell quickly to Philip. A new political dispensation was now organized: Philip was elected *archon* of the Thessalian League, a position less than royal but more than honorary, giving him a powerful influence in Thessalian affairs. It was probably as such that he kept control of Pagasai, which his forces had conquered, and Magnesia, the area north along the coast occupied by his army during the siege of Pagasai; he could claim that it was 'spear-won' land. The Thessalians made a formal request that he return it to Thessaly, but he did not bother. Philip also collected another wife, Nikesipolis, a niece of Jason of Pherai and a cousin of the expelled tyrants, presumably as a conciliatory gesture to that city.[18]

An *epimeletes* called Agathokles was installed to administer some or all of Perrhaibia,[19] the northern section of Thessaly, the neighbour of Macedon and Elimaia. Control of the area was Philip's forward defence if things went wrong again in Thessaly. The land's several cities were possibly omitted from Agathokles' remit; he would thus have responsibility for the rural areas, acting also as an early warning system for Macedon, and presumably collected local taxation. It is notable that Agathokles was a Thessalian, not a Macedonian, but he was appointed by Philip.

When he was finished Philip marched south, presumably intending to join forces with the Boiotians. At Thermopylai he found the pass held by the Phokians along with contingents from Athens and Sparta and other Phokian allies, including the former tyrants of Pherai. Having looked, he turned round and went home.[20] Philip's priorities were clearly his own, even though he fought Onomarchos in the name of Apollo of Delphi. He was uninterested in the 'Sacred' war as such, being mainly concerned to control Thessaly to prevent its use by his enemies. Similarly Athens was involved at Thermopylai not because the city was keen to support Phokis, but because it was at war with Philip and Thebes, whose junction would pose great dangers. Both veered away from a direct conflict.

The Athenian fleet commanded by Chares, which had threatened Philip's ships at Neapolis in Thrace earlier, was active again. Chares seized and colonized Sestos on the Chersonese side of the Hellespont, and roused the Thracian kings, where Kersobleptes made an alliance with Athens.[21] This was what drew Philip away from Thermopylai.

The situation in Thrace was complex. Kersobleptes menaced Amadokos, who joined Philip; Byzantion and Perinthos were also involved. Philip's arrival in strength disrupted the complex conflict, and he immediately defeated Kersobleptes, imposing severely restrictive peace terms. Later he besieged Heraion Teichos, a small town close to Perinthos, which would seem to have been in Athenian hands – at least the Athenians reacted vigorously, voting for a fleet of 40 triremes to go to the town's rescue.

But Philip fell ill, the expedition by the Athenians was abandoned, and Heraion Teichos was left untaken.[22] The result was that Philip had fastened an even firmer grip on parts of Thrace than before, but he had not damaged the real enemy, which was Athens. Philip had been kept fully occupied in fighting Athens' allies and clients for the past two years, which was why these allies had been recruited in the first place. Athens itself had sent out only small expeditions, which were generally successful, at Neapolis, Thermopylai and the Chersonese. The real problem was that Philip kept winning, and eventually there would be no allies left. Athens would then have to do more than send out fleets and occupy defensible posts. Less visible was another effect: Philip was steadily consolidating his power both in Macedon and in the surrounding lands. When the war with Athens began, he had been confined to traditional Macedon, from Mount Olympos to the Strymon River; now his southern boundary lay across the water from Euboia, and his eastern was approaching the Propontis.

From Macedon these acquisitions pushed likely enemies well away from the homeland, but there was still another Athenian ally very close by. While Philip was involved in Thrace and Thessaly, the leading city at the Chalkidian League, Olynthos, had begun negotiations with Athens, and had publicly declared friendship between the two cities. This was in violation of the treaty of alliance Olynthos had made with Philip in 355, and was probably provoked by Philip's increasing power and his defeat in 353 in the first war in Thessaly.[23]

Philip reacted by protests and attempted negotiation, accompanied by threats. This had the opposite effect to that intended. The League became allied with Athens and, as a direct threat to Philip personally, Olynthos granted asylum to his two surviving half-brothers, Arrhidaios and Menelaos. Philip's illness in the Thracian campaign in 352 will have reminded everyone that he was both mortal and irreplaceable. It was only a step from there to the thought that, by replacing him, any threat to Olynthos would cease, particularly if the new Macedonian king had a good reason to be grateful to Olynthos. Certainly if Philip was suddenly eliminated, a new succession crisis would erupt (his own sons were still small children), Thessaly would go its own way, the Thracian kings would be released, the Illyrians would be less fearful. The appearance of his half-brothers at Olynthos after a decade in which they had been out of sight indicates a new phase of the war.[24]

Philip was at war with Athens very unwillingly. He had avoided direct conflict so often that it looks very much as though *not* fighting Athens was Philip's preferred policy. He had generously released Athenians he captured in the fight against Argaios and at Potidaia; he had avoided Athenian expeditions off Neapolis, in Thessaly, at Thermopylai and at the Chersonese. His release of Athenian prisoners must mean he hoped for peace. He did not like it when Olynthos made peace with Athens, but he did not react until that city sponsored his half-brothers.

To understand what Philip was about it is necessary to look more comprehensively at his overall intentions and aims. This is difficult. We have nothing on the subject from Philip himself, nothing from his ancient biographers (of whose work we only have fragments), and what he may have intended has been hidden by what he actually achieved, and by what his son accomplished.[25] The basic issue concerns his aims towards Greece and Persia. In 346 the Athenian pamphleteer Isokrates urged him to attack Persia.[26] This was probably the first public comment on this, but Persia had been attacked by Greeks repeatedly in the previous half-century: by Xenophon's men in 401, by the Spartan king Agesilaus in the 390s, by Pammenes in 355, and it was Jason of Pherai's ambition in the 370s. That is, almost every successful Greek ruler had aimed to attack Persia, so it was perhaps the widespread presumption that Philip would also do so. He assisted Pammenes in 355, and gave refuge to the Persian rebels the year after. The weight of public expectation may well have been that he would turn against Persia when he was able.

Persian military power was concentrated in its cavalry, its warships and its wealth. The cavalry fought in the traditional way which Philip knew he could beat with his newly disciplined horsemen; the empire's wealth allowed it to hire innumerable Greek mercenaries, and he knew he could beat them; its sea power, however, was out of his reach. Macedon, even enlarged, was simply not large or rich enough to support both a full-scale army and a navy able to combat a Persian fleet of up to 400 warships. But the Athenian fleet was large enough and skilled enough to defeat any Persian force. If he intended to attack Persia the fleet of Athens had to be on his side.

Attention to Greece was the first essential, for earlier attacks on Persia had been regularly thwarted by trouble in Greece. If Philip aimed to attack Persia, it was first of all necessary to ensure that Greece was on his side (as Isokrates implied) or that Greece was firmly and reliably neutral. The most powerful Greek state was Athens. Everything led towards a policy of alliance with Athens.

Athens did not cooperate, being persuaded that he was an inveterate enemy, but Philip was clearly determined to avoid an all-out fight if he could, and aimed to recruit Athens as his ally if possible. An Athenian alliance would do two things: together they could dominate Greece; and the Athenian navy would protect his communications and Greece's seaward flank in any Persian invasion he mounted. This is the best explanation for his actions; if he had wanted merely to dominate Greece, Thebes was as good an ally, and he was allied with that city already; Athens' fleet was unique in Greece, and this was the one military asset Philip did not have. I conclude that, from round about 350, Philip's ultimate intention was to attack the Persian Empire, preferably in alliance with Athens.[27] (The suggestion that Philip was allied with the Empire at some point is to be dismissed, as is the story of Persian envoys at Philip's court.)[28]

In 350 Philip campaigned in Epiros, defeating Molossian king Arybbas, uncle of his wife Olympias, and probably taking Parauaea, along the Epirote border, as a result. Olympias' brother, Alexander, was taken to Pella either as a hostage or to preserve his life from the possibility of Arybbas' anger. Alexander had a good claim to the Molossian kingship, Arybbas having succeeded Alexander's father in that post. Philip already had a son of Kersobleptes as a hostage at his court, not so much a threat as a requirement to good behaviour by his father.

It was while he was in Epiros that the Olynthians received Philip's half-brothers.[29] They were no real threat to him, for by this time he had two sons, Arrhidaios, whose mother was Philinna of Larissa, and Alexander, son of Olympias: the former was about seven, the latter six, in 350. There were also two daughters. In addition he had at his court Amyntas, the son of Perdikkas, who had a claim, and was now adult. Philip's succession was thus assured, but his half-brothers were clearly a nuisance. When he returned from the Epiros expedition, Philip could turn to deal with Olynthos.

The menaces he had uttered against the Olynthians had no effect. Olynthos was the most important city of the Chalkidian League, counting for about half of its full military strength; the rest of the League consisted of about 30 cities, mostly small and weak. In 349 Philip attacked, at first ignoring Olynthos, in order to destroy the League by capturing other members. Most of them could not resist and fell either without a fight or after only a brief resistance.[30]

The Olynthians were not intimidated. A contingent of Athenians commanded by Chares arrived to bolster the defence.[31] The winter was spent in diplomacy and intrigue by both sides. Philip was in all probability partly responsible for the rebellion of Euboia from Athens;[32] it is quite possible that Athens had something to do with a rising against Philip at Pherai, instigated by the former tyrant Peitholaos.[33] Evidence is poor or non-existent in both cases but both risings were so very convenient for both sides that it is difficult to believe they were coincidences. At the very least one might assume that the initiators of the events were taking advantage of the preoccupation of Athens and Philip with Olynthos.

Philip had no real trouble at Pherai, but it took time and effort to remove Peitholaos and settle matters in Thessaly again. Athens had more difficulty in Euboia, where Kallias of Chalkis recruited mercenaries and eventually defeated the Athenian forces sent against him. Athens had to accept a treaty by which the Euboian cities left the Athenian league and formed a league of their own. In the meantime the Athenian commander of their forces in the Chalkidike, Charidemos, was able to mount a campaign of his own against the cities which defected or fell to Philip the year before.[34]

Philip abandoned the method of picking off the smaller cities to exert peripheral pressure on Olynthos. This might have been designed to indicate that he was prepared to see the league continue if it would only make, and keep, a peace with him. Now he ignored the smaller cities and concentrated on Olynthos itself. To do so he had to defeat the league army in two battles, and then lay siege to the city. This also allowed him to accept the surrenders of other cities unable to receive support from Olynthos, and he came to the conclusion that only the complete elimination of Olynthos would end the war. When the Olynthians asked for terms he offered none. The Athenians, preoccupied in Euboia, sent some help with Charidemos at the start of the campaign of 348, but it was not enough. The Olynthian cavalry surrendered; it was outside the city, and was probably outnumbered and defeated; it was commanded by men opposed to the war in the first place, and there is a strong suspicion of treason. The siege tightened and when Mekyberna, Olynthos' port, was taken, Athenian ships and men could not enter. Olynthos eventually fell after a hard fight, was sacked and destroyed, and its people were sold.[35]

Philip's methods in this war are reminiscent of the whole approach he was using in the wider war with Athens. In both cases he used a combination of diplomacy and force, and displayed a good deal of reluctance to get to grips with the main enemy, preferring to tackle subjects or allies first, and only when absolutely necessary attacking the principal enemy. The Olynthian war was a replica of the Athenian war on a small scale.

Philip had knocked aside most of the underpinnings of the Athenian alliance by this time. All northern Greece had been brought under his direct control or indirect influence, from the Propontis to the Ionian Sea, from Illyria to the southern border of Thessaly. The one Athenian ally in a position to provide substantial aid and to block an advance southwards was now Phokis, and its resolve was crumbling, along with the evaporation of the stolen Delphian riches.

Philip used diplomacy first. Messages went to Athens, suggesting peace negotiations, even while the siege of Olynthos continued. One came by way of the Euboians, arriving while the third Athenian expedition to help Olynthos was being prepared;[36] an Athenian on private business in Macedon returned with a message from Philip, in effect asking to make peace. The issue became a serious one in Athens, where the man who proposed negotiations, Philokrates, was prosecuted for making the suggestion. His acquittal was a sign that negotiations were now possible.[37] Athenian opinion was not yet fully committed; many Athenians felt they still had alternatives to peace.[38]

These were attempted during 347. An expedition was sent to the Chersonese, where Kersobleptes was contacted and several forts were built on the Propontis and inland.[39] Philip was distracted once more by events in Thessaly, where Halos rebelled against control by Pharsalos; Philip sent Parmenion to besiege it.[40] His control of Thessaly was obviously less than complete, and the country was taking up much of his time. There is no sign that the rising by Halos was Athens' doing, but it was a coastal town, and accessible from the Athenian-dominated sea. The fact that Philip was involved in war with Athens may not have been missing from the Halians' calculations.

Philip's ally Thebes was doing badly in its continuing war with Phokis, and during 347 Philip sent a small force to help the Boiotians, and together they defeated the Phokians in a small battle.[41] Athens made attempts to rouse other Greeks to what some saw as the danger of Philip, but was generally unsuccessful. Sparta was interested, but the Arkadians were not.[42] There was no reason for these cities to play Athens' game. If they wished they could point out that Athens was allied with the condemned party in the 'Sacred' war, and that Philip was the only ruler to have made a serious dent in the Phokian power on behalf of Delphian Apollo. In fact, the Arkadian cities' major problem was Sparta, whose ambitions to revive its predominant position in the Peloponnese were a threat to every Spartan neighbour. So, if Sparta was Athens' ally, Athens' policies were automatically suspect.

The lack of success in recruiting allies was compounded by the news that Phokian resolution was failing. Phalaikos, the general in command, was deposed in favour of a board of three generals who, after initial successes, were beaten by the joint Macedonian-Boiotian force. Phalaikos resumed command. A suggestion had been made that the Phokians should hand over their forts at Thermopylai to Athenian garrisons, but Phalaikos cancelled that idea. An offer from the Spartan king Archidamos to install a Spartan garrison was also refused. It was not only Arkadians who were suspicious of Sparta and Athens.[43]

Athens' various ploys had all failed by early 346; there was to be no grand alliance of Hellenes against barbarian Macedon; Kersobleptes had taken the forts in Thrace but had done nothing more, being fully aware that Philip had him in his sights once more. The Phokians were exhausted, and Phalaikos' insistence on holding Thermopylai himself demonstrated quite clearly his lack of trust in his distant and barely active allies. In March 346 the Athenians in Assembly voted to appoint ten ambassadors to go to Macedon to negotiate peace.[44]

Phalaikos was dismayed when this news arrived. If Athens made peace he and the Phokians and his mercenary army would be left alone to face the Boiotians, the Thessalians and Philip's Macedonians, and the money from Delphi was almost finished. At Pella, the Athenians found embassies from Phokis, Thebes and Sparta present. Philip had gathered into his hands all the strings needed to contrive a settlement of both wars. The negotiations took time, not least because the ten Athenians all insisted on making long speeches to Philip, who then replied at similar length. Then the envoys had to travel back and forth to Athens to get the terms agreed.

While they did so Philip went off to Thrace to coerce Kersobleptes. During this expedition he took over the forts near the Chersonese that the Athenians had set up the year before and which were in Kersobleptes' control.[45] When he returned to Macedon, the Athenian envoys were waiting for him at Pella. It had taken the Athenians a month to decide to accept the peace terms more or less as negotiated, and they had given their ratifying oaths.[46] But the Phokians were excluded, and so were Halos and Kersobleptes.

Athens thus abandoned friends and allies, and Philip abandoned his Theban ally. That relationship was based on mutual enmity towards the Phokians, but no other mutual interests existed. Philip had helped Pammenes reach Asia with his soldiers, but this was a personal matter, and he was no doubt quite happy to see Thebes giving away 5,000 soldiers. Thebes' policy towards Phokis was purely destructive; if Thebes had its way, the result of the war would be the total destruction of the Phokians. This only made Phokians fight the harder; it also gave Philip the entry he needed by offering milder terms. The peace agreed in 346 between Philip and Athens was therefore the first of a series of agreements between the various parties, which loosened and destroyed the existing alliances. Thebes fully understood what was happening; as Philip travelled south, the Thebans mobilized their forces.[47]

Part of the treaty, called by the Athenians the Peace of Philokrates,[48] was an alliance of Philip and Athens, an arrangement which Philip must have hoped would smooth affairs all round. The joint authority of the greatest naval and military powers in Greece would surely dominate Greece effectively and calm affairs down everywhere else. This was not much to the liking of many Athenians, notably the orator Demosthenes, but it was part of the price for peace. In Athens' view, the war was being lost; their ally Phokis was failing. Peace was necessary, and Philip insisted on an alliance to go with it.[49] Philip might be keen, but Athens was not. While Athens deliberated, Philip dealt with Kersobleptes, and it seems also reached a final agreement with Phalaikos.

As the Athenians were returning home with Philip's own ratification, his army was marching through Thessaly to take control of Phokis and of Thermopylai.[50] He owed it to his allies, the Thessalians and the Boiotians and the Delphic Amphiktyony, to see that Phokis was punished, if possible without forcing Phalaikos and his army to go to extremes; he also had to prevent the Athenians from intervening on behalf of their allies, without annoying them so much that they broke the peace terms. He was balancing all these conflicting interests, and the most interesting aspect of it all is that he was being careful to do so, whereas it would have been all too easy to impose a military settlement.

Phalaikos had garrisoned Thermopylai, and had 8,000 mercenaries under his command. These men understood that they could be beaten by the Macedonian army, which was reinforced by the Thessalian levy, and if they fought, the Boiotians would join in. They also understood that they were liable to exemplary punishment for the sacrilege at Delphi, so any terms Phalaikos could extract which would let the men go free would be acceptable to them. That this would leave Phokis prostrate before its enemies was not their concern.

The terms were that the men could go free, with only what they could carry, without weapons or horses. This might have made them vulnerable to killing as outcasts, but these were tough men, and no doubt they would arm themselves again quickly enough. The men accepted these terms; the Phokians, no doubt by prearrangement through Phalaikos, then surrendered to Philip, who now occupied Thermopylai.[51]

Philip handed over to his allies, the Amphiktyons, who had been the aggrieved party over Delphi, the decision over Phokis' punishment. The Boiotians dealt with three cities of their league which had fallen to the Phokians, and had effectively seceded: Orchomenos, Koronai and Korsiai were destroyed, their inhabitants sold.[52] The Amphiktyons voted to expel Phokis from their organization, giving the seats thus left vacant to Philip. They then voted for the elimination of all the Phokian cities and the imposition of a great fine.[53] The Athenians did not send representatives to the meeting, but it seems that Philip argued for leniency. The agreed punishment was harsh enough, but the original proposal had been for all the Phokian men to be killed. Philip's pressure was thus effective, but then he was all-powerful at that meeting anyway.[54] He presided at the Pythian festival in the autumn, the first of the new era of Delphian freedom; then returned home. He had achieved a remarkable diplomatic triumph, settling a ten-year war which had ravaged all central Greece and at the same time ending an even longer war with Athens. The Athenians were not happy about the fate of Phokis, but they learned to live with it. They agreed that the alliance with Philip should continue, though with a similar lack of enthusiasm.

Philip had been king of the Macedonians for just 13 years. His achievements had been considerable, but it will not do to exaggerate them. His first six or so years had been spent in recovering what had been lost to Macedon in the previous generation. Beyond that he had made three major conquests: Thessaly, Chalkidike and the Amphipolis-Philippi area.

The kingdom was still in a developing stage. The several measures Philip had taken had not yet consolidated fully into a well-developed state system. His one major institutional innovation had been his army, the necessary instrument of defence, and then of aggression. But he had been careful. His long war with Athens had been conspicuously unfought, and one reason for this caution was an understanding of the kingdom's weakness. He picked his enemies very carefully, and had not yet fought a really major enemy. After the necessary defeat of Bardylis and his Illyrians in 358, Philip had fought only one large battle – the Crocus Fields – and otherwise had concentrated on sieges, small captures and well-placed marches, all combined with careful and inventive diplomacy. He had established Macedon as one of the great powers of Greece, alongside the traditional great powers, Athens, Thebes and Sparta, but only as one of the group.

4

Cold war, 346–340 BC

Having hoisted himself and his kingdom to the position of a great power in the Greek world, Philip found that there was no problem in that region which did not concern him. Athens was the only other Greek state in this situation. None of the other Greek states could stand beside these two: Sparta had been reduced by Thebes' victory in 362, Thebes damaged by the Phokian war. The conclusion of peace in 346 had not solved the problems between Macedon and Athens, any more than the Common Peace of 360 had solved the problems of Greece, and the alliance of the two did not hide the tensions. The six years following the peace were a time of diplomatic contest and manoeuvring for advantage, the sort of situation we have come to call a cold war.

The contest resumed even as Philip was about to ratify the peace agreement, when Athens refused to assist Philip in his move against the Phokians.[1] This gave Philip a free hand, and no doubt the Athenians refused for the very good reason that they had deserted their ally and scarcely wished to be in at the kill, but it showed the alliance of the two great powers as no more than a paper agreement. In addition Athens gave shelter to refugees fleeing from destroyed Phokian and Boiotian cities.

Philip was absent from Macedon, first in Thrace and then in Thessaly and Greece, for much of 346, returning only in the autumn. There was, no doubt, an accumulation of local problems at home for him to deal with; it may also be that his absence alerted his Balkan enemies to sniff out a possible prey. The following year, for no known immediate reason, Philip went on a campaign into Illyria, probably against the Ardaei and the Dardani. It seems that they were allied; and the potential power of the pair attracted Philip's attention. Until now he fought the Illyrians when they attacked; now he was pre-empting any attack. The campaign was largely successful: both kingdoms were defeated, and the Dardani reduced to dependence on Macedon. The Ardaei were certainly beaten in battle, but seem not to have been made subjects.[2]

The removal of the threat of a Phokian invasion, meanwhile, had its effect on Thessaly. Pherai's rulers had been attempting for three decades to make themselves lords of all Thessaly, and the city was still ruled by men who resented the restrictions Philip's control brought. The city twice refused to supply troops to the *archon* – Philip – first for the Phokian campaign, then for the Illyrian. In the first case they would, like Athens, have been fighting against their friends and allies, and were thus perhaps excused; in the second case they could argue that an Illyrian war had nothing to do with Pherai. There was trouble also in Larissa, where a tyrant seized power and issued his own coins, a mark of independence.[3] The basic reason for these problems was resentment at Philip's control, and a wish to be independent of him, now that Philip's protection was not needed.

Philip had gone into Thessaly to prevent its use as a source to attack Macedon. He tried defeating its lords, then defeating its enemies, then accepting the position as *archon*, but each step forward had not brought security. It was time to try another move. In 344 he conducted a campaign into Thessaly during which Pherai was assaulted and taken; 'tyrants and dynasts' were removed from other places; probably for the first time, garrisons of Macedonian soldiers were imposed, at least at Pherai and Larissa, and maybe elsewhere; Pagasai and Magnesia were already his.[4]

This was still not enough. Two years later, in 342, after more thought and discussion, he revived an older division of the land into 'quarters' (*tetrads*) and placed men of his own as the tetrarchs, probably the men who would command the levies when the army was called out. This would stop the local city rulers from simply failing to obey a summons. The removal of tyrants had perhaps quietened the party strife, and Philip's display of the mailed fist and the presence of garrisons had their effect. He had been intervening now for 15 years: his determination to reach a durable settlement was surely realized by now. Thessaly remained a separate state. It was not united to Macedon, and its league continued with Philip as *archon*. This seems finally to have done the trick; major trouble in Thessaly ceased.[5]

It is worth noting that the tetrarchs of Thessaly, appointed by Philip as *archon*, were similar in many ways to the *epimeletai* he appointed to various responsibilities in Macedon. We know of none by name, but the appointment of Macedonians would only draw attention to his overlordship, so it may be presumed that it was Thessalians who were the tetrarchs (as in Perrhaibia). The Thessalian cities were self-governing, just as those in Macedon. Thessaly was, by 340, well on the way to being organized in the same way as Macedon; the two lands were approaching integration as a single state.

Philip intervened again in Epiros, in the winter of 343/342. He deposed King Arybbas, and in his place installed Alexander, his brother-in-law, whom he had removed out of Arybbas' reach in 350.[6] He then turned south to mop up a small set of Greek cities south of Molossia, which he gave to Alexander. His action alarmed Ambrakia, locally the most important city, which went to war to preserve her local position.[7]

Ambrakia was not alone. To the south the Akarnanians, another league of cities, were equally bothered by Philip's sudden appearance so close to them. Both states appealed for help, and the Athenians sent a force to Akarnania; probably Ambrakia also received assistance – the city had strong ties to Corinth.[8] Philip discovered that his fairly gentle probe had stirred up a formidable set of enemies; both the Akarnanians and Ambrakia were tough customers, and Athens' help had been disturbingly prompt. Philip retired, but did not abandon the cities he had captured, and made an agreement with the nascent Aitolian league to hand over the city of Naupaktos to the league when he got it. The Aitolians were enemies of the Akarnanians, and this promise of future favour served neatly to neutralize Ambrakia and Akarnania.[9]

The appearance of Athenian forces in Philip's path in Akarnania and Ambrakia will not have come as a surprise. The peace of 346 had never been satisfactory from Athens' point of view. A substantial body of opinion in the city did not want it, and any action by Philip was liable to be interpreted as a threat. The alliance with Philip had only been accepted as a means to get the peace treaty. Athens' interests extended to every part of Greece, and wherever Philip went he impinged on those interests. The Athenians who disliked the peace were making progress in their propaganda that Philip was a threat to all Greece.

In the Peloponnese a new crisis between Sparta and Messene blew up in 344. Argos was somehow also involved – a traditional Spartan enemy, of course, and it was the traditional origin of Philip's dynasty. He intervened to warn Sparta, and may well have sent money and mercenaries to help those who had been attacked. He may also have made preparations, no doubt very ostentatiously, to go to the Peloponnese himself with a Macedonian army.[10]

The Spartans withdrew, and the recipients of Philip's favour had good reason to be grateful. It is an example of how his influence spread, but it was also something his Athenian enemies could use to turn opinion against him. Some time before Philip's intervention, the Athenian politician Demosthenes had visited Messene, which had also asked for Athenian help against Sparta. Demosthenes quoted what he had said to the Messenians in the speech at Athens known as the 'Second Philippic': beware masterful friends, he said, they became only masters. Philip, he was saying to the Messenians, is a greater danger even than Sparta. In Athens this might have sounded good; in Messenia, with Sparta next door, it made no sense. Demosthenes by then was not really talking to the Messenians, but the Ambrakians, Akarnanians and Corinthians all took the point.

Philip replied to these verbal attacks with a protest, to which was added the suggestion that, if necessary, he would consider amending the terms of the peace treaty. The Athenians then heard another denunciation of Philip from Demosthenes, who said that the only reason Philip could have for amending the treaty was to subdue Athens, and was followed by Hegesippos, who proposed that the one amendment needed was that Philip should hand Amphipolis 'back' to Athens.[11]

Nobody in Athens can have believed this would happen; but it did annoy Philip, which to the anti-Macedonian group was pleasing, since Philip angry was Philip menacing. This played towards their goal, which, as they must have realized, was another war. Philip ignored the suggestion, or perhaps he replied with a cool negative – it was hardly an issue to get worked up about from his viewpoint. Combined with the swift Athenian (and Corinthian) response to his probe against Ambrakia, this told him that his policy of peace and alliance with Athens was not working.

In developing a policy which would lead to war with Philip, his Athenian enemies were hampered by geography. Philip's direct control reached as far as the southern boundary of Thessaly; and south of that was Phokis, where the cities had been demolished and the people disarmed and scattered into villages, through which Philip could march with no barrier. Beyond Phokis was Boiotia, technically still Philip's ally, but now less than enthusiastic about it, though no friend of Athens. There was little to stop Philip marching all the way to Attika if he chose to. In searching for allies, therefore, Athens had to look to the Peloponnese, which made Philip's intervention there to deter Sparta all the more disturbing.

Philip surely understood this, and it was in his interests to try to prevent Athens acquiring any allies there. He could be fairly sure of Messenia, and perhaps of Argos, and of some of the Arkadians. He could be fairly sure that Sparta would stay neutral, balanced by Messenia. So Athens had to look to the northern Peloponnese for friends. This was exactly where two crises blew up during 343. In Elis an oligarchic counter-revolution overthrew the democracy; the oligarchs who seized power had been funded by Macedonian money, a fact rapidly known. In Megara, Athens' immediate neighbour, an internal dispute led to rival appeals being made to Philip (for money again), to Boiotia, and to Athens. This time the Athenians were quickest off the mark, and their supporters were installed in power.[12]

On the other side of Attika, the island of Euboia had been part of Athens' league until a few years before; it contained half a dozen cities with unstable political systems, some friendly with Athens, some not. Philip may or may not have encouraged revolutions in these cities, but he was certainly prepared to help one along if one party showed itself to be his supporter; generally, as in Elis, he supported oligarchs; democrats therefore looked to Athens. In 343 he intervened at Eretria to finish off an oligarchic coup. The survivors of the displaced regime had taken refuge in the fortified town of Porthmos, and Philip sent 1,000 soldiers to take the place.[13] Eretria lay close to Attika, and even those Athenians who had not been convinced by Demosthenes so far will have been worried by the appearance of a substantial force of Macedonian troops only a few miles from their own shores.

Apart from its home territory, the most sensitive point for Athens was the Straits from the Black Sea to the Aegean, through which Athens received much of her food supplies – the Hellespont, the Propontis, the Bosporos. In 343 a new set of settlers were sent to the Thracian Chersonese, where there were several Athenian holdings already,[14] including Sestos. But here a third element was now inevitably involved, for the Asian side of these waters was part of the Persian Empire.

Since the accession of the Great King Artaxerxes III Ochos in 359, the great empire had made substantial progress towards recovering its lost or disobedient territories and provinces. Ochos had extinguished the revolt of the satraps, and then he attended to the real issue, the independence of Egypt. He approached the problem systematically, dealing first with the Egyptian forward defences: Cyprus was reconquered; Sidon captured and burnt. By 343 Artaxerxes was able to mount an attack across the Sinai Desert which finally succeeded in reaching the Nile. The Egyptian Pharaoh fled upriver and his armies disintegrated. To avoid the fate of Sidon, the Egyptian cities rapidly surrendered.[15]

The Hellespontine Phrygian satrap, Artabazos, had lived at Philip's court for ten years, and could provide plenty of information about the empire. Philip therefore had a firm basis of knowledge in watching the unfolding events. The rickety state of the empire was no doubt interesting, but Philip will have noted its powers of recovery. He needed to be concerned whether he had to keep up his guard against it, for the reconquest of Egypt freed the Great King, and freed his forces also. No doubt Artaxerxes was kept informed in general terms of developments in Greece, and Artabazos had returned to Persia by 342. In 346 Isokrates had published his pamphlet suggesting a Macedonian conquest of Persia; Artabazos will have known of this.

Artaxerxes sent envoys to Greece in 344 seeking to recruit soldiers for his intended attack on Egypt. They went to Athens and Sparta, which both refused, and to Thebes and Argos, which contributed 1,000 and 3,000 men respectively. Athens' refusal was worded very rudely, which might have momentarily helped Philip to hope that the alliance was still operative,[16] but the Athenians' suggested amendment to the peace terms came soon after. Not only that, but the two cities to send troops to Asia were Philip's allies; Athens was surely pleased to see them go.

In these circumstances Philip cannot have been making any serious plans to attack Persia, despite the attraction of the Persian preoccupation with Egypt. After Egypt, Artaxerxes sent his Greek general Mentor to establish full control over Artabazos' old satrapy,[17] which was just when Philip decided he needed to establish his power firmly in Thrace. The Straits, Athens' sensitive lifeline, were what separated the Macedonian and Persian campaigners.

In 342 Philip began a determined attempt to remove two of the Thracian kings, Kersobleptes and Teres (the son of Amadokos), who had caused him trouble so often. This required a long and difficult campaign into the Thracian interior, whereas before he had kept to the coast. It took him the rest of 342 and well into 341 to succeed. The Thracian kings were then ejected, no one knows to where. Philip went on to campaign into the Haemos (Balkan) Mountains, and made hostile contact with the Triballi, the main tribe between these hills and the Danube. On the other hand, a treaty was arranged with the Agrianes, a tribe living in a strategic area near the headwaters of the Strymon, between the Triballi and the Paeonians. The details of this campaign are largely inaccessible now, but the net result was a great expansion of Macedonian territory. The conquered lands were pinned down by several Macedonian garrison towns: Philippopolis, Alexandropolis, Kabyle and others, peopled by a variety of immigrants from Macedonia and elsewhere; and generous estates went to Companions and others who became eligible to be Companions. The land was to pay a regular tax to the king – more work for an *epimeletes*. Its government seems to have been partly Thracian, partly from the cities which will have been allocated substantial territories, and partly under Macedonian *epimeletai*.

One of Philip's reasons for intervening so forcefully in Thrace was that Kersobleptes had been pressuring Greek cities in the Hellespont area. Philip also made contact with the Greek cities on the Black Sea coast – Odessos, Istros, Apollonia, Mesembria – with which he made alliances.[18] He collected two more wives, daughters of kings of parts of the interior with whom he made peace and alliances.[19] The extent and firmness of his control of the conquered lands is difficult to gauge. The Thracians were certainly beaten in battle and their kings were expelled, but this did not imply full Macedonian control, and certainly it did not mean that the Thracians were content.

Philip was now richer than ever. The loot of Thrace was supplemented by the new taxes he could collect. His control of the silver and gold mines of Macedon already provided him with more of those metals than anyone in Greece, or even of all the Greeks put together – the mines of Philippi are said to have produced 1,000 talents of silver annually.[20] (But Athens' income at this period was more than that: perhaps 1,100 talents a year under the treasury management by Euboulos and Lykourgos.[21]) Philip used his wealth in gifts and in pursuing his political aims – which his enemies, of course, called bribes. He recruited troops from among his allies, and had an army which, as was to be proved later, was now as large as any combination of the Greek cities could produce, and better disciplined than theirs. The conquest of Thrace was a notable achievement, but it might become a burden if the Thracians would not accept his rule. The Thessalians had required his attention repeatedly over a period of a decade and a half before they settled down; the Illyrians had been repeatedly fought as well, without being conquered. For Thrace to become a permanent part of his kingdom, Philip would need to pay close and detailed attention to it for at least the next ten years.

The warfare in Thrace inevitably connected with Athenian sensibilities. Athens' settlers in the Chersonese were under the command of Diopeithes, who was left in place during the next two years, and had to find money to pay his troops. He did this by raiding the territories round about, which were Thracian at first, but by the year after his arrival had become Macedonian. His presence also revived an old quarrel between the independent city of Kardia and Athens over the boundary between their respective territories. It was a nasty little disputatious area marginally concerning Philip – he put a protective garrison into Kardia at that city's request – but Athens more centrally.[22] Control of the Chersonese was crucial to Athens' prosperity, partly because of the settlers sent there, but mainly because from bases in the Chersonese the Athenian fleet could dominate the whole line of the Straits; an annual convoy of grain ships was shepherded through.

One minor dispute could have been easily dealt with if both sides had been willing. A group of pirates occupied the island of Halonnesos in the Aegean. The island technically belonged to Athens, which did nothing about the pirates, perhaps because they were very discriminating in their victims. But they attacked Macedonian ships, so Philip sent a force to remove the pirates, and the Macedonians stayed on the island.[23]

This took place probably in 342, which was the same year that Athens continued to block Philip's progress in Akarnarnia, and the same year that Diopeithes and his cleruchs revived the old quarrel with Kardia, and raided Philip's new conquest of Thrace. It is also the year Philip campaigned to conquer Thrace and his agents and troops established his supporters in the Euboian towns. There were thus many areas where Philip and Athens were in dispute – Akarnania, Elis, Megara, Euboia, Halonnesos, the Chersonese – but in none of them was the dispute insoluble, if only both sides would work for it. The problem was that the constant series of disputes convinced both sides that an overall solution was not possible, and each problem exacerbated the others. Demosthenes and his supporters now saw that war with Philip and the destruction of the Macedonian power he had constructed was their eventual aim. We do not know what Philip's attitude was, though he refused to back down in any of the disputes – his protest about Diopeithes was particularly sharp.

The Halonnesos and Chersonese issues persuaded Philip to send new proposals to Athens. He claimed Halonnesos by right of conquest, but offered it to Athens as a gift; he offered a treaty to compensate the dispossessed Athenian cleruchs from Potidaea; he offered to join Athens in suppressing pirates; he suggested widening the 'Peace' to include other Greek cities; he offered to revive the alliance with Athens, which could, he suggested, bring great benefits to the city; and he offered to negotiate the settlement of other disputes.[24]

There was little here to persuade the Athenians that Philip was serious: the suggestions about Halonnesos and Potidaia involved Athens recognizing his possession of those places; the offer of joint anti-pirate patrols was understandably seen as an insult, particularly as Philip's navy was small and so Athens would do the work; the offer of negotiations implied that Athens' case, particularly in the Chersonese, was not just. The one hopeful proposal was for a widening of the peace treaty, but this could only be done in an atmosphere of mutual trust, which did not exist. Philip hardly expected Athens to accept these proposals, and the Athenians did not take them seriously, any more than Philip had taken seriously the Athenian demand that he 'return' Amphipolis. They seem a set of proposals aimed at neutral opinion, so that Philip could claim to be working for peace, whereas Athens' rejection could then be portrayed as obduracy. There were plenty of opportunities for negotiation if the Athenians wanted them but it was easy for the Athenians to knock each idea down as it was suggested. Meanwhile both sides were busily bolstering their general positions: Philip in Thrace, Athens in Greece.

Athens had already thwarted Philip in Akarnania and Megara; Corinth was probably inclining Athens' way as a result of Philip's apparent threat to Ambrakia; Athens had a firm grip on the Chersonese, thanks to Diopeithes. All these places were populous and martial and their alliance or friendship would certainly assist Athens against Philip. More important, from Athens' point of view, was Euboia. The aim of those who had led the secession from Athens' alliance in 348 had been to gather all the island cities into a league, an aim not realizable if Eretria and Oreus were closely aligned with Philip. The leader of the league movement, Kallias of Chalkis, had hoped for Philip's support, but the intervention of Macedonian forces in 343 had meant he could not get it: a disunited Euboia was more attractive to Philip than a strong league. Kallias had no better luck with Thebes, similarly more interested in dividing and ruling its neighbour.

Kallias, reluctantly no doubt, turned to Athens. He was clearly worried by Macedon's influence in the island; and here Athens was just as equally concerned. Kallias met with a display of Athenian statesmanship which is a credit to the city. A force was put together of Athenian and Megarian troops, which joined with forces from Chalkis to 'liberate' Oreus. This city lay just across the strait from Philip's Thessaly, and was the obvious landing place for Macedonian troops. Later in the year the same services were performed for Eretria. Kallias was then able to form his Euboian League, and Athens forbore to make any menacing moves aimed at recovering its control of the island. In return Kallias brought Chalkis and the league into an alliance with Athens.[25] Kallias also put his political weight behind the policy advocated by Demosthenes in the name of the freedom of the Greek cities from Macedonian domination. He could be the more persuasive in that role since he could claim that he had only just escaped from such domination himself.

Kallias and Demosthenes went on a diplomatic tour of the northern Peloponnese and across into Akarnania, returning to Athens with promises of troops or money from Megara, Achaia and Akarnania, to add to those the Athenians and Euboians could raise.[26] Demosthenes summoned a meeting of the anti-Philip coalition to Athens for spring 340, and persuaded the Athenian Assembly – by now largely convinced that he was right, and that his policies were bearing fruit – to send envoys seeking similar alliances and contributions to Rhodes and Chios in the eastern Aegean, to Perinthos, Selymbria and Byzantion in the Propontis, and to the Great King in Persepolis.[27]

If there is ever any doubt that Demosthenes had the Assembly in his grasp by now, these measures should be convincing. The Greek cities he visited were those whose 'rebellion' in 357 had broken the second Athenian Confederacy; real statesmanship was required to appeal to Chios and Rhodes. The appeal to the Great King was another example, for Athens prided herself on her long-standing opposition to Persian power and pretensions, and had rudely replied to his request for troops only a couple of years before. Philip's successful campaign in Thrace had alarmed all these targets of the Athenian embassies. Byzantion was already in dispute with Philip, while Perinthos was close to Heraion Teichos, attacked by Philip some years before. Even if the Great King was not willing to become involved directly, he had already helped Diopeithes with a subsidy,[28] and money was one of the main requirements of the allies.

Byzantion was the city most directly involved. It had exercised some sort of hegemony in the local waters in the Black Sea, and had profitable relations with one of the Thracian kings dispossessed by Philip and so was adversely affected by Philip's actions. Demosthenes visited the city in the autumn of 341 urging an alliance with Athens, but the Byzantines were not yet actually at war with Philip, though incidents had certainly occurred which would give either side an excuse for war if one was required.[29]

Philip sent an envoy to protest Diopeithes' actions, but the general locked him up, tortured him and then demanded 9 talents as a ransom. A Macedonian herald had also been kidnapped, and his dispatches were read out in the Athenian Assembly.[30] Diopeithes' raid and the Macedonian garrison in Kardia brought the conflict in the Chersonese as close to open warfare as could be conceived. All that was missing was a declaration. Neither side was yet ready for that: Athens' alliances were not yet firm; Philip was busy in Thrace.

In the spring of 340 both sides notched up the tension. An Athenian envoy set out on the long journey to Persepolis or Susa. The meeting of the Athenian allies that Demosthenes hoped for probably did not take place, but the alliances remained; the seceded members of the old Athenian League were certainly bothered by Philip's actions; Byzantion could keep them informed. In Thrace Philip decided he needed the use of a fleet in the Propontis if he was to exert real pressure on the cities. The problem was that an Athenian fleet, larger than his, was already in the Athenian harbours in the Chersonese. Philip seized the chance to send a clear message to Athens: he marched his army into the Athenian section of the Chersonese, down the west coast and out again along the east coast, escorting his fleet through the Hellespont into the Propontis along the way. The Athenian land forces, now commanded by the competent but less provocative Chares, did not move, nor did the Athenian fleet.[31] The Athenians knew full well that their fleet now blocked the seaward exit: Philip's fleet, they could argue, was now trapped.

Philip wished to ensure that the Greek cities did not interfere with his control of Thrace. This meant persuading Byzantion and Perinthos to remain neutral or accept his authority, perhaps by a more binding alliance than already existed. Encouraged no doubt by Demosthenes' visit in the autumn, and by Chares' presence nearby, but above all menaced by Philip's power, Perinthos and Byzantion also defied him. It became necessary, so Philip decided to use force.

He wrote again to Athens, justifying his actions in the Chersonese, listing the occasions when he claimed Athens had broken the 'Peace', and offering to have the differences between them judged by arbitration. He also sent a defiant challenge, claiming that the orators of the city were not speaking in the city's true interest. He can have had no hope that this would have any effect by now; and there was no possible arbitrator. The letter (which is more or less authentic, it seems) was mainly aimed at non-Athenian opinion, like the previous year's proposal to identify and settle differences. Philip was trying to show that the dispute was actually between Philip and Athens alone, and not between Philip and Athens and her allies. It had no visible effect.[32]

It was the difficulties Philip encountered in his campaign in 340 which had a real effect. From the Chersonese he moved to Perinthos and laid siege to the city. The citizens defended themselves with vigour and ingenuity; even when Philip's rams broke through the city wall, they fought on house by house. Athens did not intervene directly, but Philip's fleet was unable to blockade Perinthos' harbour, so maybe Athenian sea power was used to threaten the weaker fleet. The Perinthians were actively supported with supplies and troops from both Byzantion and the Persians across the sea, whence the satrap of Hellespontine Phrygia, Arsites, sent help.

The Great King was at last taking a hand. The progress of Philip's arms and power, and sentiment in Greece for a campaign of 'revenge' for the long-ago Persian invasions, were a clear threat. This was the first occasion when Philip could be seriously held up by a Persian intervention.

Philip, facing defeat, blamed others. He took half his army to attack Byzantion, assuming that the city was now poorly defended. He found he had to besiege it, and to besiege Selymbria as well. None of these sieges was successful, and in the midst of them Philip deliberately provoked Athens into declaring open war by seizing the fleet of ships carrying the corn exports from the Black Sea, which had gathered at the Bosporos waiting to be convoyed onwards by the Athenian fleet.[33]

When the news reached Athens, the Assembly met and accepted that the city was at war.[34] It scarcely made any difference. The sieges went on; the Athenians continued their search for allies. The 'war party' at Athens had gained their goal; the outcome was to be rather more than a war between the Macedonian kingdom and the city of the Athenians.

5

The conquest of Greece, 340–334 BC

Until 340, the work of Philip of Macedon had been essentially one of preserving and expanding his ancestral kingdom. He had expanded the area he ruled directly by three or four times, and had established a wide territory of subsidiary states around it, and it is quite possible to interpret his work as defending Macedon; from the sieges of Perinthos and Byzantion in 340 onwards, however, the story changes. Philip embarked instead on a wider programme of conquest, and his eventual aim was the conquest of Persia.

The conquest of Thrace made Macedon a larger state than any other in the Mediterranean area, apart from the Persian Empire, now his neighbour across the Straits. The attacks on the cities of the Straits brought Persia and Athens into an informal alliance with the cities against him. This combination proved to be too strong, even for him, and the open hostility of Persia was ominous. But it was first necessary to deal with Athens.

There is never any hint that Philip intended to 'destroy' Athens – in whatever sense that word can be understood – but any further work he was to undertake, in the Balkans, against Persia, anywhere, required at least Athenian neutrality. There is no reason to doubt that Philip had wanted Athens' alliance, just as there is no reason to doubt that large numbers of Athenians came to see him and his policies as a major threat to the city's independence and prosperity. The challenge he faced when war finally came was to avoid fighting Persia, and to fight Athens in such a way as to persuade the Athenians at the subsequent peace that he was still interested in the city's friendship and alliance. Here was a bigger challenge to Philip's statesmanship than anything he had undertaken so far.

The new war between Athens and Philip was essentially a continuation of their previous confrontation, and, as before, it remained unfought for some time. In the winter, perhaps in January, Philip withdrew from the sieges, all three cities untaken. He slipped his small fleet out of the Propontis, past the Athenian ships and through the Hellespont, and is said to have extracted his army by a false message designed to be intercepted by his enemies.[1] It seems likely that he then reduced the number of his enemies by making peace with Byzantion, necessarily followed by peace with the city's allies, at least Chios and Rhodes. This is a tribute to Philip's diplomatic skills, for the sieges had been unpleasant.[2] He marched his army home by way of the unconquered territory between the

Haemos Mountains and the Danube, beating first the Scythians in the Dobrudja area and then attacking the Triballi. This latter war was a near disaster. Philip was badly wounded and the army lost its booty.[3]

The retirement from the Straits mollified Persia; when Philip recovered, he had to organize the war in Greece. His route south was clear as far as Phokis, and there he had been concerned to promote a local recovery rather than leave the country as a rural and geopolitical nullity. The initial payment of the Phokian reparation had been delayed, then, after a couple of full payments of 60 talents, the rate was reduced. One of its cities, Elateia, was restored. This was done by permission of the Amphiktyony and Philip and the evidence is that the Phokians gave the credit to Philip. He had converted Phokis into an ally.[4]

The next country south of Phokis (separated from Thessaly only by Lokris and Malis) was Boiotia. Nikaia, the city commanding the northern entrance to Thermopylai, was held by a Macedonian garrison for a time, but the lessening of Phokian enmity led to this garrison being reduced. The Boiotians became alarmed, and, in the spring of 339, as Philip was returning to Macedon, the Thebans seized control of Nikaia, expelling the remaining Macedonians. The main route south from Thessaly towards Attika was blocked again.[5]

A quarrel developed between the city of Amphissa and the Delphian Amphiktyony. A fine was imposed on the city, which refused to pay.[6] The Athenians supported the Amphiktyons; the Boiotians, Amphissa. The dispute went forward to the spring meeting of the Amphiktyons in spring 339. By that time the war was dominating Greek minds, and it became clear that, as the cities of Greece lined up, Thebes' position was crucial. If Thebes and the Boiotian League remained true to the alliance with Philip he was guaranteed an easy passage to the borders of Attika; if Thebes remained neutral, the march was much more difficult, even impossible; but if Thebes joined Athens and its allies against Philip, the way was open for an allied victory.

The Theban leaders were as aware of these possibilities as Philip or any Athenian politician. The seizure of Nikaia was not necessarily a move against Macedon, but one which opened up the possibility of neutrality for Boiotia. If the Thebans could block Thermopylai, then all their options were open. It also allowed the Thebans to protect Amphissa from the army the Amphiktyons were about to send against that city.

The Amphiktyons had to consider more seriously how to enforce their will on Amphissa. To fight the Thebans was impossible with the few forces they had, so they turned to their most prominent member and elected Philip *hegemon*.[7] This cannot have been done entirely on the initiative of the Amphiktyons, for Philip must have been consulted in advance. It gave him a cloak of sacredness in his war – though few Greeks will have been taken in. His attacks on the Greek cities of Perinthos and Byzantion had been godsends to Athenian propaganda about defending Greek freedoms; fighting on behalf of Apollo went some way to counter that.

Fighting for Delphi in this case, however, might mean driving the Thebans into the arms of Athens. Philip suddenly, late in 339, marched south swiftly and unexpectedly, and it was not until the last day or two of his march that it became clear that he was not actually aiming at Amphissa. Ignoring both Nikaia and Thermopylai, he marched into Phokis and camped at Elateia, on the road towards Boiotia.[8]

There he stopped. Thebes was his ally still, though now uneasy about it. The Athenians thought the alliance held and that Philip's army would be on their borders in two or three days – Demosthenes' description of the Athenian reaction is one of his masterpieces. By stopping at Elateia, Philip gave the Boiotians time to consider their options and their response, but he also gave the Athenians time to put their case at Thebes. Both sides sent envoys to try to persuade the Boiotian leaders. Philip sent two Macedonians, some Thessalians, some Aitolians, and others from the Amphiktyons, a coalition of envoys. Athens sent Demosthenes, who could speak as the leader of an alliance comprising Euboia, Megara, the Akarnanians, Achaia and others.

Philip's men argued for the alliance, asking for Boiotian participation or free passage. Demosthenes argued for freedom and independence, and he was the more persuasive. Thebes voted to fight.[9] The Athenian army, already mobilized, at once marched through Boiotia to occupy blocking positions in front of Philip's army.[10]

Philip's policy and presumably his campaign plans were thus undone. He was unable to penetrate the defensive screen set up by the Athenian forces, soon joined by Boiotian troops. Winter was not a good time for campaigning, and a reckoning up of potentialities suggested that he would be outnumbered. He sent messages to his allies in the Peloponnese – Arcadians, Messenia, Argos – but they agreed a pact only to protect themselves from Sparta; they had no more wish than Athens or Thebes to see him supreme over the whole Greek peninsula; they responded with no more than good wishes,[11] but would at least prevent the Spartans from joining in. It was to be a fight between Athens and Thebes and their Greek allies and the Macedonian kingdom and its allies.

It was also a fight between a committee of Greek commanders and one man who had proved in the last 20 years that he was one of the great generals. Philip waited through the winter, overcoming we know not what logistical difficulties, and in the spring of 338 brought forward his full levy, Macedonians, Thessalians, sub-kings, sub-tribes, an infantry force of 30,000 or more and 2,000 cavalry. The allies gathered in the Athenian and the Boiotian levies, receiving contributions from Megara, Corinth, Achaia and Akarnania and hired more mercenaries, so that they probably had more infantry though fewer cavalry than Philip. Overall the two were about equal; the outcome would rest on training and generalship.

Philip surprised the mercenaries guarding the pass above Amphissa by a night march and a false message which deluded them.[12] This turned the allied line, and they fell back to a new position inside Boiotia, the Kephisos River on the right and the fortified town of Chaironeia on the left; Philip's army closed up to face them. There was no manoeuvring space, no outflanking possibilities. This was not Philip's favourite means of warfare, for though he had fought battles before, he much preferred manoeuvres, just as he preferred diplomacy to war. A battle between equal-sized armies was too chancy for an intelligent general to contemplate with equanimity. This was a situation brought about by his enemies; he had the better army, capable and trained, unlike the heterogeneous force of mainly amateur soldiers facing him, but this simple clash of spearmen was not the sort of fight where professionalism was much use.

The battle took place, therefore, by Philip's decision, though on ground chosen by the allies. The Greeks were on the defensive; it was up to him to attack. He made plans, which does not seem to have happened on the allied side. The allies expected to fight at push-of-pike until one side gave way; Philip intended to use stratagems, but above all to use his cavalry. For the crucial point of a pike battle came when one line broke, allowing the enemy to get among the soldiers, whose main weapon, a long spear, was useless in a close fight.

When the battle began, the Macedonian and Thessalian cavalry was kept back. Philip, in personal command on his right wing, brought his section of the phalanx into a slow retreat, forcing the Athenians facing him to advance. A gap appeared in the allied line as a result. Philip's retreat stopped, and he ordered a charge; into the gap rode the Macedonian and Thessalian cavalry, headed by the king's son Alexander. The allied troops could not stand, and the main part of the army fled; the Theban elite force, the Sacred Band, stood its ground and had to be destroyed to a man. Casualties were fairly heavy on both sides, but the allied army was broken beyond recovery. There was no rally until the fleeing troops reached Lebadeia, 10 km away. The Macedonians, perhaps because Alexander and the cavalry were preoccupied with the Sacred Band, did not in the event pursue.[13]

Philip negotiated even in victory. The alternative would have been a series of sieges of well-fortified cities, casualties, impoverishment, probable interventions by his northern enemies, or even the Persian Empire. The allies, so recently joined, separated. Athens and Thebes were treated differently and placed in situations where they would find it very difficult to cooperate again. Thebes had to accept a Macedonian garrison, those Boiotian cities destroyed by Thebes were restored, and an oligarchic council was put in control of the Boiotian League;[14] Theban influence was thereby drastically reduced. Athens lost its empire-cum-confederacy, including control of the Thracian Chersonese.[15] The other allied cities were also no doubt punished, but little is known of the terms they were given, though garrisons were imposed on Ambrakia and Corinth, as well as Thebes.[16]

It was not only in the peace terms that Thebes and Athens were separated. Philip's army camped in Boiotia for several weeks, but Attika was not touched; Boiotian prisoners had to be ransomed, Athenians were freed. Philip treated Athens, in other words, more as an equal than as a defeated enemy. The Athenian League and colonies might be eliminated, but the Athenian fleet was preserved, and the city's economic position was undamaged. Sensibly the Assembly had appreciated this, prompted by the orator Demades, one of the released prisoners. Thebes' reduction, the Macedonian garrison in the Cadmeia, and the Macedonian acquisition of the Thracian Chersonese, meant that Attika was exposed to Macedonian power without any hindrance, and the city's food lifeline was under Macedon's control. Athens may have been treated leniently, but was no longer a 'Great Power'. There was only one of those left in Greece now.

Philip's Peloponnesian alliances had been of little use in the final crisis. He took his army there and turned on Sparta, whose enmity had been the cause of his allies' inability to join him. He deprived the city of its geographical defences, and handed parts over to his unhelpful allies. They therefore gained a major stake in continuing to support him: Argos, the Arkadians and Messenia were all gainers, and had presumably supported the Macedonian invasion with troops, as had Elis, which gained no territory.[17] By reducing Sparta's potential for trouble, Philip had liberated his allies, and in future they might assist him in arms.

Late in 338, after all this had been done, Philip called a meeting of the Greek states at Corinth. He proposed a Common Peace, to include a mechanism by which such a peace could be maintained. Earlier peace settlements, going back to the King's Peace of 387, had all failed, since there was no way of preventing a breakdown; for when one city attacked another, there was no way to stop it. Now, of course, there was, in the form of the Macedonian army. This Common Peace would be enforceable; at the same time it institutionalized the Macedonian victory.

Early in 337 the 'League of Corinth', or 'Hellenic League', was formed. It would be out of character for Philip to have dictated the terms, but the delegates were naturally attentive to his requirements. There was a council, in permanent existence, and a *hegemon* to whom the council would pass its decisions for implementation; Philip was, of course, elected as the first *hegemon*. The members of the League were under an obligation to contribute troops when needed, as requested by the *hegemon*. One source claims that the total troops which could be levied amounted to 200,000 infantry and 15,000 cavalry, not counting the Macedonian army, an impossibly high total (though the forces engaged at the Battle of Chaironeia had been 60,000 foot and 5,000 horse).[18]

The purpose of this League was, ostensibly, to maintain the peace within

Greece which had been imposed by Philip after his victories over Thebes and Athens and Sparta, and Philip was tapping into a vein of Panhellenic sentiment which was repelled by the repeated Greek wars, as he must have known; no doubt he shared in it himself. But the first action of the council after electing Philip's *hegemon* was to appoint him commander-in-chief of the joint Macedonian-Hellenic League army of conquest against Persia.[19] This had presumably been his intention all along, but only after Chaironeia did he have the power and authority to invade the empire; his intention to do so is implicit in his treatment of Athens in the peace settlement.

The League could only be a short-term solution. It froze the situation of Greece into the position of 338/337. The possibilities of political change in Greece were reduced to the minimum, but this would require repeated applications of the council's mandate to enforce the no-change rule. Philip had enforced his supremacy repeatedly in Thessaly over a period of 15 years, and in Thrace he had only just begun to do so. There was no reason to believe that proud Greek cities with histories of independence and imperial victories like Thebes and Athens would accept the situation for long, and Sparta refused to have anything to do with the League. For Philip there were years ahead in which he would need to attend carefully to the continuing quarrels, disputes, arguments and rebellions in all the lands he had conquered.

This was not his intention and it is unlikely he was much concerned about controlling the League. There is no indication in his career that he thought in such long-term ways. The League was no more than a temporary solution to Greece's political problems. Instead he was going off to fight Persia. This could be one way to siphon Greek restlessness, and if he won Greek settlements in the conquered territory would do the same, as Isokrates had suggested, but it was a case of running hard to stand still; the issues of Greece and Thrace and the Balkans would need to be tackled properly eventually.

Persian disquiet at Greek developments will have been obvious; its likely reaction would be equally clear – intrigue in Greece, subsidies to Greek cities, recruitment of Greek soldiers, military preparations in its western provinces. Persian interventions at Perinthos, and possibly at Byzantion, Athenian requests for Persian help, Persian subsidies to Diopeithes, showed that the Great King was alert to the problem. Preparations to contest the coming invasion, however, were disrupted. In 338, Artaxerxes III was murdered on the orders of his vizier, Bagoas, who had been one of the commanders of the invasion of Egypt. Bagoas killed off all Artaxerxes' sons as well, except for Arses, who became the new Great King as Artaxerxes IV. Not surprisingly Arses and Bagoas could not work together, and soon Arses and all his sons were also murdered. A distant member of the royal family was placed on the throne as Dareios III. Well warned, Dareios murdered Bagoas.[20]

This dynastic crisis occupied the two years in which Philip conquered Greece, and its effects gave Philip a golden opportunity to mount an invasion, while Persia was in disarray. Philip's return to Macedon in the summer of 337, therefore, was only the preliminary to another war. He celebrated his victory, as usual, by getting married. For the first time he chose a Macedonian girl, Kleopatra, the daughter of one of his barons. This created a gaudy family row, which involved a drunken party, public insults, the exile of Philip's heir Alexander and his queen Olympias, and later a very public reconciliation. The villain of the piece, Attalos, Kleopatra's uncle, was eventually removed from the court: it all left an unpleasant legacy, which poisoned the atmosphere of the court.[21]

Beneath this court froth, preparations for the Persian expedition continued. At some point Philip conducted yet another invasion of Illyria, against a king called Pleurias, a swift reminder of his power, and a lesson not to do anything awkward during the Persian campaign.[22] This did not interfere with the Persian preparations; indeed, the forces he used could get some warlike practice, and a reminder that Macedon was capable of both expeditions simultaneously would be even better, and Philip would leave a competent defence force behind when he crossed to Asia.

An advance force went across into Asia in the spring of 336, 10,000 men commanded by Parmenion, to whom Attalos, the awkward uncle, was attached. Paced by a fleet along the coast, this force, mainly Macedonian but including some mercenaries, marched south as far as Ephesos. The coastal cities fell to the fleet, inland cities to the army; they were liberated from the Persian-imposed tyrants, and democracies established. At Ephesos the pro-Persian rulers were overthrown as Parmenion approached; the same had happened on Lesbos and possibly at Erythrai. Not far beyond Ephesos, at Magnesia, Parmenion's army encountered a force commanded by Memnon of Rhodes, which was too strong to be fought; perhaps Parmenion's instructions were not to get into a battle at all. This was, after all, essentially a strong reconnaissance, and Parmenion's army was not strong enough to begin a serious conquest. To have got as far as Ephesos was a good start, and he had flushed out an enemy force.[23]

The liberated thanked Philip by setting up altars to him – Zeus Philippios at Eresos in Lesbos, an altar in the temple of Artemis at Ephesos;[24] this was not worship of a divinity, but it was not far distant from it. Philip had a celebratory circular building constructed at Olympia to display statues of himself and his family;[25] it may be that another of Philip's ambitions was to have himself worshipped. It has indeed been argued that this was the purpose of his invasion of Persia, where he would become the new Great King, an absolute ruler, whose governmental system would then be applied in Macedon;[26] and presumably also in Greece. This seems rather far-fetched; it may have been the result of the conquest, but it was hardly the aim. To expect to impose absolutism on either Macedon or Greece would suggest an ignorance of the expected reaction impossible to believe of Philip. The worshipping of living men was not unknown in Greek cities (Philip had a cult in Amphipolis, according to a late source),[27] but it was not taken seriously by the Greeks, and it was completely unknown in Persia.

Arrangements for governing Macedon while he was on campaign were also needed. The pattern of his campaigns in the past would suggest that he intended to return to his kingdom regularly, probably each winter. The western border was a further difficulty. Olympias had fled to her brother Alexander, now king of the Molossi, during the domestic upheaval after Philip's latest marriage. Their son Alexander had left also, but he was persuaded to return. Olympias was too dangerous to be left to plot in Epirus, but Philip could not bring her back while he was married to his new bride (who gave birth to a daughter early in 336). Instead he neutralized Olympias by giving his own daughter Kleopatra (Alexander's sister) to Alexander of Epiros as his bride. Kleopatra was as strong-willed as anyone in that extraordinary family, and could be counted on to prevent her mother dominating her husband.

The marriage was arranged for the summer at Aigai, the old royal capital. Philip staged a great celebration for his daughter's marriage, celebrating as well his own achievements. In a procession of the Twelve Gods his statue was portrayed as the thirteenth figure. It was also a prediction of what he would achieve in Asia. This collection of past, present and future events is typical of the politician in Philip, who was a master at dealing with several issues at once, but it was, as more than one historian, ancient and modern, noticed, also a display of hubris unusual in the man.

During the celebrations of the marriage Philip was murdered. His assassin was Pausanias, a man who had a grievance against Attalos, the uncle of Philip's new queen, a grievance which Philip had refused to deal with. This was another layer of events at Aigai that day; one Philip had not taken into account. He died of this neglect. Pausanias ran off, but was chased and killed by members of Philip's bodyguard.[28]

Conspiracy immediately comes to mind, probably unnecessarily. Almost everyone of any note in Philip's family and court has come under suspicion, but the main accused are Alexander, Olympias, Antipater and perhaps Parmenion; and superficially plausible cases can be constructed against all of them. There is even one theory which sees a plot by men of Upper Macedon against domination from the original kingdom.[29] None of the theories stands up very well, and the most that can be said is that no one shed tears at the king's killing. Alexander and Antipater certainly reacted very quickly to proclaim the former as king, but Antipater at least understood the dangers of an interregnum, and Alexander soon showed that he understood the issue as well.

The fact is that the murderer was Pausanias, a man who had nursed a grievance for a year and had been unable to get redress. His abuser had been Attalos, who was away in Asia and was the uncle of Philip's new wife; Attalos was also the sworn enemy of Alexander. In Pausanias' grievance-filled mind, the only available man on whom he could gain his revenge was Philip, who had refused to take action. It cannot have been absent from Pausanias' mind that killing Philip would benefit Alexander; perhaps he expected to get away with it. The question of '*cui bono*' used to accuse Alexander, is, given Pausanias' state of mind, irrelevant.[30]

Philip's private life – if that term may be used for so public a man – was disputatious enough that his death in a private dispute is scarcely a surprise. Alexander established a firm grip on the kingdom from the start. He was supported by his father's most prominent commanders, Antipater and Parmenion, though he clearly felt he might face opposition. Antipater in fact stood up before the crowd in the theatre at Aigai, which had just witnessed Philip's murder, to praise Alexander, which speech in part resulted in Alexander's being acclaimed king there and then, the audience in the theatre acting as the Macedonian Assembly.[31] It was the first uncontested succession in Macedon for over a century.

Alexander was brought up in the Macedonian court. He had observed and learned from his father, commanded part of the army on the Thracian and Chaironeian campaigns, and acted in his father's place more than once in the past few years. He was intended by Philip as his successor from childhood, and the support of Antipater and Parmenion was clearly good enough for the Macedonians. Alexander, however, did have to work hard to make sure that nothing happened to displace him. His succession might be instant, but it was not without problems.

As the news of the death of the victorious king spread, Philip's painfully constructed empire began to break apart. Its personal basis became all too clear; the succession of a 20-year-old boy was assumed to be that of someone inexperienced and incompetent, and the history of the Macedonian royal family gave grounds for an assumption that there would be trouble. In fact the Macedonian kingdom was intact and still functioning. If Alexander lived – not a matter necessarily to be assumed – he had inherited his father's political base intact. It was the surrounding subjugated lands which became restless.

Alexander spent several months in Macedon ensuring that the kingdom functioned properly, and making quite sure that his kingship was not challenged. Two members of the Lynkestian royal family were executed at Philip's funeral for their involvement in his killing, as were two pages. Since another Lynkestian brother was not executed, there had clearly been an investigation, and those involved with the murderer had been identified. This, at least officially, was the limit of any conspiracy.[32]

Olympias was allowed to return from Epirus, but soon procured the murder

of her supplanter Kleopatra and her infant daughter.[33] This made it necessary
to eliminate Attalos, her vociferous uncle, and an agent was sent to the army in
Asia to do so: Parmenion made no objection, even though Attalos was his own
son-in-law: it was Attalos' boorishness which had disrupted the royal family, and
had caused Pausanias' grievance.[34] These killings are perhaps understandable, but
Alexander revealed an unpleasant streak of paranoia, which was to grow, when
he also ordered the murder of Amyntas, the son of Perdikkas III. Amyntas had
lived at Philip's court and had acted as his agent in some diplomatic dealings,
and was married to Kynnane, one of Philip's daughters. He may have been seen
as Philip's successor when Alexander went off to Illyria. Alexander certainly saw
him as a competitor for the kingship in the early uncertainty; his murder was a
pre-emptive move by the king in the long tradition of such killings within the
Macedonian royal family.[35]

This minor massacre cleared the air in Macedon, and Alexander felt secure
enough to look abroad, where movements of rebellion in the name of independence from Macedonian domination were stirring. Greece was potentially the
most powerful of the restless areas, and Thessaly had to be secured, for his father's
post as *archon* was now vacant. In the autumn Alexander set off southwards. A
group of Thessalians occupied the pass leading from Macedon, explaining that
they were discussing whether to admit him, implying that the elevation of an
archon was the business of the Thessalians. Alexander showed that he had his
father's military ingenuity by evading the block and appearing in strength in
Thessaly. He contacted Larissa, his father's old mainstay in Thessaly, first of all,
and then without difficulty was elected *archon*. From the Thessalian point of
view, it was a *coup d'état*.[36]

From Thessaly he marched to Thermopylai, where his father's presidency of
the Amphiktyonic Council was rapidly conferred on him, and then appeared
before Thebes even as the city was still wondering whether to rebel or not.
Philip's garrison on the Kadmeia had thereby served its purpose. Any other
tentative movements to 'rebel' faded away and at Corinth Alexander was chosen
as *hegemon* of the league in his father's place, and appointed commander in
chief of the expeditionary force against Persia: another *coup d'etat*.[37] The Greeks
had been overawed by his speed, but were not convinced of his staying power.
Alexander had to return north to attend to other threats, and his absence gave
the Greeks time to think longer about their situation.

Macedon's northern border needed attention. The Triballi were causing
trouble and others in Thrace were stirring. Alexander campaigned there in the
spring of 335, exhibiting the speed and ingenuity already seen in Greece. Once
the Triballi had been beaten and had surrendered, others succumbed as well.[38]
Once more the Macedonian writ ran through Thrace, but again it was scarcely
a definitive conquest. The news of the 'revolt' of the king of an Illyrian group

took Alexander across to the Adriatic side of the mountains, and another stirring display of military technique was followed by another victory.[39] These early campaigns of Alexander showed both his own natural facility for command, but also the sheer professionalism and flexibility of the army he had inherited. Passing defended passes, winning two battles, a river crossing by night, great speed, all showed that almost any military manoeuvre or display was within their joint capability.[40]

Alexander spent most of 335 in the north, and some of the cities in Greece became inspired to try to recover their freedom of action. The Great King, whose soldiers were successfully blocking further advances by Parmenion's army in Asia, sent money to persuade the Greeks to rebel.[41] Athens officially refused the money; Demosthenes took control of it, and disbursed it in part to the Thebans. He campaigned to persuade Athens to 'rebel', even announcing as fact a rumour that Alexander had died in the Triballian war.[42] The Thebans were the only people to take real measures, and the city rose against the Macedonian garrison, though other parts of Greece – Arkadia, the Aitolians and others – mobilized.[43] Alexander, learning of this after his defeat of Kleitos in Illyria, made one of his speedy marches and arrived in Boiotia before even rumours of his approach.[44]

He arrived as *hegemon* of the league, and required Thebes to submit to him in that office. He was joined by troops from other cities of Boiotia, who had unpleasant memories of Theban domination. He gave the Thebans the chance to ask forgiveness, which he promised, but inside the city those who advocated independence and freedom won the argument. They then lost the fight; Alexander's troops broke into and captured the city.[45]

The news of Alexander's arrival had deterred others who had intended to join the Thebans. Athens promised to do so, but did not; the Arkadians marched, but turned back; others made preliminary moves, and now sent apologies or, in the case of the Athenians, congratulations to Alexander. Alexander, as *hegemon*, convoked a meeting of the league to decide on the Thebes' punishment. The meeting was dominated by cities which had suffered at Theban hands over the past 40 years, and they voted, not surprisingly, for the destruction of the city, just as Thebes had destroyed them.[46]

The coalition which had been forming round Thebes and which collapsed because of Alexander's swift march and sudden arrival was in fact very like the League of Corinth without Macedonian participation. Aitolia, Boiotia, Athens, Elis, Argos and Arkadia in alliance were the larger part of Greece south of Thessaly. If such an alliance had proved durable, a true Common Peace might have resulted, but durability could only come at the expense of a constant state of hostility towards Macedon. Such a grouping would be unlikely to endure for more than a year or so – but that would have suited Persia.

This set of campaigns in the Balkans and Greece is generally seen as a dazzling precursor to Alexander's later career of Asian conquest. Politically, the core Macedonian kingdom remained loyal, as had the old hill kingdoms. Beyond these lands, Thrace, Greece, Illyria, Thessaly all wished to break free of Macedonian control. Only Alexander's speed and determination, and his army, held them. This general anti-Macedonian attitude is scarcely surprising. When Philip died, the political agreements he had made automatically ended. Alexander had to make new ones. At the same time, it is probable that, had he lived, Philip would have had to campaign to enforce his domination.

Alexander's victories meant that the attack on Persia would certainly take place, and he showed himself his father's son by determining to go off to war in the east as soon as possible. Philip had already conducted a survey of the military resources of the league, and now Alexander indicated who was to provide what. The mainland cities supplied hoplites and light-armed soldiers, totalling only 7,000 men, together with 600 cavalry. A total of 160 ships were called up, equipped and manned, which accounted for about another 32,000 men, mainly from Athens and the Aegean islands. This was a large force, roughly equal in total to the Macedonian contingent (which included contingents from the surrounding subject states).[47]

No Greek city was left without the means of self-defence, and the neighbours of Sparta were not called on to contribute at all; Sparta remained a danger to all the states round about and was soon in contact with the Great King. Similarly Macedon was left with enough forces to see off any serious attack, either from the Balkans or from Greece. It was left under the viceroyalty of Antipater, who had more trouble from Olympias than he had from his neighbours. Alexander took a force of over 80,000 men, cavalry, infantry and sailors, to his Persian War.

In Macedon there was some discussion of the folly of the king in going off to war without leaving an heir to succeed him if he were killed.[48] Parmenion, who had returned from Asia during the Theban emergency, is said to have advised the king to marry and have a son before he set off (but Parmenion is cast by the ancient historians in this role so often as to invite suspicion). In fact Alexander had had time to do that and still set off in 334. He did not, and good reasons can be conjectured. His choice of wife would be contentious, as his father's choice of Kleopatra had been; Macedonian men did not usually marry as young as he was; above all, he probably did not want to. His father's marital career, and the confusion it had surely caused in the royal household, would deter any man from marriage. But it is also probable that he did not greatly care what happened to Macedon if he died. He certainly never showed any wish to return to it, and was careless of the place even as he lay dying.

The invasion of Asia took place in spring 334, two years later than originally planned. The succession crisis at Persepolis had prevented the Great King from doing much to hinder Philip and Alexander but the Persian commanders in Asia

Minor were able to make preparations. The invasion was in no sense a surprise: several contingents of Greek envoys were at the royal court, from Thebes, Athens and Sparta, and the recruitment of Greek mercenary soldiers had been intensive – there were many more Greeks in Persian service than in Alexander's. A revolt in Egypt in 337–336 had not helped, but it was suppressed quickly enough. Philip's advance force was driven back to the Hellespont, holding on to only Abydos and Rhoetion. Parmenion was in Macedon during 335, and he may have taken some men away, but the Greek mercenary general Memnon had been more than equal to Parmenion as a general, which means that Memnon was a very good commander indeed. The Persian defence was to be commanded by the satraps of the threatened provinces, and they had collected a considerable army of 20,000 cavalry, a compact force of 6,000 Greek mercenaries, and a large number of local infantry levies, who were of little use.[49]

Alexander sent his army to land at Abydos, while he went across near Troy, sacrificing before, during and after the crossing, and hurling a spear ashore as a symbolic conquest.[50] His first objectives were the Greek cities of the Aegean coast which Parmenion had visited two years before, but first he had to eliminate the threat posed by the army of the satraps which had gathered to the east of the landing places. At least three satraps – Arsites of Hellespontine Phrygia, Spithridates of Lydia/Ionia and Arsames of Kilikia – brought up their forces. Memnon of Rhodes commanded the Greek mercenaries. He is said to have advocated withdrawing and destroying the local resources, which armchair strategists afterwards pronounced the best strategy; it was rejected by the satraps, for it would only drive the local population into Alexander's arms. Their job was to protect as well as rule their provinces, not destroy them.[51]

Had Alexander marched south, this force could have followed him and cut him off from the Hellespont and his communications; he must have expected to have to besiege one or more of the cities, and the Persian fleet was on its way into the Aegean. He might find himself attacked by two land armies and by the fleet all at once.

The satrapal army was therefore Alexander's first target. He marched east to find it, and defeated it decisively at the Granikos River. The Persian commanders placed the Greek phalanx behind the cavalry, so the fight was between the cavalry forces. The Macedonians and Thessalians proved to be better in battle than the Persians, above all because of their discipline. As the Persian cavalry survivors broke and fled, Alexander turned on the Greek mercenary infantry. They fought hard, outnumbered by at least two to one and surrounded. Only 2,000 survived; these surrendered, and were sent in chains to labour in Macedonia. Alexander may have felt they were traitors to his cause, but he also knew full well that Greek soldiers alone would provide the infantry backbone for any Persian army. They had to be removed wherever they were encountered.[52]

The Persian survivors scattered. Most of the commanders had been killed, and Arsites committed suicide. Alexander sent the booty to Greece to advertise his success. A detachment occupied Arsites' government centre, the town of Daskyleion, and a Macedonian from Elimaia, Kalas, was appointed satrap.[53] This might indicate that it was Alexander's plan to take over the empire as a going concern; more likely it was a temporary measure to ensure the continuation of settled government in his rear as he marched away. Whatever plans he had for the empire, it was clearly premature to implement them when he had beaten only a local detachment of the Persian forces at the very edge of the empire. He constituted Ilion as a Greek city and remitted its taxes, while also maintaining the Persian administration at Daskyleion, and so he was appealing to Greeks of Asia. The problem of governing his conquests was thus encountered already.

The main army marched south along the coast. Parmenion had collected rapid civic submissions two years before, and this happened again. Without hindrance, Alexander reached Sardis, the main Persian administrative centre in western Asia Minor. The commander surrendered the citadel and the treasure, the satrap having died at Granikos. Alexander appointed another satrap, Asander, brother of Parmenion, for Lydia, and left a contingent of Argives as a new garrison. The Greeks of the league forces were scarcely being used, except as auxiliaries.[54] Ephesos had surrendered to Parmenion two years before, but was retaken by Memnon. The result was internal revolution. A spate of revenge killings escalated to such an extent that Alexander had to step in to enforce order.[55] Detachments accepted the surrenders of other cities.

Only Miletos was the scene of any resistance, partly because of the proximity of the Persian fleet. The Greek fleet blocked the narrow harbour entrance, isolating the city which was then taken by assault.[56] This was the only occasion when Alexander had been able to use his fleet in warfare, and, having control of western Asia Minor coast, he was not in need of supplies from Greece. He did need money, however, for his land army was very expensive, so he disbanded the fleet, thereby saving money.[57] This was rather premature, for he could have used it to advantage at the next hold-up. Marching south he met one more resisting city, Halikarnassos, which he besieged in a fairly leisurely fashion through the summer and autumn of 334. When the city finally fell he had cleared the Aegean coast.[58]

The route of conquest Alexander had followed is distinctly odd. Partly, of course, it was intended, like his move against the satrapal army, to clear enemies from behind him, though the presence of the Persian fleet at large in the Aegean rather negated that, and Halikarnassos could have been blockaded by land. The conquest route was thus aimed to gather up and liberate the Greek cities. After the victory at the Granikos River, he sent a trophy to Athens with the inscription that it was the result of a victory by Alexander and the Greeks, and there was certainly a good deal of interest and enthusiasm in Greece in his progress.

The Greek cities of Asia, in the propaganda of the anti-Persians, were groaning under Persian rule. If Alexander was thus leading a campaign to liberate them and to gain revenge for past Persian attacks on Greece and the oppression of Greek cities, he had to take the cities, including Halikarnassos, and establish democracies where the Persians had favoured tyrannies or oligarchies. Whether the cities were then enrolled in the League of Corinth is not known. There is no evidence that they were, but it would not be surprising if it happened. Some island states – Mitylene, Samos, Chios, and so on – were certainly brought into the league.[59] Either way, for the first time all the ancient Greek cities, in Greece, Asia, and the islands (with the exception of Sparta and Crete) were united under one rule.

The murder of Philip had only delayed the conquest of all Greece for a year or so. In the propaganda of the war, the main work was now accomplished, for the Persian war had begun with a campaign of conquest along the Asian coast. It was, of course, impossible to stop now, if only because any Persian reply would leave Alexander's cities vulnerable to attack from inland. But from now on the propaganda of 'liberation' rang hollow, and revenge was the motive. Insofar as either motive was actually believed by the Macedonians (who had not been harmed by the Persian invasions), they were both superseded by the desire for conquest and riches. Isokrates had distinguished three possible conquests: the Greek cities, Asia Minor 'from Cilicia to the Halys', and the whole empire. The first was accomplished, and the second at least was necessary. But from now on it was a different war.

6

The great campaign, 334–325 BC

For nine years after his capture of Halikarnassos, Alexander marched about the Persian Empire and its neighbours, fully occupied with military matters. The administration of his conquests was left to the satraps he appointed; some were incompetent or venal; others were killed in quarrels and rebellions. It was clearly no more than a stopgap.

Alexander appointed satraps in Hellespontine Phrygia and Lydia, but in Karia he reappointed the former Persian satrap, the local Queen Ada.[1] He was faced with the problem that the empire he was invading required a large number of administrators. He had also appointed garrison commanders and financial officers at Sardis,[2] and so far had only dealt with the fringe of the empire. He did not have enough skilled and trustworthy manpower to leave men behind in administrative roles on such a scale throughout the empire.

He could not ignore the fact that this was enemy territory while the Great King lived and ruled. Garrisons were needed to control the conquests, and detachments had to deal with outlying areas. Few commanders could be allowed to be detached to such tasks. Alexander had used Parmenion in that role at Daskyleion and in Ionia. These conquests were in territory largely friendly, where the Greek cities could be expected to remain cooperative, but even there he had to leave occasional garrisons.

He surely realized from the start that he was dealing with an extent of territory with which no Greek or Macedonian had ever yet had to cope; none seems to have had any idea of its size.[3] Its size began to become clear to his army during the winter of 334/333. Alexander sent a detachment, under Parmenion, inland by way of Sardis into Phrygia with the heavy equipment. He took another section through Lykia and Pamphylia himself, in one of his less glorious campaigns. In Pamphylia he was defied at three separate cities, and only at one of these did he prevail. He left some troops in a garrison (at Side), and appointed one of his closest friends, Nearchos of Crete, as satrap of both Lykia and Pamphylia.[4]

In this case he combined two areas under one man, and again on a larger scale in the Anatolian interior. After dropping off a force to besiege Kelainai, the Phrygian satrapal centre, he camped at Gordion, where Parmenion rejoined. He left one of his father's contemporaries, Antigonus the One-Eyed, as satrap of Phrygia, a huge area with indefinite boundaries. He had very few troops, and his first task was to gain the surrender of the Persian force holding Kelainai, which became his administrative centre; the surrendered troops, Carians and Greek mercenaries, were recruited into his force, and others were recruited locally.[5] Alexander received the formal surrender of the Paphlagonians on the north coast, and of the Kappadokians further east in the interior; Kalas, the satrap of Hellespontine Phrygia, was assigned to Paphlagonia;[6] a man called Sabiktas is said to have been made satrap of Kappadokia – he is never heard of again, and may not even have existed.[7]

The Great King appointed Memnon as overall commander in the west after the Granikos defeat. Now he was using the Persian fleet to begin the process of undoing Alexander's conquest of the Asian coast. He gained control at Kos, Chios and Samos, perhaps of Miletos, and laid siege to Mitylene on Lesbos. His agents were active in Greece, meeting with a favourable but cautious response. Memnon died at Mitylene and was eventually succeeded by his nephew Pharnabazos, but he was ordered to send his mercenaries to the king. Alexander had called Dareios' Aegean bluff, and moved on eastwards rather than turning west to deal with Memnon: Dareios was outbluffed.[8]

Alexander marched swiftly from Gordion to Kilikia and turned south towards Syria, only to be surprised by the full Persian royal army under the Dareios' personal command. He had marched up from Babylon and got across Alexander's rearward communications by crossing the Amanus Mountains. Strategically the Persians had trapped Alexander, who had to reverse his march, deploy his army in a narrow plain, and devise a way of using his battle-winning combination of hoplite infantry and disciplined cavalry on a battlefield which stretched up a mountainside. He set his phalanx to attack the Greek mercenaries, but concentrated much of his cavalry on the hillside. Close to the sea the Thessalian cavalry alone faced the main force of the Persian horse. Alexander commanded the spearhead of the attack directed at Dareios. The Thessalians were driven back; the phalanx nearly lost cohesion crossing the stream between the armies; Alexander's charge broke the Persian left; Dareios fled to avoid capture. Alexander kept control of his men and turned them seaward to help his phalanx. This, rather than Dareios' flight, was the decisive move, for the Persian mercenary phalanx, taken in flank, now collapsed. A general flight followed, with much killing.[9]

Dareios withdrew towards his main base in Babylonia. Most surviving Persians withdrew east with him, but others moved north, and still others went south. Amyntas, son of Antiochos, a Macedonian enemy of Alexander's, took 4,000 mercenaries to Tripolis, then to Cyprus, where he collected more troops and went on to Egypt. He claimed to have Dareios' commission as satrap, but soon outstayed his welcome; he and most of his men were killed by Mazakes, the Persian governor.[10]

Alexander moved south from the battlefield, received the submissions of the Phoenician cities of Arados and Sidon, but was held up by determined resistance at Tyre. Meanwhile a substantial detachment of the Persian survivors moved into Anatolia, recruited Paphlagonians and Kappadokians – so much for their submission and for their new satraps – and headed for Sardis. This was the political centre from which western Asia Minor had been governed for three centuries, the main route centre and the site of the treasury. Its capture would destroy the whole Macedonian governing system in Anatolia, such as it was, and contact made with Pharnabazos and the Persian fleet, possibly with Sparta and Greece, while the Greek cities of the Aegean Coast would have again come under immediate threat. This was a major emergency.[11]

The Persian strategy was apparently designed to isolate at Tyre while Asia Minor was reconquered. Egypt and southern Palestine were held, and the local inhabitants of Palestine and the Lebanese mountains were stirred up to attack his besieging forces. Dareios gathered a new army to fight him, and the fleet operated in the Aegean and Greece.

Coordination of all these was the real problem. The capture of the Phoenician cities caused the fleet, which was mainly composed of Phoenician ships, to break up. The ships of the captured cities joined Alexander, as did those from Cyprus.[12] In Asia Minor the satrap Antigonos proved to be a strategist of Philip's stature. He and Kalas joined forces, and the satrap Balakros came up from Kilikia, no doubt on Alexander's urging. The Persian attack came along three separate roads, the Royal Road in the centre, and roads parallel to it to the north and south; Antigonos used his interior lines of communication to defeat the Persian attacks separately.[13]

The siege at Tyre was thus a central event in the general strategic development of the war. It was also a major test of the Macedonian army and its commander. Besieging an island without command of the sea was, to say the least, difficult. It was not possible to leave the city untaken behind him while the rest of the fighting was in the balance. The result was determined by the arrival of ships deserting from the Persian fleet. Alexander was then able to conduct a regular siege of the island, constructing a great mole to reach it. It took six months or more, but by the time he took the city, amid hideous scenes of massacre and destruction, the crises in Asia Minor and the Aegean were over.[14]

Diplomatic exchanges accompanied all this: first an exchange of letters after Issos, then an offer by Dareios to cede part of the empire, possibly from the Euphrates to the Aegean, and the offer of 10,000 talents, ransom for Dareios' family, captured after Issos. Alexander was now compelled to reveal his overall purpose, since Parmenion (and perhaps others of the Companions) was in favour of acceptance. Alexander replied by claiming the kingship of the whole empire. This may have been simply defiance in the face of the several dangers the Macedonians faced at the time, but Alexander's appetite had probably grown as he kept winning.[15]

Dareios' strategy had failed by the midsummer of 332, but another long siege at Gaza delayed Alexander in the west. Most of 332 was occupied by the conquest of Syria and Palestine. At Gaza, Alexander sacked the city and the population was treated with great cruelty.[16] He finally reached Egypt late in 332. Garrisons were left in north Syria and Kilikia (at Soli and near Issos)[17] and others surely at Tyre and Gaza. A satrap, Menon, was appointed for Syria; when the governor of Palestine was killed in a local revolt, Menon's area was extended.[18]

These detachments, and the casualties the army suffered at Issos, Tyre and Gaza, plus the usual wear and tear of an army on the march, threatened to reduce the army's size drastically. Already from Gordion Alexander had ordered up 4,000 more Macedonians, who reached him at Sidon, and 4,000 more arrived during the siege at Tyre.[19] Most of these reinforcements came from Macedon, others from Greece. He had now given up massacring Greek mercenaries in favour of recruiting them. He left the garrison of 4,000 men in Egypt, so when he marched out of Egypt the army was about the same size as when he first met a Persian army at the Granikos.

The army spent the winter of 332–331 in Egypt. Alexander organized its government, first being crowned as pharaoh. The Egyptians, who had always detested Persian rule, welcomed him, but so did the Persian governor, who had no force strong enough to resist him. Governing authority in notably wealthy Egypt was carefully divided (as at Sardis) between a governor, a financial official and several military and naval commanders. This division of responsibilities did not actually work, for the tax collector Kleomenes of Naukratis was able to dominate the whole administration by his control of finances. He was also clever enough to keep on Alexander's good side, in part because he only wanted to get rich rather than to amass political power. He pushed on a project of the king's to develop a new city at the mouth of the Nile, where Alexander personally laid out the main lines of the city; Kleomenes, however, did not make as much progress as he claimed. Alexander also paid a visit to the Temple of Ammon at Siwah in the desert, an experience which affected him strongly, enhancing his belief in his own abilities.[20]

Dareios spent the year after Issos gathering a bigger army than before, and in preparing a battlefield. To defeat Alexander's army was to win the war, so he waited for the Macedonian attack. He sent more money to Greece, with the intention of raising a rebellion in Alexander's rear. It was the same strategy as before; as before, Alexander ignored it.

A rising in Greece was quite likely. Antipater, having sent at least 12,000 reinforcements to Alexander during 332, was clearly under strain. The governor of Thrace, Memnon, instigated a rising, for no known purpose; Antipater marched with his full force into Thrace to suppress it, for if a full-scale war developed, Macedon was in danger. He calmed Memnon with the promise that he would remain as governor,[21] which suggests it was not a rebellion by the Thracians but an internal Macedonian dispute.

Antipater's march into Thrace triggered a declaration of war by Sparta. King Agis III had made preliminary diplomatic contacts and recruited troops, financed by money from Pharnabazos. He hired 10,000 mercenaries, some of them survivors of Issos, mobilized Sparta's army, and defeated a Macedonian force in the Peloponnese. Other risings, in Elis, Achaea and parts of Arkadia, followed. These were the places which tentatively moved to assist Thebes in 335. This all took place more or less at the time Alexander was expected to meet Dareios in battle; coordination was surely intended.

Alexander was told of this war long after his victory over Dareios at Gaugamela in October 331, so the coordination was unsuccessful, since real coordination required that he be distracted at the time of the battle. From Dareios' point of view, Agis' war needed to occur before he fought Alexander; no doubt Agis did not see it that way. Antipater was apparently not strong enough to reply to Agis at once, quite apart from the Thracian entanglement, but Agis' success was very limited even so. Messenia and Argos were implacably hostile, Athens stayed loyal throughout, and Agis had to besiege the Arkadian city of Megalopolis.[22] This may have been a mistake, but it would have been a bigger mistake to leave a major hostile state in arms behind him. Antipater could therefore bide his time.

Alexander marched east from Syria in September, and met Dareios' army early in October. The Macedonian/Greek army was outnumbered, perhaps by five to one, but once again Alexander's disciplined troops were more than a match for the numerous but individualistic Iranian horsemen and the undisciplined peasant recruits. He deployed his forces defensively, but used his own horsemen to attack directly at Dareios in his command chariot. It was a very close fight, for the Macedonian defences were breaking even as Alexander's attack succeeded. Dareios' personal defeat again caused his army to break up, and this time substantial Persian forces gave up the fight altogether. He had done this at a remarkably low cost to his own army.[23]

Alexander was now in territory largely unknown to the Greeks, much of it hostile in the way none of his conquests so far had been. He was welcomed at Babylon, but it had to be garrisoned, then the Persian imperial centres at Persepolis and Susa were occupied. Part of the palace at Persepolis was burnt in a wild celebration, but a garrison had to be left there, and another at Susa. These three places absorbed 10,000 men, one-fifth of Alexander's entire army. He received reinforcements sufficient to keep his army up to strength, but Dareios was not finished, nor had the real centre of power of the empire, Media, been reached.[24] With Susa and Persepolis Alexander acquired imperial treasuries, gold, silver, precious cloths, utensils in precious metals, the loot of an empire. At Susa he acquired over 50,000 talents of gold and silver, at Persepolis over twice as much.[25] Alexander was generous with gifts, as a Macedonian king should be.

The problem of Agis, when Alexander finally heard about it, was dealt with by sending Antipater money to pay for mercenaries to supplement his Macedonian forces.[26] In the spring of 330, while Alexander was at Persepolis, and long after the decisive battle in Mesopotamia, Antipater marched south into Greece with a force said to number 40,000 soldiers. He had recruited extensively among his Balkan neighbours and the Greek mercenary markets, and had contingents from the league cities.[27] Alexander's fleet, now including 600 Phoenician and Cypriot ships – mostly the same ships which had campaigned for Persia earlier – allowed him to blockade the Spartan coasts and sever communications with Crete, the main source of Agis' mercenaries.[28]

Therefore two mainly Greek armies met in battle near Megalopolis. Antipater also had his Macedonians, to whom the credit is normally given for the victory, though without any detailed evidence. The battle was an old-style Greek hoplite encounter, nasty and bloody, with almost 10,000 killed, including Agis. This result is an indirect tribute to the military skills of Philip and Alexander, none of whose battles was anything near as sanguinary.[29]

Alexander had to face two more extremely costly campaigns, in Baktria and in India. He marched to Ekbatana, the Median capital, in summer 330, and received there a reinforcement of 6,000 Greek soldiers, sent out after the defeat of Agis. He took the opportunity to reorganize his army. The contingents of the Greek cities – the league forces – were now dismissed with thanks and a fat bonus, and invited to re-enlist as mercenaries for another fat bonus. Many elected to go home, their pay and bonuses no doubt supplemented by considerable loot.[30]

Alexander, now immensely rich, could afford to employ all the mercenaries he could find, but it was the knowledge that Antipater had prevailed over Agis which allowed him to let the Greek forces go. It was a pleasant way of thanking the Greek cities for their loyalty to the league; he had already released some Athenians he had been holding prisoner. The league council had met to consider the punishment of those league members who had joined Agis, and had referred the matter to Alexander, who was lenient. Sparta had to discharge its mercenaries and surrender 50 hostages; its losses in the fighting meant that it was crippled as a military power anyway for the foreseeable future, so there was little to gain by greater severity. It was not technically in rebellion, never having joined the league. The league system had worked, both in Greece and in Asia.[31]

Dareios retreated to Ekbatana after the defeat at Gaugamela. He gathered substantial forces, but not enough to face the Macedonian army, and few reinforcements were forthcoming. When Alexander approached, he retreated eastwards, and Alexander pursued him across northern Iran. Dareios was deserted by his remaining troops, except for the Greek mercenaries, and was murdered by Bessos, the satrap of Baktria, and the *chiliarchos* (chief administrator) Nabarzanes.[32]

Alexander's army moved forward by stages into eastern Iran, but with Dareios' death, tensions developed among the Macedonian officers, some of whom developed serious doubts as to his purpose. Since Babylon, he had taken to wearing Persian dress; he had appointed Persians as satraps, and he had Persians advising him. Their administrative expertise and their family connections made them useful.[33] The disquiet of the Macedonians grew and emerged as plots, drunken brawls and philosophical disputes. In one plot Philotas, son of the great general Parmenion, was marginally involved; both he and his father were thereupon killed. A drunken argument saw Alexander murder Kleitos the Black, who had saved his life at the Granikos. The court historian Kallisthenes insulted the king and was punished.[34]

These plots, insofar as they were serious, were part of the atmosphere of Alexander's court, where his accession had been accompanied by the killing of suspect men, relatives and enemies; others had been eliminated on suspicion during the campaign.[35] Alexander was alert always to possible plots, and was always prepared to kill pre-emptively: dead men don't plot. But in eastern Iran the threat became bigger and worse.

The uncertainty at the root of the Macedonians' mood lay in Alexander's intentions, an uncertainty which was probably present in the king's mind also. The men who set out from Macedonia in 334 had hardly expected that four years later they would be in eastern Iran. Alexander had no thought-out plans for the lands he conquered at any stage before the last year or so of his life. He was, like his father, no more than a grand opportunist. Appointing satraps, Macedonian or Persian, to the old Persian administrative regions was a temporary measure.

He may have aimed simply to become a Macedonian version of the Great King; it was what he eventually tried to be, but an empire from the Adriatic to the Indus could not be ruled from one corner, Macedon. The Persians held the empire together by recruiting other Iranians, Medians, Baktrians, Arachosians, to assist them in governing, and had conciliated the great subordinate groups – Phoenicians, Babylonians, Greeks – by letting them alone as long as they paid their taxes. The Macedonians could not rule the empire themselves, not even with Greek help. Their land was too remote from the great population centres in Babylonia, Media, Egypt and Baktria, and the kingdom was too administratively undeveloped to cope. It did not have the bureaucratic manpower, nor did its people have the necessary skills or mindset to provide a government for the empire.

The exuberant Macedonian invaders revelled in their new wealth, and Alexander was extravagantly generous with his new riches. Above all, Alexander was enjoying his life as a conqueror too much to be able to attend to such mundane and routine matters as administration and government. At times he seems to have gone campaigning to avoid such chores. He had left Macedon without providing an heir, and had milked it of manpower to conquer Persia; in the empire he was moving from challenge to challenge without providing a real government for it other than a temporary continuation of the old system; he even invented adventures, for he is repeatedly recorded as doing something because he strongly wished to do so.[36] This careless, living-for-the-moment attitude fed the soldiers' unease. He became angry when challenged over philosophical issues of government because he had no real philosophical basis for his actions.

The alternatives were awkward. In theory, Alexander could take the army and his riches home, leaving Asia in chaos; or he could annex just part of the empire – as far as the Halys River, or as far as the Euphrates, were suggestions already made; or he could take over as Great King. The first was unthinkable; the second unlikely since Alexander was already in eastern Iran; the third involved keeping the army with him, recruiting Asians to replace them, or both. The Macedonian lords no doubt preferred the last alternative, but the rank-and-file, who had left families at home and had taken the propaganda line that the war was one of revenge for past Persian attacks on Greece, saw no reason not to go home.

Alexander was temporarily rescued from the problem by Bessos, who had himself proclaimed Great King in succession to Dareios.[37] The war developed into a long series of extremely difficult campaigns. Bessos and his associates aimed to recover the whole Persian Empire, and he recruited a formidable force. He was quickly outmanoeuvred, captured and killed, but the war went on under the leadership of Spitamenes, a prominent lord in Sogdiana, north of Baktria. He recruited help from nomads beyond the northern border, and successfully lengthened the war for another year. He was Alexander's most skilful enemy, and only his death ended the fighting. A series of minor campaigns, notably the need to capture several rock-fortresses, followed. Alexander's marriage to Roxane, daughter of Oxyartes, the lord of one of these fortresses, was clearly designed as a conciliatory gesture.[38]

The human cost of this war was enormous. Alexander lost at least 7,000 of his soldiers; Baktrian and Sogdian deaths were at least ten and perhaps 20 times that.[39] The conquered land had to be held, because it was so disturbed and because Alexander intended to move on still further east, and could not allow it to erupt again in his rear. A large number of Baktrian and Sogdian soldiers were recruited to reinforce his army. Well over 30,000 men were thereby removed from their homelands and unlikely to rebel. Then Alexander left a large garrison behind, '10,000' infantry and 3,500 cavalry in Sogdia. The numbers are suspiciously round, but '10,000' clearly implies a large number of men.[40]

A considerable number of 'settlers' remained, some organized in cities. The number of cities Alexander founded has been greatly exaggerated in later sources;

it was a mark of civic pride in later centuries to claim Alexander as founder. Of those for which he was really responsible, all except Alexandria by Egypt and Boukephala in India were established in eastern Iran. Their basic purpose was to act as large garrisons, fortified centres of government, to magnify the effects of the conquest.[41] These foundations, fortifications, shifting of populations, killing, and recruiting, the deaths of Dareios and Bessos, convinced most men that the Persian Empire was not revivable. On the other hand, there is a good deal of evidence that there were local movements aimed at escaping Macedonian rule.

Alexander marched off on a new campaign, into India. This can only be described as escapism. The difficulty of the Baktrian campaign, and the plots and arguments in the high command, were indications that serious work needed to be done to order and organize his new empire. It cannot be argued that the conquest of India was necessary. The Indus Valley had certainly been part of the Persian Empire long before, but it had been independent for some time, and the only Indian troops Alexander had faced so far had been mercenaries.[42] A few recalcitrant Persians, such as Barsaentes, the former satrap of Arachosia, had escaped into India, but they had little effect. Alexander's motives for this invasion were pathetic: to see the place and emulate the mythical journeys of the god Dionysos, who was 'discovered' to have journeyed there, and to conquer the last vestige of the defunct Akhaimenid Empire.

It was as difficult a campaign as Baktria, a good deal less necessary, and even nastier. The soldiers, by now not just Macedonians and Greeks, but with a strong Iranian and Baktrian contingent as well, faced tough and determined opposition from a sequence of militant states and peoples. They fought soldiers armed with frightening new weapons, such as war elephants, scarcely met with before. In the monsoon season they sickened, their weapons corroded, and their clothing and equipment rotted. The complete absence of any evidence of Persian authority destroyed the idea of completing the conquest of the empire. At last, at the Hyphasis River, faced by another long march and then an attack on a new empire (Magadha), even Alexander could not get the army to go on. He sulked in his tent for several days, a tactic which had worked with the army before but which failed this time. A face-saving soothsayer got him out of the impasse, and the army turned south.[43]

In this 'the army' meant the Macedonians. They were outnumbered substantially by other soldiers by this time, but it was always with the Macedonians that the king negotiated, with the senior officers or with the ordinary soldiers in a public meeting. It was a military version of Macedonian society that was conquering the Persian Empire, and it was largely for the benefit of Macedon that these troops believed the campaign was being conducted. It is a measure of Alexander's failure to convince his army of the reality of empire that after eight years of marching, fighting and conquest, the soldiers still believed this. To them it was still a long raid for booty, after which they would go home rich. But with an empire to run, Alexander could not let them go home.

Alexander set the army to march down the Indus Valley to the ocean, even though he had agreed that they were to go home. He could have returned by the Khyber Pass, as he had arrived, or by one of the other passes into Afghanistan – one contingent under Krateros was sent by way of Arachosia to suppress dissent there.[44] To take the whole army that way might suggest defeat – which he felt he had suffered – at his own army's hands. The result was that the men, more or less willing to indulge him now that he had agreed to return, believing they were going home, and in complete ignorance of the distances involved, were reluctant to do any fighting. Alexander insisted; receiving yet another wound in a rash attack on a city his troops had been slow to assault.[45] The army, and perhaps Alexander himself, turned savage, and the Indus campaign is a foul record of killing and destruction.[46]

Alexander left garrisons of troops scattered the length of the Indus River, supervised by two satraps and by several of the Indian kings whom he had defeated and then made into subsidiary allies. He constructed ships to sail down the river, and more ships to sail the ocean when he reached it. A detachment went west by sea under Nearchos; Alexander took the rest on a march along the Gedrosian coast, presumably in ignorance of the fact that it was desert; a third detachment under Leonnatos marched by an inland route.[47]

Krateros' and Nearchos' forces got through with relatively little difficulty, but Alexander's force staggered from crisis to crisis, many of the men and the camp followers dying of thirst, hunger, heat or flash floods. It was almost as though Alexander was revenging himself on his army for having defeated him. The land groups reunited at a town later called Alexandria-in-Karmania (the present Gulushkird), where Alexander's group are reported to have danced and drunk their way through the rich countryside in a drunken celebration. Alexander, as keen on drinking as most and addicted to comparisons with the gods, had no objection to this Dionysiac frenzy.[48]

The rebuff he faced from his army in India rankled. He may well have become steadily more conscious of his own mortality, particularly after the appalling wound he suffered in India, which surely contributed to his early death. He was suspicious already by that time, thanks to the plots generated within the court. He now found that none of the satraps of southern Iran had bothered to send supplies to await his arrival. This may not have been their fault, though he had probably sent word for them to be provided, but he was not in the mood to listen when he emerged from the desert. He returned to the centre of his empire suspicious of everyone, and determined to take it out on someone.

The failure of the satraps to send him supplies was as much a failure of Alexander's government as of the satraps personally. He had steadily avoided the more unexciting decisions such as organizing a government, reasonably enough when the conquest of the empire was still unfinished. But then he had vanished into India, from which emerged no doubt exaggerated stories of murder, army revolts, massacres and life-threatening wounds received by the king. Some at least of his satraps thought he was dead, or would never return.

This was a consequence of the fact that he was a king specifically of Macedon. Philip's legacy had been an army more than anything else, a superb fighting force capable of defeating any other army in the world at the time. But the government of Macedon was not developed to the same sophisticated level; the Macedonian government was essentially the king, scarcely modified by the Army-as-Assembly.[49] Alexander had assumed that he could simply take over the Persian Empire from Dareios, as he had taken over Macedon from Philip, needing only to replace a few satraps. Macedon was a personal state, dependent wholly on the king, who controlled everything, judged most of the legal disputes himself, oversaw the tax collection system, and so on. The kingdom was just about big enough to be governed in such a way by an energetic king, and Philip did not delegate any of his powers, military or civil. Neither did Alexander, but this was because he did not trust anyone. Once or twice, as with Parmenion and Krateros, he sent a man off with part of the army, but he would never trust anyone with the administrative development of the empire. It was not possible to run the empire alone; he needed a system, a bureaucracy and dependable officials.

7

The united empire, 325–319 BC

The problems facing Alexander on his return from India were those faced by any conqueror: how to control the conquered population; how to reward his army; how to provide just government; how to install a working administration; how to prevent outsiders exploiting his difficulties. He also had some problems exclusively his own: how to stay alive and provide for the succession, which had now become a more than urgent matter. As if these were not enough, he planned a series of new conquests which were liable to be more like the campaigns in eastern Iran and India than the relative ease with which the western provinces had been conquered.

He had been absent from the centre for five years when he arrived back from India. In Baktria he had been in touch, but while in India no major royal decisions were forthcoming; and this from a man who would not delegate. Some news had reached him from Iran, and Krateros had been sent to deal with trouble in Arachosia, but there was more to concern him than that when he arrived in Karmania. His first concern was for supplies, which took far too long to be produced, and he began to hear rumours of misgovernment, extortion by his satraps, and so on.

His absence and his failure to attend to internal affairs had led to the progressive disintegration of the Persian Empire into its constituent provinces. The satraps had been left without supervision, and had governed according to their own requirements and purposes. They could do nothing else. The Persian satraps used the methods of the old empire, but the Macedonians and Greeks had no such tradition or training. Confusion, at the very least, was inevitable.

The Greeks and Macedonians were suddenly surrounded by more wealth and power than they had ever dreamed of. They had become rich, and as was the custom in their society, they were generous in giving presents to friends and subordinates, an extremely wasteful habit in the circumstances. With no philosophy of public service, and no ingrained respect for, or relationship with, the people they ruled, corruption and abuse were rife. Their satrapies were the size of Macedon: they had become the equivalent of kings. And where the governors went, their followers went also.

In Karmania, as soon as he arrived, Alexander was told of the abuse of power by the local satrap Astaspes. Dissembling until his troops had recovered, the king waited a week, then had Astaspes executed for 'rebellion'.[1] What Astaspes had actually done was to rule his satrapy without supervision; every other satrap was in his position.

A reinforcement of 6,000 men arrived from Ekbatana, commanded by a group of officers, some of whom had been involved in the killing of Parmenion and had reaped much unpopularity. Officers and men were accused of a catalogue of crimes by men of the army and by Medians who had accompanied the march. Two of the officers, Kleandros and Sitalkes, were executed; another, Agathon, may have been; a fourth, Herakon, was acquitted, but later convicted of similar crimes in Susiana, and executed there. Their troops were also punished, by decimation.[2]

The satrap of Susiana, Abulites, was accused of not sending Alexander supplies. He had retained this post after surrendering to Alexander; his son Oxathres was satrap of Paraitakene next door, and Abulites had extended his power over the Uxii, another neighbour. This conjunction suggests that the concentration of family power was the real issue: father and son were both executed, Oxathres reputedly by Alexander personally.[3] Other Persian satraps had been appointed in Iran, several, like Abulites and Astaspes, to the satrapies they had governed previously. Perhaps originally a temporary measure to keep the area quiet while the conquest was finished off, Alexander's return meant a reckoning.[4]

The Persian satraps had Macedonian and Greek officials alongside them, one to command the garrison, and one to take charge of finances. The satraps did not like this system, which reflected on their loyalty and probity. Some accepted it as the price of conquest and proved loyal: Phrat__aphernes in Parthia was one, and sent supplies to Karmania soon after Alexander arrived, convoyed by his son Pharismenes;[5] Atropates of Media was trusted to suppress the previous satrap who had been disloyal.[6] In Persis, of all sensitive places, the satrap Phrasaortes died while Alexander was in India. Orxines, a high Persian aristocrat, took over without permission: Alexander was out of touch, and there was no alternative source of authority, but he was executed for his presumption.[7] This was clearly unjust: it was Alexander's responsibility to provide for the unexpected death of a satrap, and Orxines may have simply been operating the Akhaimenid system. Orxines was an enemy of Alexander's favourite, the eunuch Bagoas, whose intrigues certainly contributed to Alexander's suspicions.[8]

The Persian satraps who were removed were replaced by Macedonians. This process, and execution of the Persian nobles, was a blow to Alexander's hopes of a combined Persian-Macedonian government. But it was not just the Persians who were delinquent; Macedonians were as liable to be disobedient and disloyal. Alexander's own boyhood friend, Harpalos, his treasurer, absconded to Greece with a large sum of the money entrusted to him.[9] In Egypt, Kleomenes of Naukratis had used his position to establish control over the whole government machine, and became extremely rich as well. Alexander, perhaps unable to remove him from a distance, and pleased that he was pushing on the construction of Alexandria, may have cooperated by making him the satrap.[10] Orxines was executed for taking emergency control of a vital satrapy; Kleomenes was promoted for usurping authority; this was a travesty of government.

Alexander ordered the satraps to disband their own mercenary forces.[11] This would disarm potential opponents and reduce the burden on the population. But some of the discharged soldiers became bandits, others returned to Greece, where they assembled at the great mercenary market at Cape Tainaron in Sparta, waiting to be employed. The consequences of Alexander's order had not been thought out.

One reason for the order might be a rebellion by a group of Greek mercenaries in Baktria, who had believed a rumour of Alexander's death in India. They seized Baktra, the satrapal capital, and elected one of their officers, an Athenian called Athenodoros, as king. They soon dissolved into quarrelling groups: some wanted to return to Greece, but the election of a king suggests that others wanted an independent state.[12] South of Baktria, in Arachosia, Krateros, on his march from India with the elephants and some of the Macedonian troops, he encountered rebel Persian officers, Ordanes (or Ozines) and Zariaspes. He arrested them. He brought them to Alexander at Karmania in chains; they were executed.[13]

Establishing control over the governors was fairly easy; the execution of a few swiftly sorted out the rest into those who had always been loyal and those who fled, who were thus the disloyal ones. The army was another matter. Alexander required a large professional and efficient army, to keep order, overawe and punish rebels and potential rebels, and carry out further conquests. His troops were now a mixture of Greek mercenaries, Persians and Indians, and his own Macedonians. It was the Macedonians he had to control or conciliate. They wanted to go home, to display their wealth and their scars and boast of their exploits. Alexander could not allow this, since if they all went home he would be left only with his former enemies in arms. The answer was a balance between the two groups. A squadron of Iranian Companions was recruited, and some were brought into the royal squadron.[14]

The ceremonial and procedures of the court became more elaborate, and Alexander tended to wear Median costume. Behind all this was the need for a much more elaborate governmental system than Macedon had had, but he was accused of succumbing to Persian culture.[15] He organized a great marriage ceremony in which 100 or so of his senior Macedonian officers married aristocratic Persian women, an obvious attempt to unite the two military and ruling aristocracies. Supposedly 10,000 of his men were married to the concubines and mistresses they had acquired on their travels in an attempt to persuade the men not to go home to Macedon. He himself took two more wives (in addition to Roxane), daughters of Dareios III and Artaxerxes III.[16]

This was partly a deliberate policy of developing a source of military support alternative to the Macedonians; a counter to the phalanx, Alexander called it.[17] The Macedonian soldiers, the rank and file anyway, resented it, making their feelings quite clear.[18] They had to be conciliated, for he could not yet do without them, but this was not easy. Alexander paid off the soldiers' debts, an action costing his treasury at least 10,000 talents.[19] He also recruited 30,000 Persian youths and drilled them in the Macedonian fashion.[20] The Macedonian soldiers were paraded for those too old or disabled for further service to be discharged, but they mutinied, believing he needed them still. He called their bluff and told them to go. There was reconciliation, but he did discharge half of them, sending them home under the command of Krateros, a man they trusted.

Krateros' other task was to replace Antipater as regent in Macedon; Antipater was to join Alexander in Babylon to give an account of his viceroyalty, bringing more Macedonians with him. It is often assumed that Antipater saw this as a threat to his position, or even to his life;[21] the evidence for this consists mainly of Antipater's failure to set out on the journey, but he had to wait for Krateros, who moved very slowly.

Greece was a further problem. The gathering of mercenaries at Cape Tainaron was a potential difficulty; their presence was a good reason for sending Krateros and his tough veterans home to Macedon, where they would be a standing deterrent to Macedonian enemies for a time. The mercenaries were often political exiles from their cities, and other men were exiled by civic coups, some brought about by the Macedonian conquest. Isokrates' idea to solve this was to settle such men in conquered lands in Asia. Such settlements had to be organized by someone, that is, the king, just as Philip had been the organizer of the settlements of Philippi and Philippopolis, or Athens had organized the settlements in the Chersonese. This does not appear to have occurred to Alexander. Having established a few cities, mainly in the east, he made no further attempt to found more.[22]

Instead he now ordered that all Greek exiles be allowed to return to their cities of origin, and had the announcement made at the Olympic Games in 324, where representatives from all Greek states were present. This would involve almost everyone in Greece in continual civic disputes for the foreseeable future. Some cities would accept it, but most would refuse or avoid compliance; its purpose was surely to distract and weaken the members of the league. It was the antithesis of good government. Antipater in Macedon was put in charge of enforcement; Krateros would have to take over the task when he got to Macedon. Neither man was a diplomat; it is likely that they would need to resort to force; two major Greek powers, Athens and Aitolia, refused point-blank to comply.[23]

At the same time another announcement was made, that Alexander, as *hegemon* of the league, required that the cities acknowledge him as a god. This is likely to be, in effect, a request by Alexander that the cities acknowledge his achievements, and this was the only way in which it could be done. It was one stage beyond Philip. Alexander took it seriously, but in Greece it provoked some ridicule, at least among his enemies, but many of the cities, including Athens, did as he asked.[24]

As if to emphasize the delicacy of the whole situation in Greece, Harpalos turned up at Athens with his stolen wealth. He was a well-connected man, a friend of Alexander, and a member of the old Elimaian royal family. One of his brothers, Philippos, was satrap in India; his cousin Kalas had been Alexander's first appointed satrap, in Hellespontine Phrygia.[25] Harpalos' defection was thus a serious matter, threatening trouble in Macedon, and now in Athens. He fled from Alexander's justice with 5,000 talents from the treasury, and he had 6,000 mercenaries with him. Athens had refused Alexander's order to allow exiles to return to Samos; the city was thus threatened with Antipater's punishment. Harpalos was therefore the focus of a whole group of anti-Macedonian elements – mercenaries, Athens, the former hill kingdoms of Upper Macedon. The Athenians were wary of becoming even more involved in Macedonian internal affairs; and Harpalos took his money and his mercenaries to Tainaron. He left the mercenaries there and returned to Athens with the money, and this time was admitted as a supplicant. The Athenians, with a cynicism fully in accord with their recent history, confiscated the money, and then let Harpalos escape from jail.[26] Clearly this was not the moment for Antipater to leave Macedon without a ruler.

These measures by Alexander, crowded into a brief period of little more than a year, were designed to shake up entrenched special interests. Return of exiles, discharge of veterans, recruitment of Persian troops, replacement of Persian satraps with Macedonians, deification, operated on the administration of his empire in all its aspects and threatened the powers of men who blocked his intentions. The problem was that such men had a lot of local power, and were very reluctant to be removed, nor did their supporters wish to see them go. This applied to Antipater, to the Athenian democratic regime, to Kleomenes in Egypt. It all looks like an alternative to a thoroughgoing renovation of the imperial administrative system, which would take a long time. And Alexander wanted to go on campaign again.

Mortality came close in the autumn 324 when Hephaistion, his closest friend, died. He had been appointed *chiliarchos* (chief administrator) of the empire, though his abilities were not up to the job – or so his enemies said. Alexander showed extravagant grief – everything he did now tended to be extravagant – and indulged himself in a campaign against a tribe of obstreperous hillmen as a death offering.[27] In the spring he made preparations for a campaign against the independent and richer parts of Arabia;[28] after this he would arrive in Egypt, where Kleomenes would surely be investigated, at the very least.

A campaign was Alexander's standard response to difficulties, but it was hardly constructive. The empire was too big already, and had many problems needing to be tackled before more expansion was undertaken. For the king to go off on a long voyage – he intended to circumnavigate Arabia, which might take months – in the midst of these troubles meant that the problems would be worse when, or if, he turned up again.

This behaviour pattern had been visible even at the start of his kingship, in 336, when he had refused to marry and produce an heir in the two years before the start of his campaign. He was good at fighting, and clearly enjoyed it more than anything else, but he used it to evade responsibility. This was a failure to grow up. In many ways he was a perpetual adolescent; his superstition, impulsiveness, carelessness with money, extravagant grief over the death of Hephaistion, unwillingness to see that other work needed to be done, love of fighting, all show this. Whether he would ever have grown up is unclear; it would have needed a surrogate father to admonish and guide him. Antipater, coming fresh to him, might have been the man, if Alexander would listen. But neither got the chance.

In the midst of the work of preparation for his Arabian expedition, Alexander became ill, and on 10 June, 323, he died.[29] Conspiracy theories surround this event: one has it that Antipater organized the assassination all the way from Macedon and involved half the imperial administration in the plot. These can be dismissed as the imaginings of the desk-bound historians and over-imaginative novelists.[30] Alexander suffered repeated wounds during his lifetime, and more than one brought him near death; he drank too much;[31] he developed a fever, during which he continued to drink too much; he believed he was a god; Babylon in high summer was hardly the healthiest place on earth; he disregarded his doctor's counsel, a man he had trusted completely ten years before; he was faced with huge problems which he planned to evade by going on campaign; people all around him were continually demanding of his time and energy. It is hardly surprising he died. As a final act of irresponsibility he is said, when asked to whom he left his kingdom, to have replied: 'to the strongest', and then, 'I foresee a great funeral contest over me'.[32]

These remarks may be *ben trovato* – Alexander is also said to have been speechless by this time – yet they do fit well with the man's life, and he certainly never designated a successor. He was a superb military commander, a master of all the detail of warfare – logistics, planning, training, fighting – and capable of adapting his military methods to the most unexpected situations. He successfully conducted sieges, great battles, hill campaigns, contested river crossings and even defeated the nomads of the steppe on their own territory. He was ruthless, and caused the deaths of hundreds of thousands of people.

But this was only part of his duties. As king he had to be a politician and administrator as well. In the first he was clever and devious and determined, as ruthless as in his warfare, but liable to stir up trouble rather than solve problems. As an administrator, despite his capability in military logistics and planning, he was a failure, relying far too much on personal persuasiveness and force. This was his father's method, but something more was required. His legacy was thus exclusively his fame and his army, seductive lures for his successors, many of whom took a long time to appreciate what was missing.

For the moment, the absence of an heir was the major concern of his men. The only male relative he had left was his half-brother Arrhidaios, who was mentally unfit to rule. Alexander had at least one son, Herakles, by a liaison with Barsine, the widow of his old enemy Memnon of Rhodes (and daughter of Artabazos). The boy was no more than two or three years old in 323.[33] His official wife Roxane was pregnant again, having had a miscarriage a couple of years before;[34] he had recently married two more wives, emulating his father: Stateira, a daughter of Dareios III, and Parysatis, a daughter of Artaxerxes III Ochos, so connecting himself with the two recent Persian dynasties. Neither is ever heard of again: Roxane is said to have killed Stateira and, it is assumed, Parysatis.[35]

Beyond his son and his half-brother, Alexander's relatives were few. He had a sister, Kleopatra, the widow of King Alexander of Epirus, the mother of a son and daughter, and two half-sisters, neither married: Thessalonike, daughter of Nikesipolis, and Kynane, daughter of Audata. For those intent on continuing the Argead royal family in ruling Macedon, therefore, there was only one male possibility, Arrhidaios, though he was widely seen as a half-wit. Or there was Roxane's child, which at least would be a child of Alexander, though it could only be considered if it was male. No competent adult was available.

It was clearly necessary for someone to secure control of the administration and of the army as rapidly as possible. The breakdown of the empire while Alexander was in India was reminiscent of the troubles Macedon went through before Philip, and the situation was on a continental scale this time. The solution was obviously some sort of regency. The paucity of available royalty must have suggested to more than one Macedonian noble that the kingship was available to any man who had the necessary support – as Alexander had said: 'the strongest', but any man who made a move to claim the throne would immediately become the enemy of all the rest. In the event none tried, not immediately, at least.

Perdikkas was *chiliarchos*, and had possession of Alexander's signet ring. This put him in control for the moment at Babylon, and after some trouble and negotiation he was able to install himself as regent. Arrhidaios, now renamed Philip, and Roxane's baby, if it was male, would be joint kings.[36] The process mainly involved Perdikkas negotiating with Krateros and Antipater, but at one point the army in Babylon almost fell into a civil war. The result put off a decision about the actual kingship for years: Roxane's son (as it proved to be) could not rule for 16 years at least, and Arrhidaios not at all.

For the moment, by controlling Arrhidaios, who became King Philip III, Perdikkas was more or less certain of his position. He eliminated Meleagros, an infantry commander who had conducted an attempted coup, and distributed offices to the senior Macedonians. Most of them were given satrapies. This ensured control of the provinces, but they were also removed from Babylon, leaving Perdikkas in exclusive continuing control of the kings and the administration. He kept with him a few trusted Macedonians, making Seleukos his second-in-command.[37]

The army suddenly ceased to demand to return home, for one casualty of the new regime was Alexander's policy of recruiting Persians and employing Persian aristocrats in high positions. The army was given a deciding vote on Alexander's plans and, not wishing to go on campaign again, voted to abandon them. The Macedonians were again supreme. Atropates continued as satrap of part of Media; Phrataphernes probably also lost some of his Parthian satrapy; Roxane's father Oxyartes retained his satrapy of Paropamisadai, safely distant. Alexander's administration in the Indus Valley had scarcely survived his departure, and India was in effect abandoned. All this was done with the approval of the Macedonian army in Babylon. Had a king made such decisions, such approval was not needed; for a regent it clearly was, even with only one-third of the army present. The cancellation of Alexander's plans also involved the cancellation of the replacement of Antipater by Krateros, which was presumably part of the bargain made between the three men. All but one of the officers married to Iranian women at Susa the year before repudiated their wives; many of the soldiers married at the time may have done so as well.

The news of Alexander's death, and the confusion over the succession, brought two wars, in Baktria and in Greece. In Baktria a large number of the Greeks left as settlers or garrisons decided that Alexander's death was a good moment for them to go home. Some had been involved in the rebellion two years before, but this was a much more formidable development. Now they were defeated again. The new satrap of Media, Peithon, and a Macedonian force, captured many of them; Perdikkas ordered them killed, to prevent Peithon recruiting them,[38] but some survived and returned to Baktria. Philip, the Baktrian satrap appointed by Alexander and reappointed by Perdikkas, seems to have survived the revolt.[39] The majority of the malcontents in the east had now been removed one way or another, and Baktria now became a major field of Greek (as compared to Macedonian) colonial settlement. There were already some cities in the region, founded by Alexander; the settlers developed more.

The death of Alexander was also the death of the *hegemon* of the Hellenic League. In theory someone such as Antipater could have been elected, but events moved too fast. Athens produced Harpalos' gold, and the Athenian general Leosthenes, who already had good contacts at the Cape Tainaron mercenary camp, used the money to hire a mercenary army. Many of the men at Tainaron had been with Alexander, and many others there had been opposed to him; recruitment cannot have been difficult among the unemployed men, and was certainly arranged quickly. Both Athens and Aitolia had objections to the restoration of exiles and made an alliance.[40] They were joined by others, but not by the Boiotians, still pleased at the destruction of Thebes. Sparta stayed out, and so Arkadia and Messenia were neutral. The Aitolians seized control of Thermopylai, and were joined there by the Athenians, who also mobilized their fleet. Antipater came south, but at the first meeting he was deserted by the Thessalians in his army and withdrew to stand a siege in Lamia. At one point he offered surrender, on terms, but Leosthenes insisted on surrender without terms, which would mean enslavement or execution. Antipater held out.[41] In effect the Macedonian European empire had dissolved.

Antipater sent out appeals for help to the nearest Macedonian forces in Asia. The satrap of Hellespontine Phrygia, Leonnatos, crossed the Hellespont with his forces; Krateros, in Kilikia, did not move until he received the news that Perdikkas was marching north from Babylon. Krateros was, it seems, concerned to maintain control of Kilikia, a key nodal point in the empire; Perdikkas' march north was for the purpose of establishing control in Kappadokia, which would ensure better communications. Krateros was not being reluctant to support Antipater; he was doing his job. Leonnatos meanwhile joined with Antipater and broke the siege of Lamia, but died in the fighting. Leosthenes was also killed. Antipater withdrew through Thessaly to Macedon. For the moment it seemed that the Greeks had won their war.[42]

The Macedonian commanders had one eye on what the Greeks were doing and the other on the situation within the Macedonian command structure. The Macedonian barons began to operate as near-independent lords, making alliances among themselves. Antipater offered one daughter to Perdikkas and another to Krateros. This second offer was to induce Krateros to help him, but it also implied the making of an alliance in Macedonian politics; in the circumstances this could only be directed against Perdikkas. Leonnatos had received a still more tempting offer, from Olympias, of the hand of Alexander's sister Kleopatra; he accepted but was killed soon after.[43] Krateros took up Antipater's offer and moved west, leaving a large infantry unit, the Argyraspides (Silver Shields) in Kilikia. He sent a fleet under the command of Kleitos to the Aegean, and took his army towards the Hellespont. Kleitos' fleet defeated that of Athens at Amorgos in June, and then joined with Antipater's Macedonian fleet. Together the two fleets met that of Athens again and overwhelmed it.[44] Krateros crossed the Hellespont to join Antipater and claim his bride, and together the two men brought their armies back south into Thessaly. At Krannon the Macedonian army met the allied Greek army in battle and beat it. The defeat of the Greeks from Baktria and those in

Europe took place within about three months of each other.[45]

Antipater dealt separately with the defeated cities; most quickly surrendered. Athens was treated to a Macedonian military occupation and given an oligarchic regime; democratic leaders were killed, the *cleruchs* on Samos expelled, and the remains of the fleet confiscated.[46] Aitolia, a league of upland cantons which had only recently developed into an important state, proved most obdurate; the Aitolians methodically removed their population to the hills and defied a Macedonian invasion. Antipater and Krateros made plans to treat the land by a mixture of ravaging, extermination and deportation, but events elsewhere interrupted that process. They had not captured many Aitolians anyway. The Macedonians withdrew.[47] The League of Corinth was not revived, being replaced by a Macedonian domination enforced by the garrisons in the Peiraios, Corinth and elsewhere.

By mid-322, therefore, the empire of Alexander had been restored. Macedon dominated Greece, and the Macedonian army dominated Asia. The governing system, such as it was, continued with the appointment and reappointment of the satraps, and there were two kings supervised by a regent. The two possible main competitors for Perdikkas' authority, Antipater and Krateros, were fully occupied in Greece, first by settling affairs after the battle of Krannon, and then by the continued resistance of the Aitolians.

Perdikkas had come north from Babylon to install his protégé Eumenes, Alexander's former secretary, as satrap of Kappadokia. Leonnatos in Hellespontine Phrygia and Antigonus the One-Eyed in Phrygia had been instructed to conquer the land for Eumenes, who had few troops, but neither had bothered, Leonnatos having been quickly distracted by the Lamian War. Perdikkas came to do the job himself, which involved a substantial battle,[48] and intended to discipline Antigonos because of his dereliction. Antigonos, summoned by Perdikkas to explain himself, fled to Antipater and Krateros and explained that Perdikkas had great plans to discipline everyone else as well. He cannot possibly have known Perdikkas' plans, but he was preaching to men already suspicious of the regent: Krateros and Antipater welcomed the allegation as justification for their own political stances.[49]

Perdikkas was a poor politician, rousing far too many enemies at the same time. His power made him every Macedonian baron's enemy, but he was clumsy. The men in Greece were joined by Ptolemy, the satrap of Egypt, who had defied Perdikkas by taking Alexander's body for burial at Alexandria rather than to Aigai as Perdikkas intended. Perdikkas made his personal ambition clear by repudiating Nikaia, Antipater's daughter, and marrying Kleopatra, Alexander's sister. He was manoeuvring himself into a very strong dynastic position, similar to that from which Ptolemy of Aloros had made himself king. He turned to deal with Ptolemy, who proved to be a military match for him. In the camp at Pelusion, after a disaster in which 2,000 of Perdikkas' soldiers drowned in the flooded Nile, a group of his officers, led by Seleukos, his second-in-command, banded together to assassinate him.[50]

Krateros and Antipater crossed into Asia Minor, as did Antigonos separately. The first two were opposed by Eumenes, who proved to be a masterly commander; he met Krateros in a battle in which Krateros died.[51] The deaths of both Krateros and Perdikkas cleared the air, and Antipater was now the Macedonian with the greatest prestige. At a meeting of the top men held at Triparadeisos in Syria, Antipater was made regent, and Antigonos was to have charge of the kings, with Antipater's son Kassander as his *chiliarchos*. This arrangement did not last long, for Kassander distrusted Antigonos and persuaded his father to take the kings under his own control. Antipater was the obvious man to be regent, given his rank and experience, and he took the two kings to Macedon with him when he returned there. He was by now almost 80 years old, the last of Philip's generation in a position of authority, which gave him a certain moral authority, as did his control of the persons of the kings.

There still remained Eumenes and his army. Antipater, instead of going after Eumenes himself and using his prestige and authority to bring him to terms, which, as regent, he surely should have done, commissioned Antigonus as '*strategos* of the royal forces', or perhaps as '*strategos* over Asia', to do the job, with Perdikkas' former army.[52] It was, of course, the policy Antipater had always used: force first, and diplomacy nowhere. Eumenes could probably have been brought in by diplomacy, for his strongest political belief was loyalty to Philip II and his family, but no real attempt was made to persuade him.

A new distribution of satrapies was necessary as a result of the several deaths. The murderers of Perdikkas were rewarded with Babylon (Seleukos) and Susiana (Antigenes); Antigonos was confirmed in Phrygia and his other lands in Asia Minor, as was Ptolemy in Egypt.[53] Antipater was not very interested in all this. He had control of the kings, of a major part of the Macedonian army, and the kingdom itself. These he clearly identified as the crucial elements in the government, but, not having been on the great campaign with Alexander, he had no real conception of what Asia was like, and this aspect afflicted the judgement of other men. The legacy of Alexander was also the shared experience of his long anabasis.

Perdikkas had been beset from the start of his regency by his fellow Macedonians' suspicions and ambitions. He was clearly not a man to attract loyalty, and most of the men he favoured betrayed him in some way: Peithon, Seleukos, Antigenes. But he had accomplished the main task he had, by assuming the regency, set himself, which was to maintain the unity of the empire. And yet the first cracks in that unity appeared because of his policy, in the form of the failure to discipline Ptolemy of Egypt. Under Antipater the empire of

Alexander still held together, but the basic problem, the growing autonomy of the satraps, was ignored. Alexander had tried to discipline them, but had died before succeeding; now they were killing each other. This was in no way unusual in a period of royal succession in Macedon. Philip II's assassination had been accompanied by the same set of events, and Alexander's death had produced the usual set of murders which followed the death of any Macedonian king. The elimination of some commanders had winnowed out the field, leaving the one old man in charge. Or so it seemed.

The settlement at Triparadeisos put Antipater in power, but he was no longer up to the job. His conduct of the Lamian war had been barely competent, his gullibility when Antigonos accused Perdikkas of plots was culpable, and his acquiescence at Triparadeisos was that of a lazy old man who couldn't be bothered any more. As regent he may have had authority, but he immediately returned to Macedon. It was simply not possible to run the empire from there, as even Alexander had realized. By appointing Antigonos to the command in Asia, Antipater abdicated responsibility for the major part of the empire, and lifted the most ambitious man around to a post with the greatest potential. Antipater knew Antigonos' great ambition, and refused to let him have the persons of the kings, but he did not follow that thought to its obvious conclusion. When he died, in 319, only a few months after Triparadeisos,[54] there was no Macedonian left with his personal authority, and in that year the unity of the empire broke down definitively.

World view II: 319 BC

Between 325 and 319 BC most of the lands between the Adriatic Sea and the Indus River were under the government of one man, first Alexander, then Perdikkas, then Antipater. For that brief period Greece, Macedonia, the Persian Empire and the Indus Valley were theoretically united. The end of that period is a good point from which to consider other areas. Alexander's last plans included the conquest of Arabia and possibly an attack on Carthage; an embassy from Rome was at Babylon in the last year of his life, presumably to find out what he intended for Italy. And the thwarting of his invasion of India was surely something he would try to overcome at some point.

Arabia, Carthage, Italy, the Ganges valley: these are the areas still outside the empire which were known to be functioning and recognizable states. If appetite grows up by what it feeds on, then Alexander, beginning by seeking 'revenge' for the Persian invasions of Greece, had ended by aiming to conquer the world: his final plans were aimed therefore at the achievement of that ambition.[1]

His soldiers, after his death, swiftly voted to abandon the plans, when Perdikkas asked them.[2] This was one of the key moments in the disintegration of the empire. The ambitions of the great men were now directed against each other: only an active king could exercise control over such men, preferably by sending them on to conquer more lands. There were areas technically part of the empire but actually outside it. Perdikkas identified two, Kappadokia and Paphlagonia in Asia Minor, both supposed to have tendered their submission to Alexander in 334, but by 322 they were independent. It took a full-scale battle and several thousand casualties to bring Kappadokia into the empire.[3] As an empire, Alexander's was a very ramshackle affair, much more so than its Persian predecessor.

The Roman embassy to Alexander is not a well-attested event, but Rome was at the least very interested in what was happening.[4] In the 40 years since the accession of Philip II the city's power had grown substantially. A war with her Latin league partners produced a reorganized league which guaranteed clear rights to the league cities, yet also liberated substantial military manpower under Roman direction. Like Alexander's system, this was a polity which was either aggressive or suffered internal divisions. As a result a process of expansion began and brought Rome close to the position of the greatest power in Italy by the time of Alexander's death. True, two years later, in 321, Rome suffered a setback in a war against the mountain confederation of the Samnites, but still maintained control over the Campanian cities, which were threatened by the Samnites no less than Rome. Controlling both Latium and Campania, Rome held the richest and most populous areas of peninsular Italy: a substantial geographical base for the city's growth.[5]

The Greek cities of southern Italy were also threatened by inland Italian states, and appealed for help to their mother cities in old Greece. Taras had twice been assisted, first by King Archidamos of Sparta in 342 and then by King Alexander the Molossian in 333. Both had some success until they died in the fighting.[6] The main cause of the troubles in southern Italy was the slow collapse of the Syracusan monarchy. Dionysios II was not as ruthless as his father, and in 357 Dion, his uncle, returned from exile and drove him out. Dion was then murdered, and the tyranny broke down. In 347 Dionysios II returned to Syracuse, but by this time the opposition was emboldened, and he was able to re-establish himself only in Syracuse. The opposition appealed for help to Corinth, Syracuse's mother city.

Instead of a king and an army, Corinth had sent one man, Timoleon, who turned out to be a statesman of uncanny power. He removed Dionysios, deconstructed the Syracusan kingdom, repelled a Carthaginian invasion, set up the Greek states of Sicily in local independence, and then retired to live as a private citizen, dying in 337 or 336 BC.[7] It was an extraordinary performance, which took place at the same time as Philip was uniting Greece. Only time would tell if it had any long-term success: Sicily was liable to these great reversals, and ambitions for conquest by Carthage, or for monarchical rule among some of the Greeks, were by no means over. In 325 one such ambitious man, Agathokles, had been driven into exile. He intrigued to return, and in 319 he did so. Syracuse was always the powerhouse of the Greek Sicilian empire and monarchy, and Agathokles was territorially even more ambitious than Dionysios, and just as brutal.[8]

This was part of the essential background to Philip and Alexander's plans. The expeditions of Archidamos and Timoleon in the 340s were surely in their minds, for the tyrants of Syracuse were always liable to intervene in old Greece, and Sparta was Macedon's most inveterate enemy. With both cities distracted and with Alexander of Epiros also interested – he sailed to Italy in 334 – the Macedonian kings had no worries about intervention from the west while conquering the east.

Given all this activity in their political neighbourhood, the Romans were sensible to send an embassy to test Alexander's intentions: Rome's actions in Campania, Agathokles' actions in Syracuse, Alexander of Epiros' work in southern Italy, could provide excuses for Macedonian invasions in the name of the liberation of Greek cities, or even for revenge for the death of Alexander's sister's husband.

Alexander's brutal campaign in India may well have been in the minds of his soldiers when they rejected his plans, for a campaign in the west would have been equally unpleasant and difficult. The conquest of most of the Persian Empire had required three battles (Granikos, Issos and Gaugamela), three major sieges (Halikarnassos, Tyre, Gaza), and the Baktrian campaign. It had been necessary only to defeat the Persian royal army to gain control of the whole empire from the Hellespont to eastern Iran; the resistance of Baktria and Sogdiana had been, so it might seem in retrospect, a warning of what was to come in India. In the west, things were different. The campaign would have been against individual cities and tribes, each of which would resist, very like that in India, and probably even nastier. Alexander might have been welcomed in southern Italy, but not in Syracuse, and neither Carthage nor Rome would be easy victims. Carthage could be expected to put up the same sort of resistance as her daughter city Tyre, and each central Italian city and tribe would be likely to resist Alexander as some had resisted his brother-in-law; nor would the Samnites give in easily. In India the result had been many Macedonian, and even more Indian, casualties, and the destruction of an established political system and society. A Macedonian campaign in the west would be just as unpleasant and destructive.

The Indus Valley heaved with trouble after Alexander left. Two of his satraps were murdered even as he marched through the Gedrosian desert, and India was largely ignored in the redistribution of posts at Babylon. At Triparadeisos the Paropamisadai remained with Oxyartes, Roxane's father, but India itself was assigned to the Indian kings Poros and Taxiles, because they were irremovable, at least by Antipater.[9] The mess was about to be cleaned up by a man who the Greeks claimed was inspired by Alexander. Chandragupta Maurya may have met Alexander in the Punjab, according to later legend.[10] More importantly, he was a political opponent of the Nanda dynasty in Magadha, which had largely united the Ganges Valley under its rule. This would have been Alexander's next victim if he had managed to persuade his army to march east. The Nandas' position was brittle, and proved to be as vulnerable as the Persians had been. By 321, when Perdikkas was failing, Chandragupta had overthrown the Nanda king in a *coup d'état*, and by 317 he had taken control of the Punjab from Poros and Taxiles. Only six years after Alexander's death, all northern India from the Khyber Pass to the Ganges Delta was united into a single empire.[11] If Alexander had implemented any of his presumed plans for India it was just about this time he would have turned to deal with Chandragupta. Well might his soldiers have quailed at the prospect.

The effects of Alexander's actions thus extended well beyond his formal boundaries: westwards to the Atlantic and eastwards to the Ganges Valley. His career inspired Chandragupta to great deeds, and soon Agathokles in Sicily would emulate him. It was one of the influences behind Rome's expansion in the next generation, if only to pre-empt a possible Macedonian invasion. When Octavianus reached Alexandria, three centuries later, he had Alexander's sarcophagus opened to inspect his preserved corpse.[12] Alexander's influence spread through time as well as space; his achievement has been a benchmark for every conqueror since.

In the completely separate political system of China, where Alexander was unknown, the preliminary stages had been accomplished in a process by which another unifying empire would appear during the next century. The border state of Qin, the westernmost of the complex of states along the Yellow River, had begun to expand. Its soldiers were hardened by constant border warfare. Two highly capable rulers, dukes Xian and Xiao, ruled from 385 to 338, and carried through reforms which increased the availability of military manpower and the effectiveness of the government system. Its nearest neighbour, the kingdom of Wei, was seriously damaged by a war with Qi to the east in the 340s, and Qin and Qi helped themselves to parts of Wei's lands in the decades following. The Qin state was beginning to turn its honed military power on to the interior cities – just as Macedon, whose troops were toughened in fighting Illyrians and Thracians, turned on the Greek cities. Not for nothing is this the 'Era of Warring States' in China. Qin emerged as one of the three or four Chinese great powers, just as Rome was about to do in the west, and by similar means: a disciplined war-making machine and an internal need to keep on conquering. In contrast to the Macedonian empire, however, Qin constructed an effective and well-established government system.[13]

8

Antigonos the One-Eyed, 319–311 BC

Antipater's death removed the only man who could pretend to be the ruler of the whole Macedonian Empire, no matter how feebly he had exercised that rule. He nominated Polyperchon as his successor as regent,[1] a man few respected, and left Antigonos with a dangerously vague commission as general in Asia. Both appointments were frequently ignored or rejected by others. Polyperchon was undermined by Kassander, Antipater's son, who had been named as *chiliarchos* by Antipater in his will, but had expected the chief post.

This emptiness at the centre, and Antigonos' ambitions, meant that the many satraps had to play their own hands; no super-satrap had the authority or the power to control them. Some may well have been working largely for themselves from the start: Antigonos is one obvious suspect, Ptolemy another, Peithon a third; they might aim at cutting themselves a slice of the empire, and going into independence, or they might aim for the whole. Some changed from one variety to the other, as conditions changed. Some took the lesson from Alexander's spectacular career that it was enough to have an army and to win battles. It was a most confusing period, until the small fry were eliminated.[2]

Antigonos' initial task was to suppress the last of Perdikkas' supporters, including Alketas, his brother, and the satrap of Kappadokia, Eumenes. Both were at large in Asia Minor, though Alketas was swiftly driven to defeat and suicide at Termessos.[3] Antigonos also drove out other local satraps, Arrhidaios of Hellespontine Phrygia and Kleitos of Lydia. These had been put in place by Antipater to confine Antigonos.[4] These were prominent men: Arrhidaios had been briefly regent before Triparadeisos, and Kleitos had been the commander of the victorious fleet in the Lamian War. Kleitos emulated Antigonos and fled to the regent. Antigonos now refused to accept Polyperchon's promotion, interpreting his position as '*strategos* over Asia' in the widest possible terms. He became the effective ruler of all western and central Asia Minor soon after Antipater's death, and having been given Perdikkas' former army, by recruiting and by enlisting his former enemies' forces, he became the commander of the largest army east of the Hellespont.

Polyperchon was challenged by Kassander, who seized control of the Macedonian garrisons in Greece. Kassander never showed any ambition to rule the whole empire, but he did insist that he was entitled to have a version of

Antipater's authority, by hereditary right. So now it became clear that one man was making a play for one section of the empire, and historic Macedon at that, basing his claim on the fact that his father had ruled it. Antipater's long stint as Macedonian viceroy (334–319) had certainly predisposed a section of the population to accept Kassander's claims. Antigonos, whose interest at the time was in reducing Polyperchon's authority, considerately sent Kassander some troops. Kassander also contacted Ptolemy, who had married his sister Eurydike.[5] Kassander and Polyperchon neutralized each other, and Antigonos could move east against Eumenes.

Polyperchon sent a new commission to Eumenes to recruit a force in the name of the kings. Eumenes persuaded the Argyraspides, whom Krateros had left in Kilikia, to join him in the name of the regent and of the kings. These 'Silver Shields' were a fearsome set of old soldiers who undoubtedly understood that Eumenes was playing on their emotions and their loyalty to the Macedonian royal family. He had an empty tent set up in which he communed with the spirit of Alexander, whose empty throne was the object of obeisance and incense-burning before meetings. The old soldiers accepted this. Eumenes, after all, did have a deal of legality on his side, and the display of the royal dress and insignia was a reminder of the legitimacy of his command.[6] It had become increasingly clear that his opponents – Antigonos, Kassander, Ptolemy – aimed at either removing the kings to whom these men were loyal, or at carving off bits of the empire which they had been instrumental in conquering. The Argyraspides were both a formidable fighting unit and a powerful symbol of the sentiment for unity of the empire.

Ptolemy as satrap in Egypt had begun by acting as a loyal subject. He quickly removed Kleomenes, which helped bring him popularity in Egypt. He expanded the empire by an expert mixture of intimidation and persuasion in Cyrenaica, thereby fulfilling part of Alexander's western plans.[7] He insisted that Alexander's wish to be entombed in Egypt be respected, despite Perdikkas' intention to bury him at the traditional royal cemetery at Aigai. Both were using the issue for their own political purposes, but Ptolemy was acting in accordance with Alexander's wishes when he persuaded Arrhidaios to head for Egypt rather than Macedon.[8] None of this was a sign of ambition for independent rule.

The decisive break in Ptolemy's loyalties came after the murder of Perdikkas. He had been, he felt, unjustly attacked and so had defended himself, and Perdikkas' death could be seen as the execution of a man whose ambition had flown too high, causing the deaths of Macedonian soldiers. After the murder, at a conference of the leaders, Ptolemy was offered the regency. If he took up the offer he would have to leave Egypt to someone else, he would enter into a political contest with Antipater, who was approaching, and he would have had to try to control these rambunctious Macedonians. He refused the job, remaining instead as satrap in Egypt. It was, in a quiet way, a declaration of independence.[9]

Ptolemy was one of the most successful political operators of the time. His control of Egypt – a country prone to taking against foreign rulers – was fully accepted by the native Egyptians. He was a conscientious administrator. His diplomacy was almost always clever and subtle; his military ability was of no great account, but his political timing was usually good, and his geopolitical understanding was always spot-on; his mistakes and defeats never threatened his essential base. These qualities might have ensured that, as regent, he would have at least delayed the collapse of Alexander's empire. Instead he was one of its prime destroyers.

Ptolemy's decision to hold Egypt in defiance of the rest of the empire made it necessary for him to put the defence of his satrapy first. Egypt was vulnerable to attack primarily from Syria; it had been conquered three times in the recent past from that direction, and threatened by Perdikkas. The Persian conquest had been delayed by Egyptian control of Phoenicia and Cyprus; Ptolemy's solution was the same: to move his defence forward. In 319, at Antipater's death but before Antigonos' victories over Alketas and Arrhidaios, Ptolemy moved into Syria, taking control as far north as Phoenicia. He evicted the satrap, Laomedon of Mitylene, who took refuge with Alketas in Asia Minor; a poor choice.[10] Ptolemy contacted the kings in the several Cypriot cities. Phoenicia and Cyprus were the traditional sources of wood for Egyptian shipbuilding. Ptolemy had thus reconstituted the Egyptian kingdom as it had been under the last independent pharaohs. Kassander and Ptolemy were pitted against Eumenes and Polyperchon in the contest between fragmentation and unity. Antigonos was leaning towards the first two, though operating essentially for his own ambition. By helping Kassander he was undermining the imperial idea personified by Polyperchon, whom he had refused to accept as his superior. By pushing out other satraps from their offices in Asia Minor he was building up his own local power, at first returning to a position similar to that held under Alexander. He was challenged over this by Eumenes, who had a commission from Polyperchon which was very like that which Antigonos had received from Antipater. By working for the continuity of the empire, Eumenes therefore set himself against both Antigonos and the fragmentizers. When Laomedon fled to Alketas, he was making the point that both Ptolemy and Antigonos were working against the unity of the empire.

Antigonos marched after Eumenes, who retreated into Syria, and this forced Ptolemy to retire to Egypt. Ptolemy appealed to the Silver Shields, but they remained loyal to the kings and Eumenes.[11] Eumenes moved eastwards and this forced Seleukos in Babylonia to declare himself. He came out against Eumenes, though he was probably just as unenthusiastic about Antigonos.[12] Eumenes marched on farther eastwards, and at Susa joined with a group of eastern satraps who had just succeeded in blocking the local ambitions of Peithon of Media.

Media was the most important satrapy in the east and Peithon had developed ambitions of his own to control the east. This forced the other eastern satraps, in Baktria, Arachosia, Karmania, Persis and others, to resist him.[13] To these men the continuation of a unified empire was preferable to either Peithon's type of ambition or that of Antigonos, which by this time looked very similar to that of Peithon. The Alexander tent came in useful; Eumenes established a precarious supremacy over the easterners. To their confederation, he brought his forces, probably a bigger persuader than the imaginary Alexander. Peithon, Seleukos and Antigonos joined forces in reply.[14] By now, the contest was for the control of the whole empire.

The armies of Antigonos and Eumenes campaigned against each other in Iran throughout 317 and into 316; the campaign, therefore, took two full years, from the start in 318. They fought complex battles and intricate campaigns, until in the spring of 316 Antigonos got the upper hand. One of Eumenes' many allies betrayed him; at the battle of Gabiene the Argyraspides' baggage (including their families) was captured by Antigonos' cavalry. They then handed Eumenes over as ransom. He was executed.[15]

In the west the unifiers suffered repeated defeats. Polyperchon turned to the Greeks for help, issuing a proclamation in which he purported to restore the freedom of the Greeks by returning to the system of Philip and Alexander, instead of the military occupation instituted by Antipater;[16] this was designed to cut the ground from under Kassander's position. But Polyperchon's fleet was destroyed by that of Antigonos, and Kassander outbid him for Greek support by removing the garrison from Athens and establishing a regime sympathetic to him in the city, under a philosopher, Demetrios of Phaleron.[17]

From his Athenian base, Kassander moved to Macedon, gained control of King Philip III, and was welcomed by the Macedonians.[18] Holding this base allowed him to return to re-establish his domination over Greece. Polyperchon, with King Alexander IV (now six years old) and Roxane, moved to the Peloponnese. Philip III was married to Eurydike, the granddaughter of Philip II (his own niece), and was wholly under his vigorous wife's control. She sided with Kassander and organized the proclamation of Kassander as regent for her husband.[19] Polyperchon contacted Olympias who was in Epiros, and handed the young Alexander to her; she invaded Macedon. The army which Eurydike had raised to combat old Olympias was wholly unwilling to fight such a war and at once changed sides.[20]

Olympias thereby gained control of Philip III and Eurydike, whom she had killed. She then set about murdering Kassander's people, killing a good hundred of the Macedonian baronage.[21] Opinion in Macedon, which had generally welcomed her return, swiftly changed. Kassander drove her into the city of Pydna, which he besieged. In 316, she surrendered, and Kassander left her fate to be decided by his army of Macedonians in an Assembly; she was executed soon after.[22] Roxane and Alexander were kept alive, strictly secluded at Amphipolis.[23] Kassander married another of Philip II's daughters, Thessalonike, daughter of the Thessalian Nikesipolis and half-sister of King Alexander.[24] This was a studiedly ambiguous gesture, either a protection for Alexander (and Roxane) or positioning himself within the Macedonian royal family as a claimant if the boy died. It certainly helped his relationship with the Macedonians and the Thessalians, and by the end of 316 Kassander had made himself lord of Macedon and overseer of Greece; Polyperchon survived, but without either of the kings he had little power.

Antigonos was proving to be lethal to the satraps put in place at Triparadeisos. In addition to those he had accounted for in Asia Minor, he now eliminated some easteners: Peukestas, the betrayer of Eumenes, was deposed from Persis, and Seleukos was soon to be driven out of Babylonia as Antigonos returned to the west. The commander of the Silver Shields, Antigenes, one of Perdikkas' murderers and satrap of Susiana, was now himself murdered.[25] Peithon, the most dangerous of the easterners, was detected in, or merely accused of, an ambition to increase his power, and was executed.[26]

Antigonos, like Antipater, had not experienced the great fighting in Baktria and India; he ignored the east; most of the surviving satraps were reinstated; some of the Argyraspides were sent to the east, to get them out of the way.[27] Antigonos turned west again, and now his actions revealed the extent of his ambition. In Babylon he demanded that Seleukos produce his satrapal accounts. Such an inspection was guaranteed to discover, or invent, malfeasances. There was no apparent set of rules on finance in the satrapies, so discrepancies could be found easily; the audit was the preliminary to Seleukos' arrest and execution. Seleukos, without forces to resist, fled. He was able to take his family and an escort of 50 troopers; the journey was thus perhaps arranged already. Antigonos' behaviour in Iran had been warning enough.[28]

Only the king or his regent had the right to demand that a satrap display an account of his stewardship, so Antigonos' demand implied that he was setting himself up in such a position. He was still '*strategos* over Asia', and no doubt this was the formal ground for acting against Seleukos, but his power now stretched from the eastern satrapies to the Hellespont and to the border of Egypt. He was bound to try to subordinate the remaining independent satraps.

Seleukos fled to Ptolemy in Egypt to whom he explained what Antigonos was doing.[29] To both it was clear that Antigonos aimed to reconstitute the Alexandrian empire under his own rule. It will have become clear to Ptolemy that, despite his tacit alliance with Antigonos against Eumenes two years before, Ptolemy himself would be now due for elimination.

Ptolemy was convinced by Seleukos' tale and his explanation of events in the east. Seleukos sent envoys on to explain the situation to Kassander and to Lysimachos of Thrace, the only westerners still outside Antigonos' control,[30] thereby doing to Antigonos what he had done to Perdikkas. Kassander was soon convinced, and Lysimachos, who might well be a target before Kassander, joined in. One of the items of news which Seleukos could reveal was the scale of the wealth Antigonos now controlled: a war chest of 25,000 talents, picked up by the occupation of imperial treasuries at Ekbatana and Susa and Persepolis, and an annual income of 11,000 talents.[31] He had also recruited a large part of Eumenes' former army. None of the allies could compete with this scale of wealth or manpower, not even Ptolemy with the reserves of Egypt, and Kassander and Lysimachos were positively poor by comparison; Seleukos, of course, was destitute.

But they were all satraps, legally appointed at the conference at Triparadeisos, which was earlier than the Antigonos' commission as *strategos*. They issued a joint ultimatum based on their legal rights, which Antigonos could not gainsay; the men who were aiming to dismantle the empire were thus proclaiming their loyalty to it against the man who aimed to restore its unity. Their demands were that Antigonos should distribute the cash he had acquired more equitably, and, since so many satrapies were vacant, he should agree to further redistribution. The implication was Antigonos' followers or clients would not receive preferment, and that Seleukos would return to Babylon. Antigonos' reply was the alternative suggestion that a negotiation should take place on the basis of who had what now. The offers of negotiation on both sides were actually declarations of war.[32]

Antigonos' eastern settlement was essentially to ignore it: most of the satraps who had joined Eumenes were left in place. In Babylonia Seleukos was replaced by Peithon, son of Agenor, who had been satrap of part of India until driven out. A new satrap for Media, Nikanor, replaced the executed Peithon, and was given a vague viceroyalty role to supervise the easterners. This was exactly what those eastern satraps had objected to before. Antigonos would find little support east of Media, and if circumstances went wrong for him, the eastern satraps were likely to come out against him. It was one of the elements which led to his eventual defeat.

The eastern satrapies were numerous – Areia, Parthia, Arachosia, Susiana, Persis, Baktria, Sogdiana, Paropamisadai – and individually did not count for much in terms of military or political power. Most of the men in office did not play a great role in Alexander's wars, but several of them had been in office for up to ten years by the time Antigonos defeated Eumenes. They had been largely untroubled by central government authority and had developed strong local roots. They operated successful administrations, that is, they operated very much as Philip II had in Macedon, or as the Persian satraps had. An assertion of satrapal power by Peithon or Antigonos would be resisted. Even if these men had few troops at their disposal, in combination their forces were substantial, and the Median and Baktrian cavalry was formidable.

Antigonos returned to the west fairly slowly. The joint ultimatum was delivered in the winter of 316/315, and in the spring he reached Syria. Ptolemy had reoccupied southern Syria when Antigonos and Eumenes had moved off eastwards.[33] Antigonos selected this as his first target, and moved in. Ptolemy made Tyre his main point of defence. Antigonos took a leisurely year to capture the city, while elsewhere in Phoenicia he built a new fleet. His next target was likely to be either Egypt or Greece, probably both.[34]

Antigonos also issued a proclamation by which the Greek cities were to be freed of their occupying garrisons, and sent agents all through Greece to spread the message, and recruit mercenaries. He was copying Polyperchon's gesture, but was a good deal more effective in implementing it.[35] This was a serious threat to Kassander's position in Greece. Antigonos tried to undermine Kassander within Macedon itself by proposing to put him on trial for the treatment of Roxane and King Alexander, and complained that Kassander had been founding cities illegally.

Antigonos' basis for all this was a deal he had made with Polyperchon, who agreed to transfer the regency to Antigonos in return for being named as Antigonos' commander in the Peloponnese. This may have been cynical, but it was consistent with Antigonos' new position of power. The two sides in this conflict were each using the concept of the unity of the empire to appeal for support, showing that there was powerful public support for that unity. Antigonos used his army as a Macedonian Assembly to ratify these proceedings.[36] Legality of a sort was important, even to Antigonos.

Seleukos, with a fleet provided by Ptolemy, sailed along the Phoenician coast, flaunting his defiance in Antigonos' face. He contacted possibly anti-Antigonid satraps in Antigonos' home territory of Anatolia, based himself in Cyprus, and persuaded the satrap of Karia, Asandros, to join the coalition. Asandros must already have been apprehensive. A substantial Antigonid force under Antigonos' nephew Polemaios was in Lydia, presumably as a defensive move, but it obviously threatened any independently-minded satrap in the region, and Asandros was such a one. Kassander sent an army into Anatolia, by way of the Black Sea port of Amisos, under a general called Asklepiodoros, who moved south into Kappadokia. His mission was presumably as a distraction, but Kappadokia had been one of the satrapies claimed in the allies' ultimatum.[37]

The timing of events in this war is difficult, but it would seem that much of this happened while Antigonos was involved in Phoenicia.[38] Once he had the ships the siege was easily finished, and in summer 314 his fleet sailed to the Aegean. In strategic terms Antigonos occupied the centre ground and could choose to attack in any direction. The strongest of his enemies were Ptolemy and Kassandros, and he opted to tackle Kassander first. If he won he would control King Alexander IV (if he survived), plus Macedon and Greece. These were still the main sources of military manpower, and it was consistent with his assumption of the regency, and his clear enmity towards Kassander. The decision required that the situation in Anatolia be cleared up first. This decision may well have been a strategic error; if he had eliminated Ptolemy first, there would be no distractions in his rear; a defeat of Ptolemy would have driven Seleukos out of Egypt, and it was Seleukos who was, despite his lack of obvious power, his main enemy. Antigonos was fully conscious of the problem, and met Ptolemy at an Egyptian place called Ekregma for negotiations. They failed. Antigonos was not prepared to agree to Ptolemy's terms.[39]

Antigonos marched from Syria into his old satrapy of Phrygia and his old capital at Kelainai in the spring of 313. His nephew Polemaios had pushed Askepiodoros out of Anatolia, and was sent against Asandros in Karia, where Kassander had sent other troops to assist his ally. Kassander's forces were defeated, and Antigonos came in with his main army and polished off the conquest of the whole area. This took some time, for it involved intrigues, captures, escapes and betrayals, but by the end of 313 Antigonos was in control. Ptolemy sent troops to help Asandros, making it all the more important for Antigonos to control the area.[40]

Antigonos' fleet gained control of the islands in the centre of the Aegean. These were formed into the League of the Islanders, with Antigonos as patron.[41] This was the first real test of Antigonos' proclaimed 'freedom' of the Greeks. Its implementation was a good omen for the Greek cities; Antigonos placed no garrisons in the islands, unless requested to. In Karia, also, one of the reasons for Asandros' failure was the preference of the Greek cities of the coast for Antigonos over him.

Antigonos sent another nephew, Telesphoros, into the Peloponnese, where Kassander's position crumbled,[42] though Athens held firm to Kassander's cause under the philosopher tyrant, Demetrios of Phaleron. Polemaios was sent with another force into Euboia and Boiotia.[43] Kassander had recently restored the city of Thebes, which was not a move calculated to win him support from the rest of the Boiotian cities; Antigonos had made this one of his main complaints about Kassander.

By the end of 313 Antigonos had made progress in recovering control of Anatolia, and in gaining power in Greece. Kassander held only the Mounychia fortress in Athens south of Thessaly. But Antigonos' policy of not garrisoning the cities he took from Kassander left his position in Greece precarious, and he made no impression on Kassander's base in Macedon or on Lysimachos in Thrace. Meanwhile, Ptolemy, who had shifted his Egyptian capital from Memphis to Alexandria during 313, used his fleet to suppress a revolt in Kyrene, conquer

Cyprus, and launch attacks in Kilikia, where Antigonos stored a large part of his treasure.[44]

Antigonos wintered his army at the Hellespont, where he could menace Lysimachos across the Straits, though Byzantion refused to join his alliance.[45] Threatened from that direction and by Polemaios from the south and with the Aegean dominated by Antigonos' fleet, Kassander offered to negotiate, but Antigonos spurned this, not yet strong enough to dictate terms.[46] He was encouraged by this evidence of chinks in the alliance's armour. Polemaios pushed northwards into Phokis during the winter, but neither there nor at the Straits could the allies' defences be penetrated.

Antigonos' army in Syria was nominally commanded by his teenage son Demetrios, with several experienced Macedonian commanders assisting him. Ptolemy, with Seleukos as one of his commanders, threatened a full-scale invasion of Syria. This was intended to achieve several goals, for Ptolemy to recover southern Syria and draw Demetrios' army southwards out of northern Syria, his main base; and secondly, to allow Seleukos to get to Babylon. Ptolemy also hoped that a battle would seriously damage the Antigonid forces. It seems unlikely that they expected to do more than inflict a severe defeat on Demetrios, but even that would reduce the pressure on Kassander.

The subsequent battle of Gaza proved to be the decisive encounter in the war, with disproportionate effects. Demetrios commanded only a fraction of his father's army, about 18,000 men; Ptolemy's army had been built up to about 20,000 men. He had been recruiting steadily for years, mostly Macedonians and Greek mercenaries, but he also mustered a few units of Egyptians – the only time in a century his family did this. Demetrius and his advisers faced two old soldiers of Alexander, of somewhat more cunning aspect than they were. Demetrios had a force of 43 elephants, intended as the decisive weapon. This threat stimulated the defensive inventiveness in their opponents.

The two phalanxes faced each other, and both sides massed most of their cavalry on the eastern wing; Demetrios' elephants faced a solid phalanx of infantry and archers, protected by a carpet of spikes and chains. The battle therefore became one between cavalry. Demetrios' cavalry charged and mixed it with Ptolemy and Seleukos' horsemen. The elephants charged, but were stopped by the spikes and chains, which they would not walk on. The archers then shot down the mahouts and aimed at the elephants' eyes, maddening the beasts and driving them away into the Antigonid army, which broke and fled, as much from their own rampaging elephants as from the Ptolemaic pursuit.[47]

Demetrios acknowledged defeat after his army disintegrated and Ptolemy captured Gaza city. He retired as far as northern Syria before recovering control of a serious number of soldiers.[48] Ptolemy, conscious that he had beaten only a part of Antigonos' forces, moved his army carefully northwards. Tyre was held against Ptolemy, but only briefly; the garrison was unwilling to stand a siege and forced surrender.[49]

Ptolemy gained more than just territory. He took over most of Demetrios' hoplites, Greek mercenaries who were not in the business of fighting to the death. They were sent into Egypt as colonists, a very useful reinforcement of the Greco-Macedonian element among Ptolemy's subjects.[50] Ptolemy did not need to recruit Egyptians again.

The next result was that the allies opened up a new front. From the battle-field – this was clearly prearranged and would probably have happened even if Demetrios had won – Seleukos took a small force on a ride past Demetrios' disintegrating army, through Syria and Mesopotamia (where he collected more troops from Antigonos' garrison at Karrhai) and into Babylonia to reclaim his lost satrapy. Antigonos' satrap, Peithon son of Agenor, had been killed at Gaza, which will have loosened the command structure. He reached Babylon with about 3,000 soldiers, three times the number he started with. This expedition was undoubtedly Seleukos' own idea; Ptolemy was never so audacious, and he did not even risk any troops – all of them were Seleukos' (or originally Antigonos') men.[51]

Seleukos was central to the opposition of the allies to Antigonos. He had apparently been content to be satrap in Babylonia until his expulsion, and undoubtedly saw this as unjust and sought revenge. His first aim was to recover his satrapy, but that would now never be enough. He remained the most determined of Antigonos' enemies, but he was, in Babylon, the most vulnerable of the coalition partners.

Even at the time, it must have been clear that, as a result of Gaza and Seleukos' return to Babylon, Antigonos' grasp at Alexander's empire had failed. He recovered Syria during 311,[52] but he could not get into Egypt. He could threaten Kassander and Lysimachos, but not penetrate their strongholds; now he had lost Babylonia. Then from Greece news arrived that his nephew Telesphoros, who had been made a subordinate of Polemaios', had rebelled,[53] financing his rising by looting treasures from the sanctuary at Olympia. This rebellion did not last long, but it prevented any operations by Polemaios in Greece for a time. Antigonos was on the defensive.

From Media, Antigonos' viceroy Nikanor came down though the mountains with an army of 10,000 infantry and 7,000 cavalry to evict Seleukos. He was ambushed in the marshes of the Tigris valley by Seleukos' much smaller army, and Seleukos captured and then enlisted most of his army.[54] Suddenly Seleukos was a formidable force, with an army of 20,000 men, and solid local support in Babylonia, where Antigonos' regime had not been liked. Antigonos' governing methods were not conducive to his popularity, and it is noticeable that his soldiers were very willing to join his enemies: he had now lost well over 20,000 men to Ptolemy and Seleukos.

Antigonos was fighting on four fronts – Syria, Babylon, Greece and the Straits. Demetrios was sent on a flying raid against Babylon city, part of which he seized, but he encountered a stubborn defence commanded by Seleukos' general Patrokles. Antigonos had given him a strict time limit; he had to withdraw when he did not succeed at once.[55] Antigonos could hit out in all directions but score in none. Fought to a standstill, he made a peace with his western opponents. Kassander and Lysimachos seized the opportunity created by Telesphoros' brief rebellion to negotiate. Agreement was quickly reached and then Ptolemy hastily joined in. The terms were that all should hold what they had, and that Antigonos' Tyre proclamation of Greek freedom should be accepted as common policy.[56] It was a peace of sorts, but not one anyone expected to last. Antigonos had not modified his ambitions. Above all, Seleukos was not included, either because he refused to be involved or because Antigonos refused to include him.

None of the participants was satisfied, but the fact of the truce indicated a mutual exhaustion. Antigonos was thwarted, Kassander and Ptolemy had lost territory, Lysimachos was very vulnerable. Some of the Greek cities had recovered a degree of autonomy, but were coming to realize that this involved accepting a relationship with a great man akin to subordination. Several of the more important cities were a good deal less than autonomous: Athens still had a Macedonian garrison backing up the dictatorial rule of Demetrios of Phaleron, Corinth had a Macedonian garrison on its acropolis under Polyperchon's control. There were still potent limits on the freedom of the Greek cities.

The cities of the eastern Aegean coast adapted well to this regime, for it was a distinct improvement in political terms on the methods the Persian Empire had used on them. Some of the grander cities – Ephesos, Miletos, Rhodes among them – began to enjoy a period of great economic prosperity at this time. Much of this was a result of Antigonos' even and consistent approach, based on his proclamation of Greek civic freedom, which he conscientiously applied, so setting the pattern for everyone else.[57] The preoccupation of the great men with combating each other, therefore, permitted Greek cities to work themselves into political situations of less onerous supervision, and largely prevented them from fighting each other. In some cases states went further. The Aitolian League emerged as a local power in Greece fit to stand beside, or rather against, Macedon. Attacked without result by the joint forces of Antipater and Krateros in 322, and again by Kassander later, the League had emerged more solid than before, and was looking to expand.

The main power in the Greek peninsula was still, however, Macedon. Partially drained of its men of military age by Alexander for his great campaign,[58] it was still capable of fielding tough armies under Antipater and his son. Kassander was able to extend his power into Greece and across the western mountains into Epiros, and seems to have had little trouble with his northern boundary. Thrace, now a separate satrapy, was both a protection and less of a potential problem than before, and Thessaly was now almost indissolubly united to Macedon.

There was one other clause in the peace of 311. Kassander was given the title '*strategos* over Europe', a non-existent office, in imitation of that which Antigonos had held in Asia. Polyperchon was thus demoted even further and subordinated to Kassander; there is no sign that he had been consulted. Kassander's new title meant little, but was an apparent acknowledgement of Antigonos' claim to the regency, and that all these campaigning satraps were only really doing it on behalf of their king, Alexander IV. The boy was now 12 years old, and would reach his majority in at most six years. At that time he could claim power. Kassander's office of '*strategos* over Europe' would therefore expire by 305.

Antigonos' career had been one of seizing opportunities: first his capacity for government and command had been shown in the aftermath of Issos, then his capacity for intrigue brought him to the usefully vague position as '*strategos* over Asia'. He exploited this to campaign against Eumenes, gaining Asia as a result. But his acquisition of great military and financial power scared his contemporaries into a coalition. The defeat of Gaza began the slow destruction of his power, though he controlled huge territories still. This did not dent his control of the Persian treasure and of Alexander's empire from Babylonia to the Aegean, nor did his enemies make much progress against him, but it did suggest that the restoration of Alexander's empire by one man's efforts was going to be impossible.

9

The new king, 311–306 BC

The peace of 311 did not last. It is likely none of them expected it to, and Seleukos was excluded from the start, so fighting never stopped. The war in the east continued for several years, ending in a formal peace in 308. Had Antigonos won, he could have turned with all the more power on his western enemies, and they certainly understood this, so that the truce in the west broke down fairly soon. Antigonos was unable to concentrate for long on his eastern war, and his central position became converted into over-extension, where his enemies were able to attack unexpectedly wherever he was weak.

His nephew Polemaios had been promoted by Antigonos in the past, and was successful in Karia and in Greece during the last war, but now he saw Antigonos' own sons, especially Demetrios, overtaking him, and aimed to create an independent realm of his own in Greece. He contacted Kassander, who naturally encouraged and helped him, and subverted Antigonos' governor in Hellespontine Phrygia.[1] For Antigonos, this took precedence over the war with Seleukos, and he took the opportunity to move against Ptolemy's outposts in Kilikia. The war in the west was on again, after only a year, but little effort went into the fighting at first.

Antigonos' son Philippos speedily dealt with Hellespontine Phrygia.[2] Antigonos contacted Polyperchon, who was still in Greece with an army and had control of Corinth and Sikyon, in an attempt to distract and possibly remove Kassander. Herakles, Alexander's son by Barsine, now about 17, was delivered to Polyperchon, along with money, some troops and an alliance with the Aitolians. He used the boy as a figurehead in an attempt to take Macedon away from Kassander. After a tense armed confrontation, Kassander persuaded Polyperchon to kill his protégé and set himself up as a local tyrant as Kassander's man in the Peloponnese. This marked the end of Polyperchon's importance.[3]

Ptolemy meanwhile reacted to the attacks on his Kilikian posts by a wide-ranging naval expedition. First he fastened his control on Cyprus by eliminating the last of the local city kings, and placed his brother Menelaos there as viceroy.[4] He cruised along the coast of southern Asia Minor seizing control of a string of towns and forts and cities – Korakesion, Phaselis, Xanthos, Patara, Kaunos, Myndos – which established his full control over the eastern Mediterranean from Cyrenaica round to the Aegean, apart from Phoenicia. Large numbers of soldiers were to come from Pamphylia and Pisidia in Ptolemaic service, funnelled through these towns.[5] Korakesion was strongly fortified and became the seat of his power in the area.

In the Aegean, Ptolemy based himself on Kos, and contacted Polemaios who rather trustingly visited him; Ptolemy decided he would not be a useful tool, and killed him.[6] He seized a strategic post at Itanos at the eastern end of Crete, which he fortified, and then moved across to the Peloponnese. He had issued a rival 'freedom' proclamation to counter that of Antigonos many years before, but the Greek cities were suspicious of him. He seized control of Corinth and Sikyon, and then asked for contributions to his expenses. This confirmed all those Greek suspicions; they made polite noises and his local support faded away.[7]

The Macedonian royal family had provided the main casualties in this conflict. The peace of 311 was in fact a disguised invitation to the jailers to eliminate any members of the family they held. None of them, having been independent rulers for a decade, was prepared to submit again. Kassander's appointment as '*strategos* over Europe' was to last only until Alexander IV reached his majority; within a year he had arranged for both Alexander and his mother to be murdered. (The exact date is not clear, for he could scarcely announce it right away, but 310 or 309 seem most likely.) Only Polyperchon had taken Herakles seriously as a candidate. During his naval campaign, Ptolemy contacted Kleopatra (under Antigonos' control in Sardis), with a proposal of marriage. She escaped briefly, but was captured and murdered at Antigonos' orders. By 308, there were no members of the old Argead royal family left alive,[8] but Alexander IV was assumed to be king still by the general public.[9]

The war between Antigonos and Seleukos ended in 308. Seleukos secured control of Susiana before Demetrios attacked Babylon in 311, and afterwards he was able to make a quick campaign into Media, where Nikanor, Antigonos' governor, was quickly eliminated.[10] Seleukos made contact with the eastern satraps, the men who had opposed the ambition of Peithon to control them, and had felt the same about Nikanor. Seleukos, unlike Antigonos, had been with Alexander all through the eastern campaigns, and was able to reassure them. One source implies that Seleukos travelled as far east as the Paropamisadai, but this seems unlikely, for Seleukos was under attack in the west, when Antigonos freed himself of his enemies there.[11]

The course of the fighting between the two in 310–308 is largely unknown, except that it took place in Babylonia and Mesopotamia. By his quick eastern expedition Seleukos had eliminated the possibility of being attacked from the Iranian side, and was also able to draw on Iranian manpower. The final battle, the only one recorded in any detail, was a two-day affair: the first day was a draw, after which the two armies withdrew for a night's rest. Antigonos' army settled down, but Seleukos kept his men armed, and attacked before the other army was ready.[12] Seleukos was able to drive Antigonos' forces out of Babylonia and from much of Mesopotamia, and Antigonos was persuaded to agree to a peace agreement. The terms are not known, but some can be deduced.

Mesopotamia was divided between the two men, who fortified their holdings. Antigonos developed a line of towns – Edessa, Karrhai, Ichnai – as a forward defence for the vital Euphrates crossing at Thapsakos, which was now becoming called simply Zeugma – 'the Bridge'. Seleukos' towns were further east, blocking the routes along the Euphrates and across the Mesopotamian steppe at Nisibis, and Dura-Europos. A wide area of no-man's-land was left between them.[13]

By the end of 308, Antigonos' situation had deteriorated, but it was also made clearer. He controlled Asia Minor and Syria, together with part of Mesopotamia. Seleukos was for the moment fought to a standstill, and turned to the east again. Ptolemy's adventure into Greece was only partly successful: he held Corinth and Sikyon, Cyprus, and several places in Asia Minor, but he had been driven out of Syria. Kassander had rebuffed the attempt to remove him from Macedon with little difficulty. Polyperchon was finished.[14]

Seleukos returned to the east in 307, staying in the eastern satrapies and India for the next four years, confident that Antigonos would keep the peace. The result of the defeat in the two-day battle, and of the fortifications they had both made in Mesopotamia, produced a balance, and Antigonos never really was interested in that area anyway. Seleukos was successful in establishing his authority over the easterners. One satrap, Sibyrtios of Arachosia, had survived from 324 until Seleukos' campaign.[15] Stasanor of Baktria-Sogdiana had apparently developed territorial ambitions of his own;[16] Seleukos probably removed him. The new satraps he appointed are unknown. Demodamas, one of Seleukos' commanders, is known to have campaigned along the Iaxartes;[17] perhaps he was the Sogdian satrap. Seleukos created none of the resentment roused by Antigonos, presumably handling the situation with tact and finesse. He spent three years or so organizing and campaigning in the east, before heading on to India. There was clearly a lot to do, and the satraps he found in place had been unable to do it. Some sort of central direction was obviously required, despite the satraps' wish for independence. The presence of Seleukos' victorious, and large, army was no doubt decisive.[18]

Ptolemy had installed a long-time governor in Cyrenaica, a Macedonian called Ophellas. He aspired to independence, and became allied with Agathokles of Syracuse in a campaign against Carthage. Agathokles was more than a match for him in intrigue and betrayal, and took over his army, mainly made up of Greek mercenaries, in particular Athenians.[19] Perhaps Ptolemy was not sorry to see Ophellas go, but it is a sign of his governmental method that both Menelaos in Cyprus and Ophellas in Cyrenaica were left in place for long periods.

Ptolemy's basic problem was a shortage of Greek and Macedonian soldiers.

He had filched the imperial navy in 315, and captured and recruited 8,000 of Demetrios' soldiers after Gaza, and he recruited vigorously in the main recruiting grounds for mercenary soldiers, old Greece and Anatolia. These men were expensive, but he had control of one of the richest countries in the world; and by importing Greeks to man the local government system of Egypt, he was able to establish a bureaucratic regime which would allow him to tax the Egyptian population consistently and heavily. He made gestures towards Egyptian political and religious expectations, honouring the native priests and giving grants for temple building and repair, but his attention was fixed almost continuously on the threats from outside and on the need to be ready to meet those threats. He always had to balance the need of the country against that for strong defences, the need of Greek civil and military manpower against the Macedonian inheritance of personal governance he brought with him, and against the wellbeing of the Egyptian population whose labour upheld the whole structure. It was mainly Greeks who were available for recruitment, plus men such as Karians and Pisidians who were Hellenized by their service, but it was the Macedonian city of Alexandria which was his capital. The city was always called Alexandria-by-Egypt, a Macedonian foundation next to, but not part of, Egypt.[20]

Ptolemy emerges as a cautious, careful man, moving slowly and deliberately to fasten his grip firmly on Egypt by means of a detailed system of government, and forming a series of forward defensive positions to protect it. This policy made it all but impossible for any man to recover the unity of Alexander's empire. He was not going to publicize a decision implying the destruction of Alexander's empire, but his actions forced the conclusion that he aimed for independent rule from at least 320. He was one of the rocks on which Antigonos' attempt to revive the united empire was wrecked.

The other main obstacle to a restoration of imperial unity was Kassander. Like Ptolemy, he put his own ambition before the imperial heritage of Alexander and his own father, Antipater. His father's rule had predisposed Macedonians to accept Kassander, though what they really wanted was the old royal family. Kassander kept Alexander IV alive for years, and eventually had him and his mother killed secretly. The elimination of the royal family left the Macedonians with Kassander, if unenthusiastically; he was at least married to the last member of the old family, Philip's daughter Thessalonike, and the Argeads would therefore continue through their children.

Kassander ruled as a traditional Macedonian king, moving about the kingdom, dispensing justice, and in war personally leading the Macedonian levy. His policies were necessarily defensive, for the Macedonian home forces were seriously reduced by Alexander's levies, and Kassander did not have access to the military recruitment areas available to his enemy, nor did he have the money for a bigger army. His policy in Greece was like his father's; more markedly military than either Philip or Alexander had felt necessary. There is no sign of any serious expansion of the Macedonian state, nor was there any elaboration of the administration. Thessaly and the old inland kingdoms were integrated with core Macedon.[21]

Ptolemy and Kassander were therefore both building on their inheritances from the past in organizing and ruling their lands. Ptolemy had a country with an age-old tradition of rule by royal control, exercised through a bureaucratic system designed to extract tax revenues. This was adopted by Ptolemy and adapted to his requirements, staffed by imported Greeks, and the whole defended by an expensive Greco-Macedonian army. Ptolemy – it seems characteristic of his careful, pragmatic ways – took over the system he found in existence, improved its efficiency, and staffed it with men he felt he could rely on. For all his apparent conciliation of the native Egyptian population, he clearly did not feel he could rely on them or trust them.[22] Similarly Kassander, probably without having consciously to decide it, accepted the old Macedonian system. There was, after all, no real point in changing it, it must have seemed, for the old system had obviously worked.

It was Antigonos who had to develop a new governing system. He was the one man of the three who ruled a geographically extensive territory with no settled traditional or unified governing system, except insofar as they had been part of the loosely governed Persian Empire. Antigonos aimed to expand his territory and at the same time had to be constantly on guard against attacks, so he had to rule in a much more detailed, perhaps oppressive, manner. Such a huge area could not be ruled by methods of the Macedonian kingship. His lands were widely spread, and widely various in geography and society, so the bureaucratic methods appropriate in Egypt did not apply either.

In legal terms Antigonos was the regent for the king. In practice he exercised royal powers, controlling the royal lands, appointing the officials, commanding armies. His lands had been conquered, or as Alexander insisted from the first crossing of the Hellespont, were 'spear-won', implying that the king had unrestricted power over all the lands and all the peoples. He could impose any administrative system he chose, in theory. Probably few of his subjects concerned themselves with Antigonos' theoretical legal and constitutional position: he had the power, and that was what counted.

The sources of the administration he developed were thus partly Macedonian and partly Persian. There was first the theory and practice of kingship as he had seen it in Macedon. Antigonos was almost 50 when Alexander put him in control of Phrygia, the first time he administered anything bigger than a rural estate. The administrative system he knew was Philip's: a group of men who were given a variety of tasks – diplomatic, military, judicial and administrative – as and when needed. This was also the essence of Antigonos' central administrative system. The group were his *philoi*, 'friends', which became a formal rank under later kings.

The second source was the Akhaimenid Empire, which had ruled his lands for two centuries. When he took over Phrygia some men remained in office in the satrapal administration, and all he had to do was get them working again. As his area of authority grew, he appointed satraps to his conquests. It seems probable that the old satrapies continued, but it also seems that the satraps became called *strategoi*, a title suggesting purely military responsibilities. Alexander had appointed men to separate military and financial duties in each satrapy, and this may be what Antigonos did, with the exception that the satrap and the *strategos* became a single military and administrative official. A separate financial official, no doubt appointed by, and answering directly to, Antigonos himself, was also put in place. Antigonos was in power long enough to fix a firm administrative system in place, but it seems that the flexibility of Philip's informal system prevailed; the Akhaimenid system was also fairly informal, at the level of the ordinary farmer and townsman, so a fusion was not difficult.

In addition to the conquered Persian lands, Antigonos had also under his control, albeit not quite directly, a large number of Greek, Phoenician, Karian and Lykian cities. These were accustomed to a large degree of autonomy, even under the former Persian regime, and there is no sign that Antigonos wished to change this. Indeed he made it a hallmark of his rule to respect their 'freedom', though by doing so he effectively restricted that freedom. The cities administered themselves, so he had a third administrative system to use as a pattern.

Antigonos, a busy man with little time for reflection and well set in his ways, did not develop a new government system to be applied throughout his realm, but over time an administration did evolve which was competent and provided a degree of security to the inhabitants. It also produced a substantial and reliable income for Antigonos. Above all, he had to work with an existing system; it could change only slowly and piecemeal if it was not to break down altogether.

Like Kassander and Ptolemy, Antigonos' administrative system grew out of the preceding situation. It had a stronger military flavour than theirs, with strong Macedonian elements to it, and there were Akhaimenid elements also.[23] The one thing common to all these rulers was their relationship with the cities, often Greek, within or next to their territories. Some of the kings had clearly felt that the best way to deal with such cities was to crush them; and several had been captured and destroyed in the previous century, notably by Philip II in the Chalkidike. The cities themselves were usually unwilling to be subordinated to the kings, but the kings were usually too strong for them.

At the same time Philip and Alexander had founded new cities as a means of extending their control into new areas. Alexander left groups of soldiers in various places, as garrisons or colonists; or perhaps it was that the garrisons developed into colonies as time went on. Garrisons are obvious tactics for military rulers, and are often only temporary, but it took a good deal of effort and expense to found a city, always intended to be permanent. Alexander's later reputation as a city founder was exaggerated by the retrospective attribution to him of many places which had been garrisons. The establishment of a new city brought considerable renown to its founder, and it was a powerful political statement, but took time, attention and money.

The Macedonian rulers after Alexander all founded cities. Ptolemy had a head start for he acquired responsibility for the new city of Alexandria, founded ten years before his appointment as Egyptian satrap; some progress was made by Kleomenes in its construction, but there was still much for Ptolemy to do, including the construction of Alexander's tomb. By 313 the city was sufficiently built up to become the location of his court – a construction period of about 20 years. Ptolemy ruled a densely populated land. The Greeks who took up positions in the military and civil administration had to be spread throughout it, but Ptolemy had no wish to see them organized as autonomous cities; he founded just one city himself, in the south, calling it Ptolemais.[24]

Seleukos found groups of Greeks and Macedonians scattered throughout his lands, usually former soldiers settled in old Persian centres or new Macedonian garrisons. He organized several of these places as new cities, each with a defined territory, a set of public buildings, including city walls. Each city also had a garrison established in an adjoining citadel; he established cities, but also ensured that he retained control. Some of these places were organized while he was in the east campaigning in Baktria and India, and he inherited Alexander's foundations as well: at Alexandria at Kandahar, Alexandria-Eschate and Merv, in Margiane.[25]

In later years cities developed in Media. At the western end of the royal road were Ekbatana, the old Median capital, Laodikeia at modern Nihavend, Konkobar (now Kangavar) and a fourth at modern Khurra; and along the great road were cities at Rhagai (near Tehran) and Hekatompylos.[26] Media was the supervising satrapy for the whole east, a region called the 'Upper Satrapies', but the cities were units of administration within but separate from it. A similar situation is best seen in Syria, where the four great cities, Antioch, Seleukeia, Apamea and Laodikeia, and half a dozen other cities between the coast and the Euphrates, divided up the whole of Syria between them. There was never a satrap of Syria in the Seleukid kingdom, since it was governed through the cities. These city regions were called by the city's name with the addition of the ending 'ene' – so, for example, Apamene.

This is the governing system eventually organized by Seleukos, work continued by Antiochus I after him. There were two main elements, city regions and satrapies, but each was directly connected to the king, the satraps by their very appointments, and the cities through an *epistates*, a *philos* of the king appointed as his liaison with a particular city. The responsibilities of the two were, of course, different; the satraps were largely military men with governing duties in rural areas; the cities ran themselves; both had the duty of collecting and forwarding the royal taxes.

The contrast with the Macedonian personal monarchy is obvious; the Seleukid state, from the moment Seleukos united Media, Susiana, Persis and Babylonia in the aftermath of the defeat of Nikanor – that is, within a few months – was far too big to be governed by the king personally, hence the need for satraps. It was also different from the system of Ptolemy in Egypt. Babylonia might have been a suitable place for a detailed bureaucratic regime, but it was a land divided among self-governing cities.[27] Seleukos therefore developed an answer to the administrative problem, and also solved his other major difficulty, a shortage of skilled Greco-Macedonian manpower. The cities he founded were designed to support a Greco-Macedonian landowning class whose duty it was to supply soldiers for the royal army and administrators to the royal court and bureaucracy, as well as run their cities. These were the people who formed the citizens of the kingdom.

It took time to devise this system and found the Greek and Macedonian cities all through the kingdom. Seleukos, until 300 or so, did not have the manpower to plant many cities, nor the access to the Mediterranean needed to attract people from Greece, but he made a start with his Iranian cities and a new imperial capital, Seleukeia in Babylonia, and with the frontier towns in Mesopotamia. Eventually he took over the system developed by Antigonos, and then he was able to organize the first truly Hellenistic kingdom, later to become the pattern for the others, including Macedon and, ultimately, for Rome.

Seleukeia-on-the-Tigris in Babylonia was one of a series of new, great cities founded by all Alexander's successors on the model of Alexandria-by-Egypt. All these great lords copied Alexander's one great city, and added other smaller cities. Kassander repaired some of the destruction perpetrated in Greece; he refounded Thebes, gathering up the surviving citizens, as early as 316 – though as usual the rest of the Boiotians were unwelcoming – and in Macedon he founded Kassandreia to replace the destroyed Potidaia, on the western finger of the Chalkidike, and Thessalonika (named for his wife) at the head of the Thermaic Gulf.[28] Both cities were populated by gathering inhabitants from nearby towns and cities, a process called synoikism which saved a founder from the need to search for colonists. The results were substantial cities, which developed quickly into immediate financial and military assets. The work was also overtly political: Thebes had been Alexander's victim, Potidaia Philip II's, Olynthian survivors were collected for Kassandreia. Kassander was indicating his claim to be an alternative to the Argead dynasty while by marrying Thessalonike linking himself with it. (No wonder Antigonos, having developed similar but greater ambitions, complained about Kassander's cities.) Kassander's brother Alexarchos was captivated by new ideas of perfect societies; he was allowed to found his own city, Ouranopolis – 'city of heaven' – on the Athos peninsula, close to the site of a city, Akanthos, destroyed by Philip II in his conquest of the Chalkidikian League.[29]

Lysimachos struggled to make his satrapy of Thrace a worthwhile office. The Thracians, conquered by Philip II, had not wished to continue as Macedonian subjects, and it was all too easy for Antigonos to raise rebellion in Lysimachos' rear when they were in conflict. Lysimachos founded a city, called Lysimacheia to nobody's surprise, at the root of the Thracian Chersonese, where it replaced Kardia, which had always suffered from Thracian and Athenian attacks. So long as it was supported by royal favour, this was a successful city.[30]

Kassander did his founding work early in his rule, in 316 and 315; Lysimachos not till 309, and between these dates, both Seleukos and Antigonos founded cities. Antigonos was rather more active in this field than his competitors, but then he was considerably richer, had more manpower, and in many ways was more in need of urban centres in his lands. Most of his foundations were small, basically garrisons, and tended to have names derived from Macedonian towns – Pella, Ichnai, Beroia. He was also responsible for some bigger projects, which can be recognized by being named for him. There was an Antigoneia in Syria (which did not last), another in the Troad, by the Hellespont, was a synoikism, which changed its name to Alexandria later, and there were three Antigoneias in Hellespontine Phrygia, an area liable to rebellion. Like Kassander, he refounded a destroyed city – Smyrna – by facilitating the return of its scattered citizens.[31]

Antigonos' cities were concentrated in the north-west, near the Straits, and in Ionia, where Smyrna, Teos, Lebedos and Kolophon were all revived or refounded. Three urban centres established in Phrygia were at the intersection of a major north–south route with a major east–west route – Dokimeion, Synnada, and the city he used as his governing centre, Kelainai. Dokimeion was founded by Dokimos, a slippery Macedonian who changed sides very easily; nearby Themisonion was founded by another Macedonian, Themison; Antigonos was clearly quite amenable to such work; those cities were deep within his own territory and not liable to become independent principalities. Antigonos' greatest city, where he spent his last years, was in northern Syria, on the Orontes.

Seleukos had had to defend Babylon against more than one attack by Antigonos' forces, and assisted its recovery after their ravagings, rebuilding the city's public buildings. He also began the construction of a new city of his own, Seleukeia-by-the-Tigris, north-east of Babylon, and planned on a scale to rival Alexandria-by-Egypt. It was about two-thirds the size of Alexandria, but Alexandria had a huge palace area. This work was probably begun as soon as

Seleukos had returned to Babylonia in 311, and continued throughout the war with Antigonos and after.[32]

The founding of cities was part of the competition these men had with one another, and they were emulating, or competing with, Alexander. The use of Alexandria by Ptolemy as his capital was a clear statement of his assumption of part of the mantle of the dead king; Kassander's refoundation of Thebes and his foundations on the sites of destroyed Chalkidikian cities were a repudiation of the policies of Philip and Alexander. Antigonos only founded a great city of the Alexandria and Seleukeia type in his last years. Neither Kassander nor Antigonos had been on the great expedition, so their relations with Alexander's memory were tangential, where Ptolemy, while he was intent on subtracting Egypt from Alexander's empire, was able to link himself convincingly with him, even to the extent of writing a version of the expedition as his own memoirs.

Seleukos was the most insistent on claiming the heritage of the dead king. Between 308 and 303 he was campaigned in the east, where Alexander's hardest wars had been fought, a task Antigonos had avoided; this was clearly a policy directly aimed at Antigonos, and his new city at Seleukeia-on-the-Tigris was the only one of the cities these men founded on an Alexandrian scale. For those attuned to the symbolism behind the doings of these great lords, it will have become clear by 308–307 that Seleukos had developed an ambition to restore the unity of the empire of Alexander. To make this quite clear, certain stories were being circulated, such as that he was born in the same year as Alexander, or that he had worn Alexander's diadem when he had rescued it from the river in Babylon.[33]

Antigonos was free of the war with Seleukos from 308, and Seleukos' eastern expedition mean he was no longer an immediate threat. Antigonos now broke the western stalemate. In 307 Demetrios, in command of a fleet, captured Athens, claiming to restore the city's freedom, removed Kassander's garrisons, and ejected Demetrios of Phaleron. The Athenians overwhelmed both son and father with thanks and honours, and Antigonos sent in money and food, and timber for use in the Athenian shipyards.[34] The capture of Athens produced a solid block of allies across central Greece for him.

This substantial political position, bolstered by Antigonid garrisons placed where requested, was sufficiently deterring to block any Kassandrian riposte. Antigonos now had Demetrios take his fleet and army to Cyprus. As a major Ptolemaic base, this threatened all the Antigonid coasts from Palestine to the Aegean. Demetrios performed brilliantly. He besieged Salamis, the main city of the island, and when Ptolemy came with relief, he defeated his fleet and captured most of his army, then captured the city as well; some of the Ptolemaic soldiers were enlisted into his own service, and the captured ships reinforced his fleet.[35]

This was the greatest military/naval victory since Gaugamela and seemed to cut down Ptolemy's power and pretensions. Yet neither Salamis nor Athens was decisive, for control of these places would not win the war. The victories were nevertheless major achievements, and Salamis was used by Antigonos to claim the empire of Alexander. When the news was taken to him at Antigoneia in Syria, both he and Demetrios were proclaimed as kings.[36]

This was a political manifesto. Antigonos was stating that he was now, by virtue of the victories of his army and fleet, the legitimate successor of Philip and Alexander. And by proclaiming Demetrios as king as well, the actual victor at Athens and Salamis, he was establishing a new dynasty, replacing the Argeads with the Antigonids. The problem was that victories do not mean a war is won, nor did the capture of Athens or the conquest of the island of Cyprus give him universal dominion. Proclaiming himself king did not make Antigonos the successor to Alexander's kingdom, and by claiming it Antigonos was actually joining Kassander and Ptolemy in refusing to restore the empire as a whole. The royal proclamation was a gesture of defiance and a confession of overall failure.

10

Antigonos' failure, 306–298 BC

Antigonos' proclamation as king took place in 306 because of the Salamis victory, but it was only the year before that the death of Alexander IV had become widely known, though it was surely rumoured before then. His death was blamed variously on disease, drugs, the commander of his guard and Kassander. Kassander staged a ritual cremation and ceremonially deposited the ashes in the Argead royal cemetery at Aigai, perhaps during 306.[1] This was one of the triggers for Antigonos' self-proclamation, for the lords had been officially acting as Alexander IV's subordinates until then. His name had been used by all of them in dating documents and on coins they issued.

Antigonos' was a personal title, not territorial, nor did it relate to a specific people. Alexander had been 'King of the Macedonians', and this was the title Kassander eventually used, but Antigonos and Demetrios were only 'king'; had he controlled Macedon, no doubt this would have been Antigonos' choice, but the plain title of king was one referring back to the Akhaimenid rulers. Antigonos' choice of title was thus designed to emphasize his claim to be the ruler of the whole of Alexander's empire and successor to Cyrus and Dareios. It was a claim his rivals denied and disputed.

The timing of the proclamation was regulated by the victory at Salamis, and he put on a particular show for the occasion. Demetrios sent one of his officers, Aristodemos of Miletos, with the news to Antigonos at Antigoneia in Syria. Aristodemos landed and walked silently and slowly to the city – a distance of perhaps 20 km. When he reached the palace, tension was great, and he broke it by shouting 'Hail, King Antigonos', and then explained the victory. Antigonos' *philoi* rallied round, a diadem was produced, and Antigonos was king. He then appointed Demetrios as king by sending him a second diadem.[2]

This was not the spontaneous event it was supposed to seem, but it did emphasize two aspects: Antigonos' monarchy was personal to him and his family, and it was connected with victory. These aspects became part of the process of king-making during the rest of the ancient world. Even Roman emperors of wholly unmilitary aspect, such as Claudius, felt the need to seal their accession by a military victory. In the Hellenistic world, the pattern was set, but power and authority was not dependent on victories. Antigonos' rivals and contemporaries were able to make themselves kings without them. In many ways it was safer not to depend on military prowess, and this was shown by the nemesis which at once engulfed Antigonos and Demetrios.

Antigonos' clearly stated ambition, revealed by his self-proclamation as king and his successes at Athens and Salamis, brought his enemies together again, though it took some time for them to come to an actual alliance. Antigonos had a window of opportunity to make good his kingship. Kassander attacked Athens when Demetrios sailed east, but came up against a united city, a revived Athenian navy, Antigonid assistance to the city, and the enmity of the Aitolian League. For a time Athens was victorious, but Kassander built ships of his own, and by 304 he had returned to blockade the city by land and sea.[3]

Antigonos followed up Demetrios' triumph at Salamis and his proclamation by a campaign designed to finish off Ptolemy. A huge army of 88,000 men, with 83 elephants, marched south along the Syrian coast, accompanied by Demetrios' fleet of 150 ships and 100 transports. But the fleet was damaged by gales, failed to establish a landing and the army's supplies ran down. Ptolemy's defences held and the invaders had to retreat.[4]

Demetrios turned to attack Rhodes, which had refused to help in the Cyprus campaign on the grounds that it was friendly towards Ptolemy.[5] This attack on a neutral Greek city was one of the great sieges of the ancient world, lasting a year (305–304). Demetrios' ingenuity was taxed to the limit, as was the endurance of his soldiers and that of the Rhodians. Ptolemy sent in relief supplies, but his own defeat two years before had severely reduced his ability to intervene. In the end, with Rhodes untaken and Athens under severe pressure as a result of Kassander's blockade, Demetrios called off the attack. Rhodes agreed to assist him against everyone except Ptolemy,[6] and he sailed off to recover ground lost in Greece.

Antigonos continued to make the political running by the attacks on Egypt and Rhodes, but both were very public defeats, and in the aftermath of these adventures his rivals took royal titles themselves. Ptolemy seems to have been the first, some time after his defensive victory, and at the earliest in January 304, possibly somewhat later.[7] Seleukos followed, even though he was in the east at the time,[8] as did Lysimachos,[9] who emerged as a major player for the first time. Kassander is said to have refrained from taking the title, but his coins give him the title of king, as does an inscription.[10] These men had been acting as kings for years, and both Seleukos and Ptolemy had been called kings by their non-Macedonian, non-Greek subjects, who were unconcerned by the minutiae of Macedonian politics. Even Athens had addressed Antigonos as king as early as 307.[11] The use of the title spread to Sicily (Agathokles), the Bosporan state in the Crimea, and even to the tyrant of the city of Herakleia Pontike.[12]

Demetrios' return recovered the Antigonid position in Greece. The alliance with the Aitolians revived, he recovered that with the Boiotians, relieved Athens, and took Kenchreai, the port of Corinth.[13] But Demetrios indulged himself in such a bombastic and egocentric way in Athens as to disgust many Greeks. He interfered in Athenian internal politics, took up residence in the Parthenon with his women, drank to excess, and accepted addresses calling him divine. Yet he was still a highly competent commander, and in the spring he moved quickly, capturing Sikyon and Corinth by cleverly disguised surprise attacks, and took control of much of the northern Peloponnese.[14]

In spring 302 Demetrios announced the re-establishment of the league of cities of Greece, a revival of the old defunct League of Corinth of Philip II. Demetrios' version is referred to as the Hellenic League to distinguish it from the original.[15] Its membership was smaller than Philip's league, but otherwise it was similarly constituted. Demetrios was *hegemon* and commander-in-chief in wartime; and by centring it at Corinth, he was attempting to recapture the idea of the old league, but it was clearly understood to be an instrument of Antigonid imperialism, and he put a garrison in the Corinthian acropolis, and strenuously conscripted military manpower. How it might have worked in time of peace is unclear, but it did institutionalize Antigonid power in Greece on a more formal and perhaps a more acceptable basis than anything Kassander or Ptolemy had tried, and it gave Greeks at least some say in its affairs.

Even before the formation of the new league, Kassander had offered to make peace. Antigonos demanded surrender, apparently convinced that Demetrios would be able to finish Kassander off anyway. Kassander refused, and renewed his pleas to the allies for assistance.[16] He was already allied with Ptolemy, who had handed over Corinth to him some time earlier, and both had been victims of Demetrios' attack at Sikyon. The attack he faced from Demetrios also clearly threatened Lysimachos. The evidence of a continued Antigonid ambition to reunite the empire and do away with his rivals was enough to bring these western allies into another alliance. Contact was made with Seleukos, who also joined in.[17] Yet again, Antigonos' ambition had frightened the others into a coalition.

Demetrios invaded Thessaly in 302, having wasted a good deal of time being initiated into the Eleusinian mysteries at Athens (forcing the Athenians to conduct the ritual at the wrong time of year for his own convenience). He had an army of 56,000 infantry and 1,500 cavalry, but did not make as much progress as he should have, given the fact that his army was double that of Kassander's in size. Kassander had established strong garrisons in Pherai and in Phthiotic Thebes, and put his main army into a well-fortified entrenched camp. Demetrios was blocked.[18]

It is a sign of the desperation of the allies in the face of the great power wielded by Antigonos and Demetrios, that they took unusual chances. Kassander sent part of his army to join Lysimachos, who crossed the Straits to invade Antigonos' home base in Asia Minor;[19] Seleukos marched all the way from the east, through the Armenian mountains, to join him.[20] It was these two, Lysimachos and

Seleukos, who had scarcely been heard of in the previous five or six years, who were to do the main fighting.

The work of Lysimachos in his satrapy of Thrace is not well known, but a general outline can be discerned from the fragmentary sources.[21] He built on the original conquest by Philip II, which had been fairly superficial, and was able to conquer the area. He fought the Odrysae, the main Thracian people south of the Haemos Mountains, and the Getai to the north, established effective control over the Greek cities of the north Aegean coast, the Thracian Chersonese, and the Straits, and founded his new city of Lysimacheia. He cultivated good relations with Byzantion, which benefited from the peaceful conditions he established in its hinterland, and which was as hostile to Antigonos as everyone else. When reinforced by 8,000 men from Kassander's forces, he was able to leave his kingdom and take a substantial army, trained and toughened, to invade Antigonos' Anatolian lands.

Seleukos, like Lysimachos (and indeed like Ptolemy and Kassander), had concentrated in the last years on developing and organizing his state in the east. It is relevant to his achievement there that he was the only one of Alexander's officers who had not repudiated his Iranian wife. Not only that, but Apama was the daughter of Spitamenes, the great leader against Alexander 20 years before. Seleukos spent as long in Baktria on this visit as Alexander had in his original conquest. What he achieved is not recorded, but he probably achieved more in terms of pacifying and organizing the land than Alexander.[22]

Seleukos had moved on, like Alexander, into India. He had an equally hostile reception. By 305, northern India was united under the rule of Chandragupta Maurya. Seleukos did not have to fight every tribe and city, but he made no progress. The two men fought a war of which details are unknown, and Seleukos clearly lost. Peace was made in 304 or early 303, and Seleukos handed over substantial territories to Chandragupta: the Indus Valley was recognized as Mauryan, along with Arachosia and the Paropamisadai (that is, the lands south of the Hindu Kush).[23]

Seleukos marched back to the west in 303 with an army which was unusually strong in cavalry, the arm most useful in the east. He also had a huge elephant force, for Chandragupta had given him 500 of the beasts as part of the peace settlement. It took all year to get them to the west, by which time there were only 480 of them left.[24] The result was that Seleukos established himself firmly in the east in strength and was able to recruit a substantial army there. When he began his march back to the west in 303, therefore, Seleukos had an unusual but potent army under his hand: he reached eastern Anatolia with elephants, 20,000 infantry, and no fewer than 12,000 cavalry.[25] To any other commander of the time this was an unpleasantly unbalanced force, but in the result it proved to be the war winner.

Antigonos had always had the advantage of control of the greater part of the surviving army of Alexander and access to the major recruiting areas of Greece and Asia Minor, and so had maintained his military superiority. He had also acquired the surviving treasure of the Akhaimenids, and so he could pay for that army as well. Neither Ptolemy nor Lysimachos had such access or wealth. The former had to recruit where he could, hence in part his lunge towards Greece, his capture of parts of southern Asia Minor and his control of Cyprus and Cyrenaica; Lysimachos' conquest of Thrace gave him access to Thracian manpower, and much of the army he took to Asia Minor in 302 will have been Thracian in personnel. Kassander was restricted to the Macedonian levy and such mercenaries as he could afford. Seleukos' reinforcement was decisive.

In the winter of 302 the decisive theatre of war was Anatolia, and Antigonos had suddenly been forced on to the defensive. Demetrios and Kassander were stalemated in Thessaly, but Kassander was holding in play Demetrios' army, which was much larger than his own. Lysimachos, with perhaps 30,000 soldiers, campaigned into Ionia and western Asia Minor and then withdrew into a great entrenched camp in the north near Dorylaion. Antigonos brought his own forces north, together with a large treasure from the store at Kyinda in Kilikia, to face him. Several of his commanders in Asia Minor had defected to Lysimachos – another indication of his inability to inspire true loyalty.[26] Seleukos marched his mobile army through the Armenian mountains, to winter in eastern Anatolia.[27] No one was prepared to campaign in the Anatolian winter.

Ptolemy, faced with the war being fought in Greece and Asia Minor, was unable to do a great deal. His military forces had hardly recovered from the Cyprus disaster four years before and naval forces were nearly destroyed at that time. This hampered his participation, though he had obviously been working to rebuild his strength. When he joined the alliance, therefore, Ptolemy was able to move into southern Syria, taking over the cities as he went in a repetition of his several campaigns for the past two decades, but this seemed unlikely to have much effect on the main event.[28]

The winter saw considerable activity by Antigonos. Demetrios and his army came from Greece to combat Lysimachos.[29] A rumour was spread in Syria that Antigonos has beaten both Lysimachos and Seleukos and was marching to fight Ptolemy with his whole army.[30] Antigonos sent a raid against Babylon.[31] None of these measures worked. Ptolemy removed his main army back to Egypt when the rumours reached him, but left garrisons in all the cities he had occupied.[32] Later he was ridiculed for this retreat, but, had there really been an Antigonid army attacking him, he had adopted exactly the right strategy: his enemy would have been tied up in a series of sieges, or blocked at Sinai and the Nile. The armies of the allies in Anatolia would then have marched south to trap the Antigonid forces between their armies and Ptolemy's somewhere in southern Syria.

The raid against Babylon was mainly aimed at bringing Seleukos into Babylonia. This would make him march to the attack out of Babylonia by way of Mesopotamia. On that route he would have faced the fortified cities established in western Mesopotamia and northern Syria in the last few years, the major river crossing at the Euphrates, and two major mountain ranges, the Amanus and Taurus, both difficult for an army to penetrate. Antigonos could have held him up at any of these passes and crossings indefinitely, but especially at the Taurus, where only a small force would be needed to block the Kilikian Gates.

Seleukos, by his northern approach march, had clearly worked this out and he ignored the Babylon raid. Instead, he crossed into Anatolia by way of the Armenian mountain routes, and camped for the winter in Kappadokia. We hear of no opposition mounted by the Medians, the Armenians or the Kappadokians to his invasion, though all were effectively independent. No doubt Seleukos had prepared the way in advance by diplomatic contacts; they were neighbours of Antigonos, and very likely were as fearful of him as was everyone else.

Lysimachos was driven back when Demetrios arrived with the main Antigonid army from Greece. Demetrios had made a truce with Kassander, but half of his army, the Greek troops who served as the army of the Hellenic League, was left behind; they simply went home, leaving Kassander supreme in Greece. The league vanished. Kassander sent more troops to assist Lysimachos, though many of the men were lost when their transports were shipwrecked on the Black Sea coast.[33]

Lysimachos played for time. He manoeuvred out of Antigonos' reach, moving from the camp at Dorylaion to another camp closer to Seleukos' approach route. Antigonos was not prepared to face the losses involved in an assault on either camp. This was the same tactic as Kassander used against Demetrios; no doubt he and Lysimachos had discussed the matter beforehand. Demetrius took up winter quarters near the Propontis, and Antigonos near Lysimachos' old camp. Antigonos still faced three enemy armies, but he had gathered all his main strength; Lysimachos was within reach of Seleukos, and the two joined in the spring.[34]

After some manoeuvring in the spring, the battle was joined at Ipsos in west central Anatolia. The allies' force was more or less equal to that of the joint forces of Antigonos and Demetrios, except that Seleukos had five times as many elephants and a superiority of cavalry. Demetrios' cavalry drove back part of the allied cavalry under Seleukos' son Antiochos, but Antiochos kept him in play and the Seleukid elephants prevented Demetrios from returning. The Antigonid infantry was threatened both by the rest of Seleukos' cavalry and by his elephants: part of the phalanx surrendered, the rest were crushed. Antigonos, over 80 years old, died fighting. Demetrios escaped.[35]

This campaign by six kings and their armies initially separated by several thousands of kilometres is even more extraordinary than those of Philip or Alexander or Antigonos and Eumenes. It reveals much about the principals: the ingenuity of Seleukos, Ptolemy's caution, the recklessness of Demetrios, the obduracy of Lysimachos, the age and slowness of Antigonos, the cunning and carefulness of Kassander. The determination of the allies is also a mark of the fear which Antigonos' ambition had animated in them, for in the past they had all reneged on such coalition agreements, and they were playing for themselves above all. The alliance could not last beyond the battle: it did not last even as long as the subsequent settlement, but then there was no reason why it should.

Three of the victors were contemporaries and colleagues of Alexander, and Kassander was a younger contemporary. All had memories, perhaps vivid, of the conqueror, and of the great empire he had acquired. Antigonos and Demetrios aimed at reconstituting that empire, and had been dragged down by their less ambitious enemies, as they might have put it. Yet Demetrios survived, and his escape was not a lone journey: he took a small army of soldiers with him, and he had control of his great fleet.[36] Once free of pursuit, he was able to count on a fair quantity of territory still under his control – Corinth, Boiotia, part of the Peloponnese, a number of the Aegean islands, Cyprus, Tyre and Sidon, amongst others – and his fleet commanded the sea. Athens, however, sent a message to inform him that a new law prohibited the city from accepting kings within the walls, and that his wife Deidameia had been expelled, though he was given his ships back.[37] Here, then, was a rather diverse kingdom to emerge from the dust and death of the battle. It was not really unusual for a king with a fleet to control widely spread territories; Ptolemy had done so for a decade.

The main beneficiary of the victory, perhaps with some justice after his whole-hearted participation in the fighting, was Lysimachos. He took over western and central Anatolia, therefore ruling a solid block of territory from the Danube to the Taurus, centred on the Straits and his new city, Lysimacheia. Seleukos took everything south and east of the mountains, though this was no more than northern Syria. Ptolemy insisted on taking over southern Syria, from the Eleutheros River to Gaza, except for Demetrios' cities of Tyre and Sidon. Seleukos therefore advanced his western border only from the middle of Mesopotamia to the Syrian coast. It did not seem a commensurate reward for his great march from the east, and for having had the battle-winning weapons, the elephants and the cavalry. Kassander, relieved of the pressure of Demetrios' army, and happy to see the disintegration of the Hellenic League, took nothing for himself, but his brother Pleistarchos was given an odd kingdom of several provinces along the southern coast of Asia Minor from Karia to Kilikia. No doubt this was a means of keeping Seleukos and Lysimachos apart, but it was a clumsy device.[38]

Ptolemy's conquest of southern Syria annoyed Seleukos, who complained, and then announced piously that he would not fight his old friend. Quite reasonably considering this as a clear threat, Ptolemy made marriage alliances with both Kassander and Lysimachos during 300. They were directed at both Seleukos and Demetrios, whose naval power impinged on all the kings, in Greece, in Ionia, in Cyprus and in Phoenicia. In reply Seleukos and Demetrios, the two isolated kings, formed their own alliance; Seleukos, his Iranian wife Apama apparently having died, married Demetrios' daughter Stratonike. On his way east for the meeting, Demetrios took over Kilikia, part of Pleistarchos' gimcrack kingdom.[39]

The recovery of Demetrios was a threat to everyone else. All the kings looked to their defences. The most creative response came from Seleukos. His basic problem had been revealed in the Ipsos campaign, when his army was counted: he arrived with only 20,000 infantry. By contrast Kassander, from a much smaller kingdom, had sent that many foot soldiers to Lysimachos and had retained as many in Macedon; and Lysimachos, Seleukos' new neighbour, had brought an army of over 30,000 infantry to the fight, and now could draw on the great manpower resources of western Asia Minor. Seleukos was poorest in manpower, despite his cavalry and his elephants. Further, he took over, in northern Syria, a virtually undefendable region, which had been marched through without difficulty repeatedly in the past 30 years – by Alexander, Eumenes and Antigonos. One reason Ptolemy always was content with southern Syria and Phoenicia was that there were no defensible fortified towns in the north in which he could anchor his power. And Seleukos' neighbours, Ptolemy, Demetrios and Lysimachos, were hardly the most friendly of kings, either towards him or each other.

Seleukos set about solving these problems with one huge measure. He founded a whole group of cities in his new province. Four of the greatest cities in the eastern Mediterranean were developed in a geographical quadrilateral, all named for members of his family – Antioch for his father, Laodikeia for his mother, Apamea for his wife, Seleukeia for himself. Each was laid out on a lavish scale, almost the size of Egyptian Alexandria, provided with fortifications, and populated partly by Greek immigrants, partly by Syrians from the surrounding countryside. He thus constituted a well-fortified region, referred to as Seleukis: two cities on the coast were developed as major ports and naval bases; two inland cities blocked the landward approaches from the south, Ptolemy's lands. Each of the four cities grew to a population of up to 100,000, and Antioch eventually to three times that.

This was not totally virgin territory in terms of cities, for Antigonos had been building his new Antigoneia close to where Antioch was founded. Seleukos trumped that ace twice over, first by founding four cities, not just one, and secondly by dismantling Antigoneia and incorporating the site into Antioch as a constituent village. He probably intended Seleukeia to be the main city of the four: it bore his own name (as did the city he had founded in Babylonia), it was on the coast, and the dynastic tombs were there. Inland Antioch was in a better position for food supplies from the surrounding plain, and was less exposed to attack from the sea, so it grew where Seleukeia did not.

Seleukos went still further. Northern Syria had a number of fairly small Antigonid settlements, and he made these into six more cities. They occupied the territory between the major group of four and the Euphrates River: Kyrrhos, Chalkis and Beroia were named for Macedonian towns; Zeugma was at the vital crossing point of the Euphrates; Hierapolis was a local temple town promoted to city status; and Nikopolis was named to celebrate Seleukos' victory, probably that over Demetrius later, which took place nearby. These places could have been a source of danger, for their Greek and Macedonian populations were originally Antigonid subjects, and they might have felt a residual loyalty to King Demetrios; the marriage with Stratonike helped to defuse that, and importing new populations would dilute that effect.[40]

It took time to build up and populate these places, but the attraction of generous land grants and a new home in a new city brought in people fairly quickly; we know of groups of settlers from Athens, Cyprus and Crete; there were undoubtedly others we do not know of; the more who arrived, the greater would be Seleukos' economic and military resources. The majority of the immigrants would be young adults, perhaps educated, with economic skills and (probably) military expertise among the men. All young male citizens served time in the army and then constituted a military reserve, unless they chose to remain in the professional army. Seleukos was thus getting a military reserve for free. He had a big enough army within 20 years to be able to challenge and beat Lysimachos. It took time to build up the new cities, but the actual time needed was less than might be imagined – just to announce that the cities existed was a political and military statement which would lodge in the minds of kings and statesmen. These fortified places now existed, even if they were still being built.

It was not Ptolemy who was the real danger; he had always wanted southern Syria as a forward defence for Egypt, but never showed a wish to go further. He certainly showed no sign of aiming at the whole empire. If he wished to move out of southern Syria he would first need to remove the threat from Demetrios' cities of Tyre and Sidon, which had already been the bases for a raid by Demetrios as far as Samaria in Palestine, probably in 298.[41] Ptolemy, as far as Seleukos was concerned, was not the most immediate threat.

The elimination of Antigonos had therefore settled nothing. Ptolemy and Kassander were still the main obstacles for any king aiming at restoring Alexander's empire; Lysimachos, who also never showed a desire to resuscitate the empire, was another. The unsatisfied kings were Demetrios and Seleukos. The former aimed to recover his father's lost territories; the latter was annoyed at Ptolemaic actions in Syria, which he claimed as his share of the spoils from Ipsos. He was boxed in by his neighbours Ptolemy, Demetrios and Lysimachos, all of them stronger in vital ways than he was. Demetrios was rescued by Seleukos for the time being, but only for his own reasons, and neither was faithful to the alliance. Demetrios was an even more disturbing element than Seleukos and seemed as great a threat to everyone as his father had been.

11

New kings for Macedon, 298–291 BC

Demetrios was a threat to every other king because he sought revenge, was inherently ambitious, had great military abilities, and possessed territories bordering on them all. His cities of Tyre and Sidon were thorns in the side of Ptolemy, but they were also coveted by Seleukos. His lands in southern Asia Minor, formerly those of Pleistarchos, bordered on Seleukos' lands in Syria, and on Lysimachos' inland; they had been taken from Kassander's brother, and some of Ptolemy's cities were his neighbours. His control of Cyprus was a standing naval threat to the coasts of Syria and Egypt, especially since neither Seleukos nor Ptolemy could match his naval strength, and Ptolemy wanted the island back. In western Asia Minor Demetrios held the city of Ephesos and others in Ionia perhaps including Erythrai and Klazomenai; this annoyed Lysimachos. Ephesos was at war with the tyrant of Priene, who was therefore on Lysimachos' side, a situation ripe for exploitation when either king felt it worthwhile. In Greece, Demetrios held Corinth and some other places, and his fleet, returned to him by Athens when the city shut him out after Ipsos, gave him mobility; and Kassander's Macedon was close by.

Athens was still the most potent city-state in Greece, and in 299 the regime in power, which had excluded Demetrios, made peace with Kassander, clearly aiming for neutrality. The city was politically unstable, with internal disputes between the men who commanded the citizen troops and the mercenaries. The commander of the mercenaries, Lachares, became leader of the city during 298, and he aligned himself with Kassander.[1] Athens was counted out for the moment, and yet at the same time was vulnerable.

Kassander had survived Demetrios' assault in 302 more or less unscathed but he lost many soldiers in the war, in Thessaly and in Asia, and those lost at sea. Afterwards he was quite unable to influence the collusive process by which his brother's curious kingdom in southern Asia Minor had been suppressed, but then his concerns had never strayed far from Macedon and Greece. He and Lysimachos were colleagues and neighbours, who had never interfered in each other's spheres and protected each other's borders; this condition remained even when Lysimachos controlled Asia Minor. Lysimachos provided a principality for Pleistarchos in Karia, after he lost Kilikia.[2]

Pleistarchos became one of a number of men, Macedonians mostly, who

controlled substantial tracts of Asia Minor. These men are referred to usually
as 'dynasts', and in many cases they did pass their estates on to their children.
Some were already in place when Lysimachos became their overlord, such as
Dokimos and Themison who had founded cities named for them. Karia was
an area particularly rich in such men, no doubt because of its tangled and
difficult geography: Pleistarchos joined Asandros, Eupolemos and Olympichos
in controlling parts of it. A dynasty founded by Lysias operated from a city in
Phrygia; later the youngest son of Seleukos Nikator became established in Lydia;
the lord of Pergamon, Philetairos, was another example.

The existence of such lordships made Asia Minor a rather different society
from that of others. These men were useful to the kings in that they controlled
considerable areas, and could usually be relied on to be active in both government
and defence. They were also obviously dangerous, and more than one of them
tended towards independence, and even kingship, in the next century. Philetairos
of Pergamon was the founder of the Attalid dynasty; Olympichos' descendants
became briefly independent. Dokimos changed allegiance all too easily in the
early wars. Asia Minor clearly required a firm but delicate royal control if it was
not to disintegrate into competing minor principalities.[3]

In Macedon, Kassander faced the same problems as his Argead predecessors.
He was frequently in dispute with the Epirote kingdom, and intervened more
than once to change the regime there – just as had Philip II.[4] He tried to dominate
Greece, if only to prevent anyone else – Antigonos, Ptolemy, Demetrios – from
doing so, but he found it difficult to reach further south than Athens: Kassander's
soldiers occupied Corinth only because Ptolemy ceded the city to him; they had
lost it easily to Demetrios. Kassander operated very much as a typical fourth-
century Macedonian ruler in his restricted range of international concerns.

Demetrios' return to Greece after Ipsos brought a restless and vengeful spirit
into a confused and complicated situation. His alliance with Seleukos a year later
provided him with an international lifeline, and his conquest of Kilikia included
the acquisition of the royal treasure at Kyinda, containing 1,400 talents. Yet he
did not interfere with a maritime expedition made by Kassander to the Ionian
Sea island of Korkyra during 298 – Agathokles of Sicily prevented him from
acquiring it.[5] But the following year the whole unstable situation in Greece was
made worse by the death of Kassander.

He is said to have died of a wasting disease, dropsy perhaps, or maybe
tuberculosis.[6] His death was followed by a series of disputes within the royal
family, as usual, and this time these disputes eliminated the whole family.
The change of dynasty had not changed Macedon; this regular collapse was
not an Argead peculiarity; it was inherent in Macedonian politics and society.
Kassander had done his best to avoid a succession crisis: he had been a successful
ruler, had associated himself with the former royal family by his marriage, and

provided three almost adult sons as his heirs, together with a capable widow to supervise them. It was not enough. At first the kingship passed without a problem to Kassander's eldest son, Philip IV. Behind him hovered his mother, Thessalonike. Her bloodline had certainly been of assistance to Kassander in his Macedonian career, as it was to be for her children as well. But Philip IV lasted only four months.[7]

In Athens, Lachares' local enemies seized control of Peiraios, while he continued in power in the city. Lachares had been an adherent of Kassander, who is said to have urged him to take this step, and his death prevented further Macedonian assistance. The result was Athenian paralysis, and, in view of the sudden absence of Macedonian royal authority, the only possible benefactor of this situation was Demetrios.[8]

Kassander had also intervened in Epiros to support Neoptolemos in the struggle for the kingship with his cousin and rival Pyrrhos. (Neoptolemos was the nephew of Olympias; Pyrrhos was the grandson of King Arybbas, expelled by Philip II.) Pyrrhos, defeated for the moment in 302, had become a soldier of fortune, attaching himself inevitably to Kassander's enemies. He had been present on the losing side at Ipsos, had escaped, and served as an officer of Demetrios until 297, when Demetrios sent him as a hostage to Ptolemy. Ptolemy took to him, gave him his daughter Antigone as wife, and helped him to get back to Epiros as king.[9] This happened soon after Kassander died, while Philip IV was establishing himself. Pyrrhos' wife Antigone soon died, and he married a second time, to Lanassa, the daughter of King Agathokles of Sicily, another of Kassander's enemies; she brought the island of Korkyra as her dowry, the very island which Kassander had been attempting to seize not long before he died.[10] Kassander's aim had been to gain a foothold from which to threaten Epiros; in Pyrrhos' hands it was a forward defence.

Pyrrhos had his rival Neoptolemos assassinated, claiming he was merely anticipating a like fate for himself,[11] but the main reason he was able to settle into power in Epiros was that there was no response from Macedon to his seizure of the kingship. Philip IV reigned for only four months before his own death. He was at Elateia in Phokis when he died, so he was probably on his way to begin the process of rebuilding Macedonian power in Greece, no doubt by assisting the 'tyranny' of Lachares in Athens. If so, the expedition stopped at once.

Philip was succeeded by both his younger brothers. Antipater and Alexander IV became joint kings, an arrangement organized by Thessalonike, who held the real power.[12] The elder of the two, Antipater, was about 16 and this gave their mother regency authority; she is said to have favoured Alexander, the younger boy, but failed to bypass Antipater, presumably being thwarted by the Assembly, which had to accept the new king. The result was paralysis at the top. The succession in Macedon was running true to form. (The similarity to the situation in Babylon after the death of Alexander the Great presumably escaped no one, but the lesson of the previous 30 years was ignored.)

Demetrios was the beneficiary. He made an attempt on Athens while it was divided,[13] but was unsuccessful. He went on to extend his power in the Peloponnese, so safeguarding his base at Corinth. He had now quarrelled with Seleukos, who demanded that he hand over Kilikia, Tyre and Sidon, all of which Seleukos claimed as part of his spoils as a participant in the defeat of Demetrios' father.[14] Demetrios had refused and spent some time during 296 in the eastern Mediterranean making sure his lands were well guarded.

Demetrios' brief friendship with Seleukos was now over. His new commitment to extending his power in Greece was one result; for he clearly required a larger base if he was to achieve anything. In the Peloponnese he clashed with Messene for some reason,[15] then he turned back to Athens. Lachares had now made himself an out-and-out tyrant,[16] which may have persuaded Demetrios that he had a good chance of a quick success. He was wrong. Demetrios had worn out his welcome in Athens years before; his attack united most of the Athenians under Lachares in resistance.

Demetrios blockaded the city, driving its population towards starvation. Ptolemy sent a fleet of 150 ships of his rebuilt navy to attempt relief. Demetrios' fleet of 300 ships blocked it. Lachares proved a less than resolute leader, and escaped out of the siege, but the Athenians fought on without him. But Demetrios won; the Athenians gave in. He sent in food but also installed three garrisons to make his control complete.[17]

Demetrios staged one of his spectacular events to demonstrate his success. It was the beginning of the festival of Dionysios. When Demetrios entered the conquered city he had the citizens gathered into the theatre, and ringed them with his armed soldiers. A pause ensued, sufficient to reduce the citizens to a quaking fear. Demetrios then entered the theatre, by way of the stage entrance as used by the tragic actors – in effect taking on the mantle of the god. The fear increased. Then he declared that he forgave the Athenians, and announced the gift of grain. The Athenians shouted their relief, and one of their orators, Dromokleides, proposed to hand over Piraios, and the Mounychia to the king as bases for his garrisons. Since he had probably occupied these places already, this was merely clothing his conquest in politeness. But he appointed his own officials in the city, including a new eponymous archon, so manipulating the calendar by beginning a new year to mark the occasion of his conquest.[18]

The concentration of Demetrios' power in Greece, and the bitter and prolonged fight made by Athens, left the rest of his possessions vulnerable, while his victory raised the prospect of his rise to substantial power again, and the paralysis in Macedon removed any local power balance. The eastern kings therefore conspired to limit potential future damage. Ptolemy's venture into the Aegean to assist Athens showed that it was not practical to challenge Demetrios in Greece, so they aimed to strip him of the territories he could use as forward bases for attacks on them. They were in no doubt that if he could, Demetrios would attack.

Seleukos seized Kilikia, moving his frontier forward, and gave him an advanced defence line along the Taurus Mountains in case Lysimachos developed ambitions, and a stretch of coastline and several cities and ports from which to develop some sea power if he wished; his new Syrian cities were now better protected. Ptolemy seized Cyprus. He had to fight for it, ironically having to besiege Salamis, where Demetrios' mother and children were living. Lysimachos mopped up the cities along the Aegean coast of Asia Minor which Demetrios held, from Abydos on the Hellespont to Ephesos. Demetrios therefore gained Athens but lost much more, and was now confined to Greece and the Aegean.[19]

The speed of these conquests is as remarkable as the coordination of the attacks. Only at Salamis was there any real resistance, probably because Demetrios' family was there. Other cities, equally well fortified, fell with no resistance. Presumably Demetrios had stripped his outlying possessions of troops in order to concentrate on Greece, leaving them vulnerable; no doubt this helped persuade Ptolemy, Seleukos and Lysimachos to launch their joint attacks. Demetrios was taken by surprise, for his family had clearly been put in Salamis for safety's sake.

Even as these reverses for Demetrios became known, a new opportunity opened up for him. The unstable situation in the Macedonian royal family had broken down. Thessalonike arranged marriages for both kings: Antipater married Eurydike, a daughter of Lysimachos, and Alexander married Lysandra, a daughter of Ptolemy, but the whole situation was uncomfortable. By 294 Antipater, irritated at his lack of power and his mother's favouring his brother, murdered her and drove Alexander out of Pella, though not out of the country.[20] Alexander appealed for help to both Pyrrhos and Demetrios, thereby demonstrating his complete unfitness to be king in Macedonia.

Pyrrhos, closest to Macedon, arrived first. His price was the western areas of Macedon, Parauaea, Atintania and the Macedonian holdings in Akarnarnia, including the city of Ambrakia, lands taken by Philip II 50 years before. He then installed Alexander as king, but only pushed Antipater off to the east, beyond the Axios River. Antipater asked his father-in-law Lysimachos for help, and he advised a partition of the kingdom. Pyrrhos agreed, and arranged it. For a time, therefore, Macedon was divided into three parts. Lysimachos cannot have been pleased at the instability, but Pyrrhos was no doubt gratified at increasing his own kingdom, and reducing Macedon to impotence. Pyrrhos engineered a fragile reconciliation between the brothers and then left. Demetrios then arrived from the south.[21]

He found things apparently settled, met Alexander, and congratulated him. The story of their meeting implies that each was plotting to kill the other, and that it was Demetrios who was successful. The killing took place at Larissa in Thessaly after the original meeting at Dion in southern Macedon, so they both had time to set up mutual assassination plots.[22] The sentiments of the Macedonians were demonstrated clearly when Demetrios presented himself to Alexander's troops after the murder. He had no difficulty in persuading them to accept and acclaim him as king.[23] Demetrios was married to a sister of Kassander, so their son, Antigonos Gonatas, was of Antipater's line, if that counted, and Demetrios had a greater presence and a more convincing royal charisma than the two boys. Demetrios moved north from Thessaly and was accepted by another Macedonian army Assembly, perhaps at Pella. Antipater, showing a little sense at last, fled to Lysimachos.[24] Suddenly Demetrios, reduced to a fleet and a few cities earlier in the year, had the kingdom of Macedon in his hands.

For once, Demetrios' impulsiveness had been successful. The result was a swift revival of the international position of Macedon. Demetrios' ability, plus his fleet and army, added to the military potential of Macedon, did this without any further effort. But there was also the matter of Demetrios' ambition and intentions. The parallel with Philip II was all too clear: Demetrios, king of Macedon, lord of Thessaly, controlled much of Greece, all of which was a good basis for even greater power. In reality, his boundaries and his position in Greece were a good deal less extensive and sound than they seemed.

Macedon was considerably smaller than it had been in Philip's reign, and even under a vigorous king its comparative power was less. Thrace was separate, and was now an adjunct to Lysimachos' kingdom of Asia Minor. Demetrios' eastern boundary therefore now reached only to Philippi. To the west, Pyrrhos was not about to give up his recent extensive gains. Kassander had maintained the kingdom as his father had ruled it, and had dominated Epiros as well as parts of Greece. Demetrios' kingdom was substantially less.

Macedon's neighbours had also changed. Lysimachos was a more formidable proposition than the satraps of Asia Minor Alexander had faced; the Aitolian League had grown in power and confidence in the last half-century; Pyrrhos' enlarged kingdom was more formidable than that of Arybbas and Alexander of Epiros. Demetrios' Macedon, therefore, was not only smaller than Philip's, it had more powerful neighbours, all of whom were instinctively wary of both him and Macedon.

Demetrios was naturally concerned with all these areas. For the moment, he established good relations with Lysimachos, who had given refuge to Antipater, and so had the potential to cause trouble.[25] Demetrios moved into Thessaly in some strength, thereby stifling any possible dissident activities, and founded a new city, Demetrias, on the Gulf of Volos, close to the site of Pagasai. This proved to be perhaps the most enduring of his works. It was also a signal of his independent kingship, for he had at last achieved a kingdom by his own unaided efforts – just as had Ptolemy, Seleukos and Lysimachos.

Demetrios had before him the examples of Antipater and Kassander, and of Philip and Alexander, as contrasting uses to be made of Macedonian power. The Argead kings had dominated Greece and used their military power to conquer Asia; the Antipatrids had been content to hold Greece and had ignored Asia as much as possible. The former policy had been glorious but terribly expensive in Macedonian manpower; the latter had maintained the internal peace of the kingdom, and allowed a recovery from Alexander's excesses.

It lay within Demetrios' grasp to adopt either of these policies, and there was no question which alternative he chose, but it is worth noting them. He was clearly consumed with a wish to emulate Alexander, with whom he was being compared in many eyes, but also to gain revenge for his father's defeat and death. His personal history was thus something of a burden for him, but it was not necessary to succumb to it. His son, Antigonos Gonatas, had the same possible futures before him two decades later, and possessed the same familial loyalty, and yet he chose to remain as a Macedonian king. By then Macedon had gone through yet another succession crisis, which damaged the land even more severely than before, but both men had the same choices, and chose differently.

To control Greece, Demetrios had to remove the hostility of Boiotia, and later in 294 he seized it by a surprise attack launched on the day after the delivery of his declaration of war to the meeting of the Boiotarchs. This not only annoyed the Boiotians, but alarmed the Aitolians as well.[26] Aitolia, the region of hills and mountains between Delphi and Akarnarnia, had developed during the previous half-century into a well-organized league, which had intervened occasionally in affairs in the wider Greek world over the previous generation. It had not yet seriously begun to expand, but it was boxed in by Demetrios' and by Pyrrhos' lands.

Aitolia allowed Kleonymos, a Spartan prince, to pass through its territory on his way to Boiotia the next year. The Boiotians seized the opportunity of his arrival (Kleonymos presumably brought some troops with him) to rise against Demetrios' control, but, like Lachares, Kleonymos did not stay to see the consequences of his actions; Demetrios moved quickly and frightened him off. The Boiotians, overwhelmed by Demetrios' speed and numbers, surrendered again,[27] but they tried to regain freedom once more in 292,[28] in alliance with the Aitolian League and Phokis, so forming a solid block of allies across central Greece.[29]

Demetrios' methods of control were clearly inefficient. He appears to have relied on his personal charm and on generosity to his political opponents to win them over, while also imposing garrisons in certain places. The leader of the Boiotian revolt in 293, Peisis of Thespiai, was appointed *polemarchos* of his own city, on the assumption that he had been won to Demetrios' support at a meeting; but a governor was also imposed over Boiotia. This was all surely designed to conciliate, but it also suggests that Demetrios did not appreciate the strength of his enemies' convictions. It was grossly inefficient to have to conquer Boiotia three times in three years. The first two conquests had been achieved above all by speed and by the arrival of overwhelming forces, and in neither case did the Boiotians believe they had really been beaten. On the third occasion the revolt was sparked by the news that Demetrios had sailed off to the Hellespont when he heard that Lysimachos was in difficulties in fighting on the Danube.[30] The Boiotians therefore had the opportunity to prepare another rebellion with more care, and make that alliance with Aitolia and Phokis. This time it took two years for Demetrios to conquer, and he had to besiege Thebes.[31] Demetrios was thus preoccupied with the conquest and control of a single Greek region for five years. It was scarcely a productive use of his time, where an investment in diplomacy might well have defused the situation much more easily.

Lysimachos' difficulties were with the Getai, whose king, Dromichaetes, actually captured him late in 292. He was released in the spring of 291, perhaps on payment of a ransom.[32] He had been fighting the Getai for some time, which may have been one of the reasons he had failed to intervene seriously in the succession crisis in Macedon. He cannot have been pleased that the crisis resulted in the resurrection of Demetrios' power; involvement in the Getic war, which seems to have begun in 294, no doubt compelled Lysimachos to accept the situation, while Demetrios' evident involvement in Boiotia similarly kept the two kings apart. When Lysimachos was captured, Demetrios mounted an expedition against the Thracian Chersonese, aiming to capture Lysimacheia.[33] He failed and the new rising in Boiotia brought him back to Greece. No one could have any doubt that Demetrios' ambitions remained alive and vigorous.

Lysimachos' rule in Asia Minor was not popular, perhaps because he was a good deal more autocratic than Antigonos had been. Lysimachos felt under permanent threat from Demetrios and Seleukos. He had to maintain a substantial army, on a lower tax base than Antigonos, who had also controlled Syria, though he had also acquired at least two of Antigonos' treasure citadels. He was unable to extend his territory in any direction since Ipsos, except into Demetrios' Ionian cities, and the defeat by Dromichaetes effectively stopped any expansion in the Balkans.

In the north of Asia Minor the peoples along the Black Sea coast had never yet been conquered by any of these rulers. The Paphlagonians had surrendered to Alexander, but it does not seem that anyone did anything about it, and Perdikkas was distracted in 321. The Bithynians, a Thracian tribe settled to the east of the Bosporos, dated their era from 297/296, having presumably succeeded in maintaining their independence at that time, presumably from Lysimachos. Their King Zipoites took the title of king, and this was later commemorated by the inauguration of the new era, but they had been independent until then anyway.

The people of the coast east of Sinope became organized as a kingdom, Pontos, under a Persian lord, Mithradates, who had been with Antigonos for a time. So were the Armenians in their difficult mountains, also under a Persian aristocrat, Orontes, who was descended from a survivor of the Akhaimenid defeat, and had successfully resisted the imposition of a Macedonian satrap.[34] Between these states, the Greek city of Herakleia Pontike, under a family of tyrants, had expanded its power and territory; the current tyrants were the sons of Amastris, a Persian lady who had been married to Perdikkas for a time, and briefly to Lysimachos at the time of the Ipsos campaign.

Along the south coast of Asia Minor Ptolemy had kept or revived his earlier power, from Kilikia west to Lykia. With all this, Lysimachos could be forgiven for feeling encircled, especially after Seleukos gained control of Kilikia and the southern exits of the passes through the Taurus Mountains.[35]

Ptolemy, having gained what he had always been after – Palestine, Phoenicia and Cyprus, and a domination of the southern Asia Minor coast – relapsed into satisfied quietness. Seleukos remained restless. He had a huge kingdom to govern, and like Lysimachos he faced potential threats from several directions. Ptolemy might decide to extend north of the Eleutheros River, so he had to be on his guard in north Syria. The great cities he was building would do that eventually, but it took time to construct and fortify and populate them. He faced Lysimachos across the Taurus, and must have feared above all an active alliance between Ptolemy and Lysimachos; in 298 Lysimachos married Ptolemy's daughter Arsinoe, though of all people Seleukos knew how little such a marriage meant in terms of real power. But the two men had the potential to push him out of his western territories without too much difficulty. His acquisition of Kilikia pushed his defence line forward, but at the cost of his friendship with Demetrios. Seleukos had become internationally isolated from 294.

It may be this Kilikian episode which ultimately lay behind the curious episode of Seleukos' second wife. He was married first to Apama, the daughter of the Sogdian lord Spitamenes, at Alexander's great wedding ceremony in 324. It was reputedly the only one of those marriages to continue after Alexander's death. They had two sons, Antiochus and Akhaios. One must assume that Seleukos already had in mind the political importance of his wife, though it was years before her Baktrian connections proved useful, and mutual affection is not to be excluded. Seleukos' establishment of control over Baktria was surely assisted by his wife's origins.

Apama was still alive in 299, but must have died in that year or the next. Seleukos married again in 298, to Demetrios' daughter Stratonike. (The Seleukids, unlike the Argeads, Ptolemies and Antigonids, developed no tradition of royal polygamy, which leads to the presumption of Apama's decease.) They had a daughter, Phila. In 294 or a little later, however, Seleukos handed his wife on to his eldest son, Antiochus. Ancient historians saw it as as a love match, with Seleukos comically ignorant of the mutual attraction of his wife and son until a doctor intervened and told him why his son was morose.[36] But the separation came soon after the diplomatic break with Demetrios (Stratonike's father), and the newly married Antiochus and Stratonike went off to rule the eastern half of the kingdom[37] – and Antiochos was the son of the Baktrian Apama. Seleukos was therefore dealing with several problems at once: his son's attraction for his stepmother, which was presumably reciprocated, though the historians ignore Stratonike's feelings; the tension caused within his household and perhaps in his kingdom by his break with Demetrios; and the need for a man he could trust in control of the eastern lands. It was a neat solution, one surely devised by a family conference beforehand, and it testifies to Seleukos' suppleness and political sense, just as his city building neatly blocked the several potential threats to his hold on Syria, while also increasing his military power, his population and his kingdom's wealth.

Antiochos' work in the east is known only from fragmentary sources, but it was a major force for the consolidation of the Greek presence in Baktria. He ruled there for more than ten years, assisted it seems by the generals Demodamas and Patrokles. Cities were founded or refounded – Alexandria-Eschate, Samarkhand, Alexandria-Margiane (which became Antiocheia) and the city at Ai Khanum. Patrokles explored the Caspian Sea. Peace was maintained with the Mauryan Empire, and invasions by nomads from the north were driven out.[38] The move of Antiochus to the east was one way for Seleukos to clear the decks so that he could concentrate on the problems of the west. Both Lysimachos and Ptolemy were also gathering their strength for Demetrios' expected move.

It is here that the significance of Demetrios' attempt at the Thracian Chersonese lies. Until 291 he had operated in much the same way as Kassander and Antipater, working to establish his power in the kingdom and in Greece. He held on to Athens and Corinth and was making serious attempts to gain control of Boiotia. His success was sufficient to persuade Pyrrhos and Aitolia to join in an alliance to oppose him, with little success. But the lunge at Lysimacheia revealed the real Demetrios. He was not just aiming to be king in Macedon; he was going to use its strength, and that of Greece, to attempt to recover his father's kingdom. He was Antigonos revived, not just another Kassander; the answer was the revival of the same alliance which had brought Antigonos down.

12

King Demetrios and his enemies, 291–285 BC

Demetrios' war with Boiotia was seen as a threat by all his neighbours; the Boiotians were helped by the Aitolians and Pyrrhos, who joined in with an invasion from Epiros.[1] Kassander had been content to rule Macedon alone, and constantly resisted Antigonos' pretensions. But Macedon was still a nursery of soldiers, and if one of the eastern kings could unite it with a greater kingdom, he would be in a position of overwhelming strength. Antigonos' ambitions to do that had brought all the rest to join together to oppose him.

Demetrios' accession marked a fundamental change in the geopolitics of the eastern Mediterranean. Macedon was now no longer a block on the reconstitution of the empire; instead it had become a means by which that reconstitution could be accomplished. Demetrios' intentions became clear in 294, even before his acquisition of the Macedonian kingship, when he gained control of Athens, the other main source of power in the area, with its commercial wealth and its shipyards, its powerful reputation, and its military potential. For the first time since Alexander, a ruler had arisen in Greece and Macedon who aimed to harness these lands' might to a programme of conquest.

And yet, matters had changed in other ways since the time of Philip and Alexander. Demetrios had a much harder job stamping his authority on Greece than any of the earlier kings – the siege of Thebes took nearly two years, and he had found it a very difficult task to conquer Athens. He was famous for his sieges, but that was because his enemies refused to fight him in open battle, and instead chose their own grounds for the fight. Any ruler of Macedon should have learned by now that conquering a Greek city was never enough. It had also to be held down, by installing a government which could be controlled – and so not a democracy – and by also installing a garrison; the more cities, the more troops were absorbed into garrisons. When Demetrios finally took Thebes, he installed a garrison and a governor, to add to those in Chalkis, Athens, Corinth and other places. This was the antithesis of the policy of Philip and Alexander.

Pyrrhos had intervened in Demetrios' Boiotian war by invading Thessaly and so cutting the land communications between Macedon and Boiotia. Demetrios quickly pushed the invaders out, but had to station 10,000 hoplites and 1,000 horse in Thessaly to prevent a recurrence.[2] The Aitolians were involved also, even though what they did is not clear. The normal military levy of Macedon-plus-Thessaly was about 30,000 to 35,000 men; Demetrios used one-third of his Macedonian military manpower simply holding Greece.

He hired mercenaries, but they were expensive; so were Macedonians, but they could be called out in emergencies and quickly sent home again. Demetrios had to impose heavy taxes on his subjects. This was new to Macedon. Philip II had relied on his control of mining revenues and port dues, but he had always spent all his money; none was left in the treasury when he died. Alexander had cash problems within a year of setting off on his great campaign. Macedon, even with Thessaly and even squeezing Greece as much as possible, could not support a big army, either in manpower or financially. The wear and tear of the previous 40 years, losses of territory, the draining of manpower, had seriously reduced Macedon's resources: the 30,000–35,000 estimate of the manpower available to Demetrios is substantially less than Alexander had had available. And Demetrios was building a navy as well. The mints in Macedon, at Pella and Amphipolis, and in the Greek cities he controlled, became exceptionally active, no doubt using all the precious metals Demetrios could get. The most productive were in cities where shipbuilding took place, a very expensive activity.[3]

Demetrios was clearly intending to finance his campaign by the loot of his conquests – as, in fact, Alexander had done – but in the meantime he had to finance his army and his fleet from the taxation of Macedon, and what he could get out of the damaged and resentful Greeks: the cities were ordered to produce large sums. One, Eretria in Euboia, got its levy reduced from 200 to 150 talents by an appeal by a philosopher from the city. These numbers are not necessarily accurate,[4] but for a smallish city, even half was a huge burden; the levies on Greece were no doubt intended to produce thousands of talents.

The enemy Demetrios would have to fight was also different. Alexander's campaign of conquest in the Persian Empire had been won by a well-trained, well-directed, tactically flexible army accustomed to campaign and fight as a unit; the enemy was a complacent aristocracy and an insecure king, whose fighting units had little military discipline. Demetrios was proposing to campaign with a heterogeneous army, mainly mercenaries who had not fought together before, against armies and cities of similar and equal discipline from the same military tradition. Alexander had conquered Persia in three battles and three sieges; the defeat of Dareios was the main object, and, once achieved, the world from the Aegean to the Indus was open to him. Demetrios was proposing to invade a succession of kingdoms equipped with armies very like his, ruled by kings with equivalent or better military skills than his. These kings, moreover, were allied to one another in determined opposition to him. In effect, he proposed to fight three Macedons, each with a professional Macedonian army, from an insecure and wasting base. The campaign, it was quite certain, would be infinitely more difficult than Alexander's.

Further, Demetrios' political instability was obvious to his enemies. Alexander had been able to rely on the loyalty of Macedon without question, counting on Antipater to defend the kingdom, hold the position he had in Greece, and feed him reinforcements on demand. Demetrios had no hereditary Macedonian loyalty to rely on, and no Antipater; he left his son Antigonos Gonatas in charge of Greece when he set off, but with few troops and no territorial backing. The slightest weakness, the smallest defeat, would set off risings among his unwilling Greek subjects and desertions by his mercenaries.

He required a much larger army than Alexander had needed. At Ipsos in 301, Lysimachos had deployed at least 40,000 men, and Seleukos 30,000. Since then both had expanded their territories: Lysimachos' army now included many of the men who had fought for Antigonos at Ipsos; Seleukos had worked hard to attract colonists who could be mobilized into his army. Ptolemy was perhaps the weakest of the three in military terms, but he had a fleet of 150 ships, and his kingdom of Egypt had major geographical advantages in defence. If the three kings could join their forces, they would outnumber Demetrios' army; even fighting them one at a time was a forbidding prospect.

Further, the lands he proposed to invade were fortified in a much more effective way than when Alexander went east. Alexander had faced fortified cities only in the west – Halikarnassos, Tyre, Gaza – and in India, but most cities were now fortified in the latest style, designed to resist attack by the sort of machines Alexander had brought with him. This was partly Demetrios' own doing, for his sieges had shown what was needed to withstand the skills and energies he deployed. His reputation as a besieger was based not on the number of sieges he won, but on those he fought; and he lost as often as he won. The new fortifications were very effective defences,[5] and every siege cost time, lives, resources and money. The generals he faced were professional strategists, and certainly Demetrios' superiors in that aspect of warfare. They were not going to play to Demetrios' strengths, but to his weaknesses, and one of these was his poor resource base. Tying up Demetrios' army in a few sieges would soon cost him the war.

There were, however, fewer tangible effects operating for him. His father's former subjects in Asia Minor and Syria were perhaps nostalgic for his government: Lysimachos' hand on the people in Asia Minor was much heavier; Demetrios might sap Lysimachos' strength by appeals to their old loyalties, but only as long as he seemed to be winning. He might attract to his side those who knew of Alexander's exploits and were keen to emulate their fathers' adventures. A swift defeat of Lysimachos' army, if it could be contrived, could well dismantle his whole kingdom. Seleukos would be tougher. The size of his kingdom, his political sense and strategic intelligence, and the proven loyalty of his people, were much more difficult to combat. The loyalty of the old Antigonid subjects of Seleukos towards Demetrios was a factor to remember, but Seleukos' vigorous colonizing work had diluted their numbers, and the new colonists owed their loyalty to Seleukos alone.

Then there were the kings' sons. Seleukos' son Antiochos ruled eastern Iran for his father, had proved himself loyal to his father, and was a capable soldier. Antiochos was also king, so if Demetrios beat Seleukos, he would still have to face Antiochos coming out of the east with an army bent on revenge – and Demetrios knew all about wanting revenge for the death of a father. Lysimachos' eldest son Agathokles was as capable a soldier as Antiochos, and probably a better commander than his father, and soon proved it. Ptolemy's eldest son, who would become Ptolemy II, was adult and more an administrator than a soldier, but the Egyptian kingdom was well fortified in the Phoenician cities and competently defended by a professional army behind the barrier of the Sinai Desert. Any objective evaluation of a plan to reunite Alexander's empire by conquering the world a second time from Macedon would conclude that by the 280s it was impossible.

But stranger things have happened. Demetrios was no fool, though perhaps shortsighted and over-ambitious. He was surely aware of the difficulties; he had, after all, grown up along with the way this world had developed. His alternative to a campaign to win the world was to become another Kassander, king of the Macedonians in Macedon only, periodically campaigning against Greeks and barbarians. After roaming the whole Middle East, he was not prepared to settle for less than Alexander's full inheritance, any more than his father had been, but he was not prepared to be as patient as his father, for the kingdoms he faced were becoming stronger and more solidly founded with every year he prepared.

His plans were on a scale fitted to his enterprise. He recruited mercenaries all over the Mediterranean, and built a fleet of 500 warships. This number included those he already had, but it was a huge programme even so, perhaps an extra 200 to 300 ships. A fleet of this size would easily outclass Ptolemy's, the only other fleet of any size. But such a fleet would require to be manned by at least 50,000 men, particularly since Demetrios built many extra large vessels – at least one had 16 men per bank of oars, another 15, many more were fives and sevens. The manpower requirement on top of the land forces, which are said to have amounted to 98,000 infantry and 12,000 cavalry, was crippling. It is widely doubted if these figures are accurate, and they do seem too great but, given the task Demetrios set himself, they are of the right scale.[6]

This all called for a huge amount of work by Demetrios, who frequently visited the shipyards to check on the work being done personally.[7] He had to watch over the gathering of the soldiers and the collection of supplies, and his mints were uniformly busy. Inevitably other tasks did not get done. He was king of a country where individual Macedonians expected to have direct access to him, but under Demetrios they did not have it. His workload was too great, but it also went against his personal inclinations; in this, he was very much a contrast with his father.

Demetrios had been rich all his life, and had habits of personal display and extravagance difficult to break away from – not that he ever showed any signs of wanting to do so. Macedonian preference was for a less ostentatious lifestyle in its kings; his display offended them. Nor was Demetrios used to dealing with the small complaints and problems of his subjects. The story is told that an old woman whom he put off by saying he was too busy to attend to her petition, shouted at him: 'Then stop being king!' This is a story also told of Philip II and the Emperor Hadrian, and as such it is suspect in all these cases – but with Philip and Hadrian the result was that the problem was attended to. So did Demetrios, but then he reneged on the reformation, whereas Philip and Hadrian learned their lesson. Demetrios is the butt of another hostile story: he collected written petitions as they were handed to him, put them in his cloak pockets, but then threw them in the river. How true such anecdotes were is impossible to judge, but their tone reflects the dislike of his Macedonian subjects.[8]

Thebes fell at last in 290, but fell into a dispute with Pyrrhos, out of which he gained another wife, Lanassa, daughter of Agathokles of Sicily, and the island of Korkyra. He invaded Aitolia next year, and went on into Epiros. Pyrrhos brought his army to assist the Aitolians, but the two marching armies missed each other, going in opposite directions by parallel roads. Pyrrhos found a Macedonian force ravaging the country, and defeated it, taking 5,000 prisoners. On the fight Pyrrhos fought a duel with the Macedonian commander Pantauches, to the admiration of both armies.[9] Demetrios returned to Macedon where he fell ill, and Pyrrhos invaded, but was quickly deterred by an army gathered by Demetrios' commanders. The result was an agreement between the two kings to keep the peace.[10]

This was hardly a good preparation for the great expedition Demetrios intended. The attacks on Aitolia and Pyrrhos were presumably designed to deter them while he was away, but victory was required for this to work. He again had the chance to become a king of Macedon only; the great force he had collected could have crushed Pyrrhos and the Aitolians, and his possession of Korkyra gave him an admirable base for expeditions north along the Adriatic or westward, but he rejected the opportunity.

Now all his Greek enemies had to do was to wait for him to leave; he cannot have been unaware of the instability of his position.

His overseas enemies had drawn together. Lysimachos, Seleukos and Ptolemy, though political enemies, formed an informal alliance to face him. That they should do so is a measure of the threat he posed.[11] They did not wait to be attacked, nor did his Greek enemies have to wait for him to leave before striking for freedom. The kings had taken note of the active Pyrrhos, who had contacts with Ptolemy. Lysimachos, whose territories bordered on Macedon, had already been threatened by Demetrios, and he had good contacts in several Greek cities.[12] Seleukos could do little in the circumstances, being too far off and without a fleet, but Ptolemy made a preliminary move by sending his fleet to the Aegean.[13] His control of the eastern Mediterranean and his alliance with Rhodes gave his fleet secure bases, and he persuaded the League of the Islanders, set up years before by Antigonos, to desert Demetrios. In a foretaste of what would happen on the mainland, Ptolemy undermined Demetrios' hold on the league by promising autonomy for the league council, a reduction in fiscal requisitions, and protection against any retribution. This was precisely what the Greeks under Demetrios wanted to hear.[14]

This development is the more interesting in that it encapsulates the attitudes and policies which became the norm in the succeeding century: the Greek cities required only their internal autonomy to be respected and subject to relatively light tribute demands to accept a king's protection and patronage. In turn the kings were relieved of the need to use force. The cities were either not garrisoned, or only lightly so. This reduced royal costs and released troops for other uses; the tribute of the cities was a useful supplement to the main taxation of the kingdoms, which was essentially based on the rural areas. This modus vivendi between kings and cities was being worked out all around the Aegean during this time: Demetrios' methods were those against which those of the other kings could be measured and were seen to be preferable. This is ironic; since it was Demetrios' father's policy of 'freedom' they were now applying, while Demetrios was a good deal more brutal.[15]

This was not the relationship of the kings and the cities they founded. These cities were never independent, and so did not have a long history of such an ideal condition to look back on. The king was their patron, their protector, their financier, their founder, and ultimately their ruler; and these conditions gave him great and continuing authority over them. The colonial cities' range of autonomy was very limited. The layout of these new cities invariably shows them dominated by a well-fortified citadel, where the royal garrison lived, separate from the citizens.[16]

These colonial cities were reminiscent of the urban centres of old Macedon rather than the cities of Greece, and the ultimate model was Philip's colonial foundations at Philippi and Philippopolis. Given who the founders were – Macedonian commanders such as Antigonos, Lysimachos and, above all, Seleukos – this is hardly surprising. Each city had its supervisor, its *epistates* (in the Seleukid kingdom), who was a means of communication between the king and the citizens. The relationship was generally polite, with kings formally requesting that the cities do things, and the cities offering formal honours to the kings, and to the *epistatai*. This clearly worked, and very few of these cities ever rebelled or struck out for independence until the kingdoms themselves failed.

Ptolemy's seduction of the Island League pushed Demetrios' seaward front back towards the mainland. A major Ptolemaic base was established on the island of Andros, close to Demetrios' lands in Euboia and Attika and Boiotia.[17] Ptolemy was in contact with the Athenian opposition, and with Pyrrhos. They planned to pre-empt Demetrios' attack by organizing their own, from several directions at once. This meant Ptolemy's naval advance in the Aegean, and land attacks by Pyrrhos and Lysimachos directed at Demetrios' power base in Macedon.

This might have been a hazardous exercise, if Demetrios really had 110,000 troops and 500 ships available, and really was firmly established as king in Macedon. The allies were fully aware that his house of cards would collapse given a firm enough shove. The size of his army, possibly exaggerated (maybe by Demetrios himself, maybe subsequently by his relieved enemies) was largely negated by his need to hold down the lands where he was unpopular; a considerable fraction of the troops was distributed in garrisons through Greece, and indeed in Macedon.

The involvement of Pyrrhos in the allied plan was clearly essential. The Macedonians liked him as a king of the type they appreciated, a bonny fighter whose fight with Pantauches had led to them singing his praises. His involvement also required that the allies reach agreement on how to divide up the spoils in advance. Pyrrhos demanded Macedon itself as his share, which was what Lysimachos also wanted. It is doubtful if the other kings would have been happy to see Epiros and Macedon united under one ruler but Pyrrhos had the whip hand, for Lysimachos could not fight a land war with Demetrios alone, and Pyrrhos could have stayed neutral. Lysimachos made enough of his claim to be allocated part of eastern Macedonia. Perhaps Ptolemy, who was probably in control of the correspondence, simply promised Macedon to both men.

This being settled, the war could begin, probably in 287. Lysimachos invaded Macedon from the east, besieging Amphipolis, and Pyrrhos came across the mountains from the west; there was also surely a campaign of subversion directed at Demetrios' forces in Macedon, for Lysimachos' ravaging should have alienated the Macedonians, yet Demetrios found that his army refused to fight. The soldiers facing Pyrrhos refused to fight to keep Demetrios in luxury, which summed up all the elements of his unpopularity.[18]

His wife Phila, Kassander's sister, committed suicide rather than go on her travels again,[19] but Demetrios himself refused to give up. He lost Macedon, but still had his fleet, most of his mercenaries, and his bases in the Greek cities. He held Tyre and Sidon in Phoenicia, useful bases from which to attack either Ptolemy or Seleukos, but Ptolemy quietly seized control of both cities, and the Sidonian King, Philokles, entered his service as a notable naval commander.[20]

In Greece, Demetrios was insecure. In June 287 Athens blew up in a rebellion, assisted by a Ptolemaic force which was landed from Andros. Demetrios was able to hold on to some forts in the countryside, and laid siege to the city, which had made serious and successful efforts to get in the harvest before he arrived. Negotiations followed between Demetrios and Ptolemy's representative Sostratos, who was advised by Kallias, an Athenian who had commanded the Ptolemaic force from Andros.

The situation in Attica was at a stalemate: Demetrios was not able to retake the city; the Athenians were not able to take Peiraios; Ptolemy was not prepared to mount a full campaign at such a distance from Egypt. Expulsion of Demetrios from Macedon had accomplished the main aim of the alliance, so peace was made on the basis that Demetrios would hold Peiraios, and Athens would be free of his political interference. The Athenians did not like it, but they could not fight Demetrios without outside help. No doubt Demetrios did not like it either, but he could console himself that he retained the essentials. Peiraios was a major naval base and port, and by holding it he had a grip on Athens' economic lifeline.[21]

This peace marked Ptolemy's exit from the alliance. He had made major gains, and now dominated the Aegean, without having committed serious forces to the war: the main fighting had been done by Pyrrhos, Lysimachos and the Athenians. The two kings amicably divided Macedon, though Pyrrhos affected to be taken aback to find he was not going to get it all. In the event he also helped Athens to resist Demetrios' siege, thus honouring his alliance with Ptolemy, an alliance Ptolemy was soon to desert.[22]

The Athenian settlement meant peace between Demetrios and Ptolemy, indeed the Athenians were actually subsumed within the treaty the two kings made. Demetrios would thus seem to have adopted his father's tactic of negotiating separately with his enemies, this time with some success. When Pyrrhos arrived in Athens, he also made peace with Demetrios.[23] Combined with Seleukos' inability to intervene so far to the west, this left Demetrios facing Lysimachos.

Demetrios launched himself on Lysimachos from Miletos. On his arrival at the city he had been greeted by Eurydike, the estranged wife of Ptolemy, who presented him with her daughter Ptolemais, to whom Demetrios had been betrothed, at least formally, since the old diplomatic changes of 299–298. He took the opportunity to marry again, then set off on campaign. He left his son Antigonos Gonatas, in command of the remaining posts in Europe, Corinth, Peiraios, Euboia, Boiotia, Phokis, several forts and towns near these cities and Demetrias in Thessaly. From Miletos, Demetrios gained control of several Ionian cities, including Ephesus and Pirene, either by being welcomed or by threats and conquest, and then marched inland to capture Sardis. He was assisted by defections of cities and soldiers from Lysimachos, but now came up against a more powerful enemy in a force commanded by Lysimachos' son Agathokles, who managed, by retaking the cities along the coast, to cut the invader off from his fleet.

Demetrios is said to have intended to reach Armenia and Media;[24] this seems most unlikely, for he had no experience of these areas, and no connections there. He certainly marched inland to get away from Agathokles' superior force. Agathokles carefully refused to fight him, except in skirmishes, but he also refused to let go of the invaders, and shepherded Demetrios and his army steadily further east to the Taurus mountain area. The old loyalties Demetrios may have counted on did not revive after the first victories; he was out-generalled by Agathokles; his army began to fade away, partly by desertion, partly by casualties and disease. Most of the mercenaries remained with him to the end, but they could not win. Agathokles manoeuvred him out of his father's territories and over the Taurus Mountains into Kilikia, Seleukos' territory.[25] At last Seleukos got into the war.

Demetrios appealed to Seleukos as a relative by marriage, and meanwhile conquered Kilikia. Seleukos, supposedly persuaded by his general Patrokles – as if he needed to be persuaded to be suspicious of Antigonos' son – gradually hardened his attitude. Kilikia was not seriously defended, though there were, as with Agathokles' army, several skirmishes. Again, no rising to his support happened in either Kilikia or Syria. Seleukos, like Agathokles, used blockade rather than risk battle against such a commander. And indeed, there was no need to risk casualties, and even possible defeat, for the poor condition of Demetrius' forces became clear very quickly. Demetrios' army reached the Amanus Hills, the boundary of Kilikia and Syria, high and difficult to cross even now: they were weary, hopeless, hungry and unpaid. Seleukos understood their physical and psychological condition and posted his own forces to surround them, lighting fires to show their presence, making it obvious that they were there and yet keeping them out of reach. There were few provisions available in the hills where they were all camped, but Seleukos' army could be supplied and Demetrios' men starved. After allowing the situation to become apparent, Seleukos came forward and stood before them, took off his helmet, and asked them to give up. It was enough. The adventure was over. They handed Demetrios over, on a promise of his life being spared (just as, 40 years before, Eumenes had been handed over to Demetrios' father). Demetrios' last act, before his own surrender, was to send orders to his son and to his men in Europe to obey no more orders from him, but to obey Antigonos instead.[26] Soon afterwards Seleukos founded another new city in the valley of the Kara Su just east of the scene, and called it Nikopolis, 'Victory-city'.

Demetrios' last adventure showed that an Alexander-type conquest was no longer possible. It may have been romantic – though Seleukos' gesture of appealing directly to his soldiers trumped even that – but it was hopeless, and was seen to be hopeless from the time he failed to bring over more than three or four cities to his cause. He was rejected by every king, by all the cities who might have supported him, and by public opinion generally. He might leave a great name behind him, but not a great achievement. This failure was the final sign that the great adventures were over. But one man still felt that the unity of the empire was attainable.

13

The last chance for the empire, 285–281 BC

In 285, once Demetrios was captured by Seleukos, the three most powerful rulers in the western world were all contemporaries of Alexander the Great, who had died 40 years before. Within four years all of them (and Demetrios, a generation younger) were dead. As is to be expected of kings who were Macedonian in origin, their goings produced confusion and conflict, but this was not wholly their fault, and two of them had already solved the old Macedonian problem of the royal succession.

The removal of their common enemy took away the only glue holding the alliance of the kings together. Ptolemy had already made peace with Demetrios; and by expelling him and his army into Kilikia, so, in effect, had Lysimachos. Seleukos cannot have been pleased to find that the disturber of the peace had been shoved over the mountains into his territory, but he overcame the problem with minimal casualties, and had acquired thereby a reasonable increase in his fame. Further, the division of Macedon between Lysimachos and Pyrrhos was hardly the result the Macedonians had expected when they removed themselves from Demetrios' kingship, and it was clearly an unstable situation.

Pyrrhos claimed he had been promised all Macedon; Lysimachos had suffered the defeats, damage and casualties, and required compensation. Neither accepted the other's argument; both wanted all Macedon.[1] Pyrrhos' growth – he seized Thessaly from Antigonos Gonatas soon after Demetrios left[2] – was not welcome to his former allies, and he began to seem as threatening as Demetrios. Nor was his new power welcome to his neighbour, the Aitolian League, which again found itself surrounded on three sides, west, north and east, by his territories. Lysimachos exploited his problems. He had assured himself of Athenian goodwill by a present of money in the crisis of their rising against Demetrios, and contacted Aitolia, both being at odds with Pyrrhos. Antigonos Gonatas held his father's old possessions, scattered along the Aegean side of Greece from the northern Peloponnese to Demetrias, together with their garrisons and a fleet of ships, and was not a negligible quantity either.[3]

When Lysimachos moved against Pyrrhos not long after Demetrios' capture, he had either the support or the acquiescence of these Greek neighbours. Without too much difficulty he pushed Pyrrhos across the mountains into his home kingdom. Pyrrhos made an alliance with Gonatas,[4] but neither was in a position to help the other. By the end of the year, Lysimachos was in control of all of Macedon and Thessaly, though Pyrrhos kept hold of his old gains in the bordering hills.

This was hardly the result either Ptolemy or Seleukos would have wished for when they allied with Lysimachos to overthrow Demetrios. In theory the union of Macedon with Asia Minor (and Thrace) produced a most powerful state, capable of fielding a huge army, and it had the potential for a big navy as well. No matter that Lysimachos was not aggressive towards his fellow kings (except Pyrrhos), he was clearly a threat; he was old, as the others knew all too well, but he had a competent and vigorous son in Agathokles. His acquisition of Macedon made him everyone's enemy.

One reason for the ease of Lysimachos' victory was contemporary events in Egypt. During 285 Ptolemy I co-opted his son Ptolemy II as co-ruler. This was either an attempt by the old man to prevent any disputes when he died, or a disguised coup by Ptolemy II. It seems best to see here one of Ptolemy I's methodical solutions to a difficult problem, in this case one of his own making. He had been married three times, had children by two of his wives, and several other children by other women to whom he was not married. Of the 'legitimate' children there were three sons by Eurydike, the daughter of Antipater, and one or two by Berenike, Antipater's granddaughter, who supplanted her aunt Eurydike in Ptolemy's bed, and later as his wife. There were daughters of both marriages, who were used in the political marriage market, and four of them married kings. By the early 280s the daughters were mainly married off, and there were three sons at the court. Berenike had another son, Magas, by an earlier marriage.[5]

Berenike's son Magas had been placed as Ptolemy's viceroy in Cyrenaica in about 300. She now intrigued with her husband to choose their son as his successor to the main kingdom.

Needless to say, neither Eurydike nor her sons accepted this, though it was clearly a decision for the king. The conflict within the court is largely invisible now, but it claimed casualties outside the family, so it was fairly unpleasant. Eurydike and her sons left the court and Egypt, probably in 286, and Berenike's son, Ptolemy of Kos, was then crowned and made co-ruler as Ptolemy II, in the winter of 285/284.[6]

Eurydike aimed for revenge. She persuaded Demetrios to marry Ptolemais in Miletos in 286; her eldest son, another Ptolemy, surnamed Keraunos ('Thunderer'), went to Lysimachos' court, where his half-sister Arsinoe (called Arsinoe II) was the wife of the king, and his full sister, Lysandra, was married to Agathokles. Partly as a result, this royal court soon became an even more murderous place.[7]

It is not clear who was in control in Egypt during the two years of the co-rule of father and son. The elevation of Ptolemy II to the kingship may have been in name only, or it may have been due to Ptolemy I's senility – he was in his eighties by then. The main point was that, despite the family dispute, the transfer of power from father to son was generally peaceful, and was certainly an improvement on the usual situation among Macedonian royalty.

The problem of the succession had the same enervating and destructive effects in Lysimachos' court, though the results were more calamitous. During 284 Lysimachos' wife Arsinoe II began to agitate for her sons to be preferred over those of Lysimachos' earlier wives. He had, like Ptolemy, been married three times. His first wife, Antipater's daughter Nikaia, was the mother of Agathokles. By his second wife, Amastris, he had no children. Amastris had been the bride of Krateros at Alexander's marriage ceremony at Susa in 324, was soon dismissed by her husband like most of her colleagues, then married Dionysios, the tyrant of Herakleia Pontike on the Black Sea coast of Bithynia, and who made himself king just before he died in 305. Amastris was of distinguished Persian ancestry, being the niece of Dareios III, and after Dionysios died, she ruled Herakleia as regent for his sons. Lysimachos' campaign against Antigonos the One-Eyed in 302 brought him to a great camp just south of Herakleia, and he made an alliance with the city, through which he could bring food and supplies and reinforcements. His first wife was dead and the military-political alliance led to the marriage of the queen and the king, apparently, at least according to one ancient historian, a love match, though this is now doubted by more cynical modern historians. Neither partner was young any more, and the marriage lasted only a short time. Soon after Ipsos, Lysimachos renounced her, so that he could marry Ptolemy's daughter Arsinoe in the diplomatic *bouleversement* of 299/298. But he kept a grip on Herakleia, and continued to respect Amastris and her sons by her first husband. She was murdered by her sons in 284; Lysimachos then effortlessly annexed the principality.[8]

Arsinoe II was thus Lysimachos' third wife. She was the daughter of Ptolemy I and Berenike and so the full sister of Ptolemy II. She was 16 when she married Lysimachos, who was in his fifties, and had three sons by Lysimachos. There was also another son, Alexander, by a woman Lysimachos had not bothered to marry. Arsinoe no doubt wanted one of her sons to be Lysimachos' successor, but it was not until 284 that, perhaps inspired by her mother's success in Egypt, she actively intrigued to displace Agathokles. Her persuasiveness was such that Lysimachos had Agathokles executed.[9]

This, of course, is the 'romantic' version, on a par with the allegation that Lysimachos' and Amastris' marriage was a love match. Unless we are to credit Arsinoe with superhuman attractiveness – she had been married to Lysimachos by this time for two decades, so a sudden infatuation is hardly likely – or Lysimachos with senility, we have to seek out other reasons for the king's actions.

The obvious reason is impatience on the part of Agathokles, particularly after his successful campaign against Demetrios. The presence of Eurydike and her sons at the court drew attention to the success of Ptolemy II in muscling into power in Alexandria; Antiochos, King Seleukos' son, had been ruling the eastern lands for a decade. Agathokles was the only one of his generation not yet with full access to royal power, though he is known to have founded a city in Mysia which bore his name.[10] None of the ancient reasons we are given are at all convincing, and it is probably best to see the crisis at the court as a sudden explosion of emotion, in which all the suggested elements – Arsinoe's ambition for her children, Eurydike's presence, Agathokles' ambition and frustration, Lysimachos' age – combined. And the deed once done could not be undone, and had continuing consequences.[11]

Agathokles' wife, Lysandra, was a daughter of Ptolemy I and Eurydike – so tangled was this unpleasant affair. She fled, along with her brother Ptolemy Keraunos, to Seleukos, where they urged that he attack Lysimachos.[12] Lysimachos now found that the main prop of his regime was gone, and the heirs to his kingdom were no more than children: Arsinoe's eldest son, Ptolemy (later called 'of Telmessos') was in his early teens.

This may well be the root cause of the apparent loss of support for Lysimachos' regime which followed. These kingdoms were still fragile political constructs. The repeated failures of the royal regimes in Macedon, and the collapse of Antigonos' kingdom, were warnings of what might happen to the other new kingdoms. The problem in Macedon was always one of the royal succession, as had been recently demonstrated yet again. This was part of the background to the transfer of political power to Antiochos and Ptolemy I by their fathers, for all the contemporaries of Alexander will have had the royal succession problem of Macedon as part of their basic political knowledge. It is a perennial concern in any monarchy, but the Macedonian system was exceptionally disruptive.

The execution of Agathokles removed the main hope for an orderly succession in Lysimachos' kingdom. The old king, in his seventies, could hardly last much longer; the succession of teenage boys, supervised by their mother, had recently resulted in great unpleasantness in Macedon (and in Herakleia Pontike). For Lysimachos' subjects it was time to look to their futures. Many of them had been Antigonos' and Demetrios' subjects, so a general desertion to an invader might be expected. Lysandra was not the only one to look to Seleukos.

Lysimachos' kingdom was a conglomerate of many different lands – Macedon, Thrace, Greek cities on the Black Sea and the Aegean, former Persian provinces. The Macedonians required the king's personal attention; this was one of the things which had kept them loyal to Kassander. But Lysimachos had killed Antipater, Kassander's son, and now he had killed his own son, then executed men who complained at Agathokles' killing.[13] Within the old Antigonid lands in Asia Minor some army officers defected to Seleukos.[14] At least one of Lysimachos' high officials, Philetairos, the governor of Pergamon and guardian of part of the king's treasure, appealed for Seleukos' intervention;[15] no doubt others did so as well. The destruction of Lysimacheia by an earthquake in 287 was later seen as an omen; even at the time it was disruptive.[16]

Seleukos was isolated diplomatically by the marriage alliance of Lysimachos and Ptolemy; Lysimachos' acquisition of Macedon made him a threatening figure, so the disruption of his court was welcome. The captivity of Demetrios and the presence at his court of Ptolemy Keraunos and Lysandra and her children gave Seleukos useful cards with which to threaten both of his rivals: he threatened to release Demetrios on to Lysimachos,[17] while Keraunos hankered for the Ptolemaic throne, which, in the process of transition, was vulnerable. The kings were close to war from 285 onwards. The capture of Demetrios had exposed the latent conflict between them. With the players in the game reduced to only three, the possibility of the reunification of the empire had reopened.

Demetrios, kept prisoner in some luxury by Seleukos at Apamea in Syria, finally succumbed to his excesses and his luxurious living in 283. Seleukos sent the ashes back to Antigonos for burial,[18] a diplomatic gesture which might turn away Antigonos' wrath. In Alexandria, Ptolemy II was joint king until the end of that year; he went through a pharaonic coronation ceremony in January 282, so presumably Ptolemy I died a few days earlier.[19] He took over full authority smoothly enough in Alexandria, but his half-brother Magas took the opportunity to declare himself king in Cyrenaica.[20] Magas' action was distinctly unpopular with his half-brother, but Ptolemy could not do much about it. The death of a king cancelled the existing treaties he had made, so whatever agreement there had been between Ptolemy I and Seleukos over Syria was now void; Ptolemy II could not afford to launch an expedition against Magas in case Seleukos took advantage of his westward preoccupation to invade Syria; equally he could not intervene in the crisis in the north for fear of Magas, who might well have ambitions to rule Egypt.

Seleukos was thus presented with a whole set of delectable alternatives, to turn to the south in order to interfere in the Ptolemaic succession with the immediate aim of seeking control of Phoenicia and southern Syria, perhaps in alliance with Magas; or to the north, to interfere in the crisis in Lysimachos' realm and perhaps to secure a good deal more. The two potential enemies were still allied by marriage, and if either was threatened, the alliance might be activated. An invasion of Syria could allow Lysimachos, whose main problem lay within his own family, to move south through the Taurus passes into Kilikia, just as Demetrios had done three or four years before; a move north into Asia Minor, while Ptolemy II was concerned to consolidate his own position, could be accomplished with little prospect of being attacked from the south. Ptolemaic policy in Syria had long been defensive, seeing southern Syria and Phoenicia as bastions for the defence of Egypt rather than as routes through which the Ptolemaic armies could invade the north. It was unlikely that the new king in Egypt would be thinking of invading his neighbour; if he did, Seleukos could encourage Magas, or back Ptolemy Keraunos for the throne. Seleukos decided to respond to the crisis in Asia Minor.

There was also a further consideration, which cannot have escaped Seleukos. Conquest of Lysimachos' kingdom would produce for him a final opportunity to reunite Alexander's empire. If he won, he would rule from the borders of India to the borders of Epiros, just as Alexander had done, with the exception only of Egypt. The prospect was surely one he felt to be irresistible. He must also have seen the inevitable result: he would need to fight Ptolemy II soon after; Ptolemy could see it too. Nor would the prospect be pleasing to the various pretenders he had at his court.

The precise trigger for the war's beginning is unknown; perhaps it just began when Seleukos was ready. He was gathering troops and supplies, according to a Babylonian source, in mid-282,[21] and the decisive battle at Koroupedion took place in February 281. Seleukos must have crossed into Asia Minor before the snows blocked the passes, in the autumn of 282. The campaign took several months but details are few. Lysimachos' son Alexander, fighting for Seleukos, gained control of the city of Kotiaion; Seleukos besieged Sardis.[22] So Seleukos penetrated into western Asia Minor, forcing Lysimachos to fight at home. At least one city, Pergamon, held by Lysimachos' treasurer Philetairos, had been promised to the invader beforehand; most other lords and cities waited to see who would win. In the end, in the one battle the two old men fought, Lysimachos was defeated and killed. The field of battle was near Sardis, so perhaps Lysimachos had to fight to save the city.[23]

Seleukos spent several more months organizing his conquests, no doubt savouring his achievement, and making decisions on the disposition of his conquests. Lysandra was consumed with a desire for revenge, but Lysimachos' son Alexander insisted on his father having a decent burial at Lysimacheia.[24] None of the family was assigned a kingdom. Presumably Seleukos was willing to provide generously for them, but not to the extent of setting any of them up as independent kings. This will have become clear as the months went by, and Ptolemy Keraunos was certainly clear by the autumn that he would get nothing.

Ptolemy II was no doubt especially concerned at Seleukos' triumph. Seleukos would not need to say or do anything to threaten him: his victory over Lysimachos did that for him. Ptolemy had plenty of relations at Seleukos' court, and he will have known of Keraunos' ambition and temperament – 'keraunos' implied loud noises and sudden actions. And in the event it was Ptolemy II who benefited most, in a negative sense, from what happened next. There is no evidence for his direct involvement, but one must harbour suspicions.

Seleukos made administrative arrangements to take over the whole of Lysimachos' kingdom. At first he did not need to do more than confirm any local officials who had stayed at their posts, and appoint others where necessary. Philetairos in Pergamon was certainly retained. An attempt was made to enforce his suzerainty over the ruler of Pontos, on the north Anatolian coast, but it failed; the lord there, Mithradates of Pontos, took the royal title to celebrate his victory.[25] The Bithynian king also survived a Seleukid attack by one of the new king's generals.[26] Neither of these rebuffs was particularly serious, but when he was approached by a delegation from Herakleia Pontike, the meeting ended in mutual annoyance, which was a mistake on Seleukos' part.[27] The lands of northern Asia Minor became even more determined on independence than before.

Arsinoe (II), Lysimachos' widow, escaped from Ephesos (where a mob had quickly formed to hunt for her) and ships of Lysimachos' fleet took her to Kassandreia in Macedon.[28] She intended to claim the kingship for her son, which made sense, but she was not wanted; it is doubtful that any Macedonians wanted another teenaged king supervised by his mother. She had no power beyond a few ships and soldiers, but she did manage to seize control of the city.[29] There was another claimant to the kingship in the person of Demetrios' son, Antigonos Gonatas, who still controlled parts of Greece and had a fleet. Pyrrhos might also revive his claim. It does not seem that anyone consulted the Macedonians, no doubt as confused as everyone else.

Seleukos demobilized most of his forces. Those he had brought from Syria were sent home, the mercenaries and his professional army retained; there was plenty for them to do in Asia Minor. The soldiers who had fought for Lysimachos could also largely be dismissed to their homes, some to various parts of Asia Minor, others to Macedon, though it is likely that there were relatively few of the latter. The mercenaries would no doubt mainly re-enlist with Seleukos, though some clearly stayed with Arsinoe.

Seleukos had next to impress his control on Macedon. By this action he would claim the kingship, but this required ratification by the Assembly. None of his competitors had succeeded in securing this consent; and Seleukos did not anticipate any dispute as to his claim. When he set out for Macedon he was escorted by former soldiers of Lysimachos, men who were probably going home. He and his court and escort crossed the Hellespont to Lysimacheia in late August or early September. Seleukos rode on, heading for Thrace on the way to Macedon. At this point, though not yet acclaimed as such by any of the Macedonians, he was de facto king of Macedon, despite Arsinoe in Kassandreia and the other competitors.

Seleukos was the last of Alexander's officers. Next to Ptolemy I, he was the most cautious but, unlike Ptolemy, he retained a full measure of Alexander- and Antigonos-type ambition, and he was on the verge of achieving what Antigonos and Demetrios had worked for, and what Kassander and Ptolemy I – and he himself until now – had worked against: the reunification of Alexander's empire. It would be astonishing if he had not wished for this more than once in the past 40 years, though he had never hinted at such an ambition. Yet when the opportunity arrived he grasped it. Now all he had to do was to reach Macedon and establish control.

In his suite was Ptolemy Keraunos, who had hoped Seleukos would assist him to a kingdom of his own, possibly Egypt, or that of Lysimachos in Asia, or Macedon. Keraunos' whole career suggests that he felt that he was entitled to nothing less than a kingdom of his own. As Seleukos rode towards Macedon, he will have finally realized that none of these was going to come to him. The prospect of the reunification of the empire will have been the talk of Seleukos' court as soon as the war with Lysimachos began. It would also have been clear to Ptolemy II in Alexandria. We do not know if there was communication between the two half-brothers, but it would not be surprising if Ptolemy II encouraged Keraunos to strike, promising support. If Keraunos gained a kingdom by himself, he would be less of a threat to Ptolemy. So, as Seleukos rode north from his late enemy's city of Lysimacheia, Keraunos decoyed him off the road to view an old open-air altar, and there, when they were apparently alone, he stabbed him to death.[30]

The deaths of kings are rarely decisive. That of Philip II did not deflect the Macedonians from establishing control of Greece and invading Asia; the death of Alexander did not encourage the disintegration of his empire, which only occurred some years later. But the death of Seleukos Nikator – 'the Victor' – marked the end of the last chance for Alexander's empire to be reunited. He had developed a viable governing system in his kingdom over the 30 years and more, with more elements of social justice and fewer elements of screwing the last drop of wealth out of the peasantry than Ptolemy's Egypt. The Seleukid system resembled that of Antigonos in lying comparatively lightly across the bent shoulders of the working population. Seleukos was less brutal than Antigonos and more reliable and consistent than Demetrios in his general policy, and unlike the rule of Kassander, Lysimachos, or Ptolemy, his death did not set off an internecine, murderous conflict within his family. Of all the successors of Alexander, Seleukos was the last to emerge as a great ruler, and was the one most likely to create an enduringly united empire; which was, of course, why he was murdered.

14

New kings, and disaster, 281–277 BC

Macedonia had no king but plenty of claimants. Arsinoe II held Kassandreia, intending one of her sons should become king as his father's successor; she had a force of mercenaries with her, but her authority extended no further than the city gates. Agathokles' widow Lysandra also had a claim through her children, though they had been with Seleukos in Asia and perhaps never reached Europe. Antiochos, still in the east, had a claim as his father's son. Antigonos Gonatas had a claim as the son of Demetrios. Pyrrhos had a claim as a former king. There was also a grandson of Antipater, a son of Kassander's brother, also called Antipater, now old enough to pretend to the throne of his uncle and his cousins. The multiplicity of claimants portended serious trouble for the Macedonians, yet it was only a more than usually complicated succession crisis.

There was also Ptolemy Keraunos. He was Seleukos' murderer, which marked him as a claimant; and like Antigonos and young Antipater, he was a grandson of old Antipater. After the murder he rode back into Lysimacheia, collecting a group of his friends on the way, metaphorically waved his bloodstained dagger, and announced himself to the soldiers and citizens as the avenger of Lysimachos. This was all surely planned. Lysimacheia, the city founded by Lysimachos where he lived for much of his reign, was the one place in his former kingdom full of his supporters. The soldiers there are said to have been Seleukos', but many of them were former troops of Lysimachos from Macedon who would be the obvious men for Seleukos to take with him into Macedon. Being assured of Seleukos' death, they acclaimed Keraunos as king. He set off to Macedon to establish his authority.[1] Despite claiming to avenge Lysimachos, he was aiming to recover only Macedon, at least for now.

Keraunos' first priority was to gain control in Macedon, which necessarily involved fending off his competitors. He could claim the ratification of the acclamation of the soldiers at Lysimacheia, but challengers would dispute this. The first of these on the scene was Antigonos, who brought his fleet north. He was met by Keraunos at sea somewhere near the Thracian Chersonese,[2] where Keraunos was victorious, using Lysimachos' fleet, some of which had been Demetrios'.

Pyrrhos was preparing an expedition to Italy and was looking for armed help: Keraunos gave him several thousand soldiers and 50 elephants.[3] These must originally have been Lysimachos' men and beasts, but Keraunos will have handed over the men he least trusted, and they would have been the volunteers. Pyrrhos also in effect recognized Keraunos as Macedonian king by this transaction, and the agreement included a marriage link, when Pyrrhos married a daughter of Keraunos.[4] Keraunos also contacted Ptolemy II, but apparently received no further encouragement.[5] The death of Seleukos was all Ptolemy required. Some contact was also made with Antiochos, who might be expected to look for revenge, but who had his hands full for the present. He sent Patrokles to save the position in Asia Minor, and clearly could not come west himself.[6]

Keraunos was thus doing very well in fending off his rivals: Pyrrhos to Italy, Antiochos stuck in Syria, Antigonos defeated, Ptolemy II not interested, and he had gained control of the Macedonian army. His most urgent internal problem was Arsinoe and her control of Kassandreia. Keraunos attacked the city, but failed to take it, then resorted to diplomacy. He offered Arsinoe marriage and the recognition of her children as joint kings with himself. Her eldest son, Ptolemy, argued against this, and when she insisted on accepting, he left.[7] Arsinoe accepted marriage to her half-brother, went through a splendid wedding and a ceremony of acceptance as queen at an army Assembly, but then saw her new husband murder her two younger sons on their wedding night. She left, fleeing to her brother in Egypt.[8] Keraunos had thus rid himself of all his rival pretenders, in and out of Macedon, using a series of methods – diplomatic, naval, military, marital, murderous – which were quite comparable in variety, success and speed to those used by his predecessors: the methods of Philip II and Alexander come insistently to mind.

One pretender who had got away, Arsinoe's eldest son, Ptolemy, returned to the fray in spring 280, having recruited help from an Illyrian king called Monounios. The invasion failed but involved a good deal of fighting inside Macedon.[9] Ptolemy now presumably headed for Egypt, where his uncle provided him with a small principality at Telmessos in Lykia.[10] This all took from later 281 to the early part of 280. As a result Keraunos was firmly king in Macedon, but not wholly secure yet. He had not removed all his competitors decisively, for Antigonos, Antiochos and Pyrrhos were only repelled. The Macedonians could be reasonably satisfied with him for the moment.

Pyrrhos had received an appeal for help from the southern Italian city of Taras and decided to follow in the steps of Spartan and Epirote predecessors and go to its assistance. So keen were the others to see him go that he was given the use of some of their troops. This was the cause for which Keraunos contributed a sizeable force. Pyrrhos asked for help from Antigonos and Antiochos as well, ships and cash respectively, but they may not have bothered to contribute once it was clear he was really going.[11] He stayed in the west for five years, and the mayhem he created on his return fully justified the measures the others took to speed him on his way. He sailed off during 280.

Antiochos may have been on his way to the west when he heard of the death of his father. He had presumably left the farther east settled and peaceful, and no doubt under a strong governor. There was certainly a satrap in office in Baktria five or so years later who was capable of sending reinforcements of elephants to the west; he was a man therefore with arms to hand, and perhaps diplomatic contacts with India.[12]

Antiochos had a lot to do when he arrived to take up his inheritance. He had been king in the east for over ten years and was scarcely known in the west, and not at all in Asia Minor. He had trouble in Syria, in Seleukis, the area of the four great new cities. The problem is not well understood, for the only evidence is an inscription from Ilion referring to rebels and trouble, but it also says Antiochos brought peace to the area.[13] This, and a journey into Asia Minor in the spring of 280, will have fully occupied his time and energy. The trouble in Syria may have involved interference by Ptolemy II, though this is no more than an assumption.[14] By the time he was free, Keraunos was in control in Macedon.

The defeat of Antigonos Gonatas by Ptolemy Keraunos had repercussions in Greece. A group of cities along the north coast of the Peloponnese formed themselves into the Achaian League during 280;[15] this was not an immediate threat to Antigonos, but it created a stronger local state less amenable to pressure. Some other cities, probably including Argos and Megalopolis, expelled their Macedonian garrisons, a sensible diminution of Antigonos' curious state; the Achaian cities may have done the same before forming their league.[16] One of the Spartan kings, Areus, suddenly emerged from his hermit state to challenge both Antigonos and the Aitolians in a revival of an ancient dispute concerning lands belonging to the temple at Delphi.

The troubles these challengers faced in 281–280 prevented them from pursuing their campaigns against Keraunos, which under other circumstances would be their first priority. This may perhaps be attributed to Egypt. Ptolemy II, by his control of the Island League, the island base of Kos, and the maritime approaches to the Aegean from Egypt, had influence all round the Aegean basin. It was in his interest to see that Keraunos was provided for, so as to neutralize his powerful claim to the Egyptian throne. A kingdom would do, preferably one at a considerable distance from Egypt and where he would be kept busy: Macedon was ideal.

Ptolemy could not assist Keraunos too openly, for this would only draw the attention of Antiochos. By the spring of 280, the problems of Syria had been mastered and Antiochos was operating in Asia Minor, where several areas, notably along the Black Sea coast, including Herakleia Pontike, sought to assert their independence. Ptolemy was able to secure control of several places on the southern coast of Asia Minor – or perhaps he resumed control of places his father had held – but he did so without provoking Antiochos to hostilities.

Even installing a garrison of Ptolemaic soldiers in Miletos[17] did not provoke a war. But Antiochos, as much as any king of the time, was capable of selecting his priorities.

It is tempting to look for the hand of Ptolemy and his money in Antigonos' troubles in Greece. No evidence actually exists but the sudden emergence of a Spartan army under Areus and the formation of a new Peloponnesian League by him, the liberation of several cities from Antigonos' control, and the formation of the enduring Achaian League, all at the moment when to distract Antigonos was materially to assist Ptolemy Keraunos, must be seen as suggesting an outside helping hand at work. Above all, Areus will have needed money to undertake his curious and futile adventure, and Ptolemy was the most obvious source for this.

The main benefactor, therefore, from the deaths of both Lysimachos and Seleukos, was Ptolemy II, who saw his royal rivals dead, his threatening half-brother distracted and fully occupied in Macedon, his Aegean rival Antigonos significantly reduced in power, and his own territories expanded by small but significant gains. His neighbour Antiochos was heavily engaged in Asia Minor, and so was less of a threat than his father had been. Ptolemy also received and gave refuge to Arsinoe II, who, at least at first, was perhaps regarded, with her surviving son, as a possible threat to Keraunos or even Antiochos; later he found an even better use for her.

Antiochos picked off many of his external enemies with relative ease partly by simply ignoring Ptolemy's provocations. Pyrrhos' request for some troops for his western expedition was probably ignored once it was known he was actually going. An agreement with Antigonos was reached, probably after some naval fighting, which was to be sealed by the marriage of Antigonos with Phila, the daughter of Seleukos and Stratonike (and so Antiochos' stepdaughter and half-sister, and Antigonos' niece). This agreement may not have been finalized until 278, but any conflict between the two kings seemed exceptionally pointless while Keraunos was king in Macedon.[18] Keraunos himself was offered and accepted some sort of an agreement by Antiochos, which can only have involved recognition of his kingship, though no doubt Antiochos had many mental reservations on this.[19] Antiochos operated in as canny a way as Keraunos and Ptolemy, if without the bloodthirstiness of the former and more openly than the latter.

Antiochos chose to rule in Asia Minor with a light hand, which meant that the incipient small principalities were tolerated. Philetairos at Pergamon controlled a substantial part of Lysimachos' treasure, and was effectively independent as well as rich.[20] He gained the goodwill of Antiochos by retrieving his father's body from Lysimacheia (Keraunos, short of cash, had demanded a ransom for it).[21] This put Antiochos under obligation to him; Philetairos' ultimate aim, as of so many in such a position at the time, was independence. In the north, Pontos and Bithynia were both independent, as was Herakleia Pontike. Herakleia had a worthwhile navy, and, along with Byzantion, Chalkedon and Teos, formed the Northern League, as a mutual self-defence. Antiochos was soon at war with both Bithynia and Herakleia, a continuation of the quarrel they had with Seleukos.[22]

By early 279 a new international equilibrium was approaching: Ptolemy II was firmly in power in Egypt, southern Syria, Cyprus and the Aegean islands, though Magas remained independent in Cyrenaica; Antiochos had brought most of his father's Asian inheritance under his own control, but he had a problem with the northern states, and had given up on Macedon and Thrace for the present; Pyrrhos had gone to the west; Antigonos Gonatas had been reduced to a few Greek fortresses and his defeated fleet; the Spartan king had gone home; in Macedon, Ptolemy Keraunos had seen off his rivals and had driven out his half-sister and her children. His acceptance by the Macedonians as their king had been decisive, insofar as a decision had been made. He defended the kingdom against invasion and extended his power over most of it; he was therefore the legitimate king in Macedon.

At this point Macedon was suddenly invaded, in the summer of 279, by a new set of barbarians from the north, Celts, whom the Greeks called *Galatoi*, Galatians. They were in the Danube area in Alexander's time, where he had briefly encountered them. They were as aggressive as he was, and answered him with defiant statements.[23] Since then more of them had moved eastwards, forming a substantial predator state centred in the area of modern Belgrade, later the kingdom of the Scordisci.[24] The preoccupations of states in Greece and Macedon prevented serious attention being paid to these developments, if indeed knowledge of them reached Macedon, the Balkan state most concerned. The involvement of the Illyrian king Monounios in a Macedonian war in 280 implies that he was not under any threat from the north at the time. Kassander had fought Galatian raiders south of the Haemos mountain range some years before[25] and a raiding band reached Thrace briefly in the later 280s.[26] There were plenty of premonitory warnings, though events in Macedon had been so all-consuming since Kassander's death that it is likely no one spared time or attention to appreciate the previous build-up of tension which the invasion of 279 implies. What actually happened was so unexpected and unusual that no one who predicted it would have been believed.

The Galatians not only appeared suddenly but their attacks were also quite without precedent, and were all the more terrifying for that. The early encounters were seen as the normal incidents of frontier warfare, if anyone thought of it, and Macedon had not suffered a serious barbarian invasion since the early days of the reign of Philip II, except that brought on by Ptolemy, son of Lysimachos with Monounios – but the Illyrians were familiar enemies, and fairly easily beatable.

From the point of view of the Galatians, the situation looked very promising.

Kassander and Lysimachos had driven off the minor raids they had met, but the fighting had not been easy. The Macedonians and Greeks may have been ignorant of much of what was going on in the north, but the Galatians clearly had a good idea of what had been happening in Macedon; the number of coins of Philip II spread through the Balkans argues frequent trade relations, and where trade goes, so goes information.[27] What they could see was continued turmoil, kings repeatedly dying or driven out (in 297 (twice), 294, 287, 285, 281) and, in 281–280, civil war. Keraunos had no friends, only enemies. His control of Macedon might look firm by early 279, but he had been king only a little over a year, had no hereditary claim to the throne, and was widely seen as an impulsive murderer and breaker of his word. To the Galatians, he looked extremely vulnerable, and it was upon the vulnerable that such raiders preyed.

Needless to say the course of events is by no means clear, for Macedon was reduced to chaos by the invasions. The Galatian attack was well planned and comprehensive. Three different invasions came, one led by Bolgios aimed at western Macedon through Illyria; a second, under Brennos, came south along the valley of the Axios heading for eastern Macedon; the third, under Kerenthios, marched against Thrace and the Triballi. They were also a migration: the warriors were accompanied by their families.[28]

Keraunos met the first invasion, led by Bolgios. He was defeated, captured and killed; this let the invaders in. His defeat and death was the occasion for moralizing comments by historians, who quite possibly invented especially unpleasant ways of having him killed in order to make the moral even more gruesomely telling. Essentially he is depicted as over-confident, which may well be the case: the invasion was, it is worth repeating, unprecedented.[29]

Half a dozen local war leaders, elected or self-appointed, are known in the next two years or so: Keraunos' brother Meleagros lasted two months, Antipater, a nephew of Kassander, lasted 45 days, a general called Sosthenes perhaps two years; Ptolemy, Arrhidaios and Alexander ruled part or all of the kingdom for uncertain periods. It is possible to put these men in sequence, but it is more likely they overlapped, operating in different parts of the country, some as kings, some as pretenders.[30] The sequence of invasions and the names of the invaders' leaders are similarly confusing, as the various Galatian bands split and rejoined in various ways. It does not seem possible to reconstruct events;[31] much that happened is quite unknown and unknowable. What is certain is that Macedon was comprehensively pillaged and burnt and looted, though the cities seem to have held out behind their walls, full of refugees and short of food. Eventually there was nothing left to steal or burn, no food to be found, and the invaders could not capture the cities. Macedonian casualties were undoubtedly appalling.

Bolgios retired with his loot back to the north, taking many of the Galatians with him.[32] Brennos remained; he may have wanted more loot, or he and

his people were maybe looking to settle; he and his band moved south into Thessaly and then beyond, leaving much of Macedon under the occupation of others of his people.[33] Royal authority had either disappeared or fragmented, and political leadership was at a premium; the only successful fighter among the many, Sosthenes, refused the royal title, but soon died; Kassandreia came under the control of a man called Apollodoros, who quickly developed into a tyrant, perhaps as the only way to keep control of a panicky city.[34] Even after Bolgios' horde had left and most of Brennos' people had moved into Thessaly, the Macedonians were quite unable to retake the land from the invaders. Had Brennos decided to stay in Macedon and make it his own kingdom, he may well have been successful.

Brennos' horde moved on from Thessaly to attack Thermopylai, where a varied collection of armed contingents, Aitolians, Boiotians, Phokians, men sent by Antigonos Gonatas and by Antiochos, and no doubt Malians and the local Lokrians, blocked the pass. He turned west to raid Delphi, but he was blocked and defeated by the Aitolians and the Phokians without reaching the sanctuary. The horde retired northwards.[35] Presumably Brennos decided that his people would be satisfied with settling in Macedon.

It was perhaps under the pressure exerted by these events that the war between Antigonos Gonatas and Antiochos I was settled with a peace treaty and marriage alliance in 278. The cause of the war is not known, but at base it was no doubt due to rivalry over Macedon. Neither king was able to establish himself in Macedon in succession to the dead Keraunos, presumably in part because of their rivalry, but the prospect of having to clear the Galatians out first cannot have been tempting. Antiochos decided that it was a kingdom too far and never made another attempt. This left the way clear for Antigonos; the Galatians had accounted for every other possible claimant.

Brennos was killed in the fighting in Greece, and his horde broke up. The survivors mainly followed Bolgios' example and retired to their homeland with their loot.[36] Another horde headed eastwards into Thrace under Leonnorios and Loutarios, either now or earlier, where the third group of the original invaders, originally under Kernthios, had gone. During 277 all these forces were still in Thrace, presumably raiding, coalescing and splitting just as had those in Macedon, and by this time, they were no doubt wondering what to do next. One group was in the region of the Thracian Chersonese. There, for some unknown reason, but possibly concerned with relations with Antiochos, Antigonos was encamped with his fleet and army, and he encountered and destroyed one of the Galatian bands.[37]

This battle, near Lysimacheia, took place in early 277; Antigonos' agreement with Antiochos had been made late the previous year. In return for the marriage alliance, Antiochos renounced any claim to Macedon, and Antigonos agreed to leave the Thracian Chersonese and the nearby cities to Antiochos. This effectively made Antigonos a subordinate ally of Antiochos', and he was in Antiochos' territory when he encountered and beat the Galatian band. He was clearly intending to use the area as his base in his new attempt to gain control of Macedon. His back was protected by the alliance with Antiochos, and he now had the prestige of a victory over the Galatians to wipe out the stain of the old defeat by Keraunos.

One way to get rid of the Galatian invaders was to enlist them: besides being cheaper than Greek mercenaries they were infinitely more expendable. Antigonos thus cleared Macedon of Galatians by recruiting them, using his own Galatians to drive out their fellows. His competitors were also removed: Antipater fled to Egypt,[38] Arrhidaios disappeared, Ptolemy also fled to Egypt. Antigonos also enlisted a Lokrian pirate leader, who succeeded in freeing Kassandreia from Apollodoros' tyranny. The siege of the city lasted ten months, which suggests a good deal of internal support for the 'tyrant'.[39] The Galatians did not actually go very far away. Apart from those who settled in the Belgrade area, others settled in Thrace and formed a kingdom inland of Byzantion, which city they laid under tribute for the next 60 years.[40] The northern borders of Macedon were as extensively disrupted as the country itself.

All this time (279–277), Antiochos was involved in his war against the Northern League and Mithradates of Pontos. It was complicated by a simultaneous crisis in Bithynia, where the succession to King Zipoites was disputed between his sons, Nikomedes and Zipoites the younger.[41] Antiochos, despite distractions such as the brief war with Antigonos, was making progress with his enemies in such disarray. Everyone also had to watch the activities of the Galatians in Thrace. The two bands led by Leonnorios and Loutarios made more than one attempt to cross over into Asia, and when Nikomedes of Bithynia became desperate, he contacted Leonnorios, hired his band to fight his enemies, and brought them into Asia.[42] The other band was in the Thracian Chersonese, and seized ships from Antiochos' governor of Hellespontine Phrygia, who had attempted to negotiate with them.[43] Once in Asia, they rejoined, drove Antiochos' army from Bithynia, and headed south into the rich lands of Ionia and Lydia. The relief of Thrace and Macedon came at the cost of extensive ravaging in Asia.

Macedon's suffering had been extreme, but it had been its own fault. The repeated disputes over the royal succession could only cause neighbours to lick their lips in anticipation whenever a king died. Previous succession disputes had always been accompanied by invasions. The Galatians were worse than usual, but something of the sort was only to be expected. Since Philip II the kings had done nothing to resolve the problem and the threat. Alexander went to conquer in Asia; Kassander campaigned over his northern border at times, but gave more attention to Greece, as had his father. Demetrios emulated Alexander.

Lysimachos, though he conquered the Paeonians, was in control of Macedon too briefly to have much effect.

Once again, Macedon's basic problem was the royal succession. By this time there were plenty of examples of what not to do – all Macedonian history showed that – and what should be done. Antigonos the One-Eyed, Ptolemy I and Seleukos I had shown that the way to ensure a smooth succession was to nominate and install one selected son as joint king before the old king died. The chosen one gained confidence and experience, the old man could relax, and everyone could get used to what the future held. Even Demetrios, hardly the most responsible of kings, had made careful provision for the succession, leaving his European lands with his son Antigonos.

This procedure relied on the senior king living long enough to produce a son, see him grow to be an adult and train him. To ensure the continuance of the kingdom was one of the duties of kings, and the lesson of Alexander's negligence in this matter was graven into the minds of his contemporaries; it was surely one of the reasons for the measures the several kings took. No doubt the absence of an accepted hereditary scheme in the new kingdoms impelled the appointment of the junior kings, but the system was the beginning of such a scheme. A species of hereditary succession existed in Macedon, in that the kings were chosen from within the Argead family, but only rarely had it worked in a patrilineal way. The resulting murderous disputes ensured that the family died out by 308. The achievement of the kingship by Antigonos II, at the third attempt, from a family owing all of its renown to its heredity, promised to remedy the problem.

The kingdom Antigonos took over was wrecked. No estimates of casualties are possible, nor any account of the physical damage. None of the cities appeared to have been taken by the invaders, though Kassandreia suffered a ten-month siege in the aftermath. Many people in the countryside survived by taking refuge in the cities; many died or were carried off into slavery, and the rural areas were surely very severely damaged. The kingdom had lost considerable numbers of men to the various expeditionary forces and reinforcements sent into the east in the past two generations. This was not necessarily a crippling loss, for the numbers of soldiers Kassander and Demetrios were able to raise were almost as substantial as those Alexander had taken with him. Yet it was certainly debilitating, and the Galatian ravaging even more so. The result, in international political terms, was to so weaken Macedon for the next generation that it had to shelter under the Seleukid wing, at least while Antiochos I and Antigonos Gonatas ruled.

It seems probable that another result was the destruction of whatever governmental institutions existed. The personal monarchy of kings before Antigonos Gonatas continued under him and his successors, but virtually all the evidence for settled administrative institutions comes from the Antigonid period. Proof is lacking, but a reasonable conjecture would be that Antigonos was faced with a wrecked country and society, in which for a long time he could not even raise much of a Macedonian army and had relied on mercenaries. He set about constructing a new system of government, to some degree bureaucratic, but building on the self-reliance exhibited by the cities in the invasion crisis. The old baronage, in so far as it had survived the earlier regime and the emigration, will have suffered disproportionately as victims of the Galatians in war. It had been the function of the barons to fight, and they had obviously lost, both their lives and in damage to their property. Antigonos had the first opportunity in centuries to start more or less anew, and seems to have taken it.[44]

This was as much a result of Alexander's expeditions as of the Galatian invasions. He had removed much of the male Macedonian population, and he had carelessly failed to provide an adult male heir until it was too late; above all, he had diverted attention from Macedon's own security to conquer an empire. The invasion of the Galatians in 279–277 was a direct consequence of Alexander's work, though not of Philip, who had been exceptionally careful to extend and dominate his northern frontier. At the same time, there were many thousands of Macedonians and Greeks, mainly descended from the participants in Alexander's adventure who were now scattered throughout Alexander's conquests, and whose lives were much enriched by their relocation; and their children had it even better.

15

The new world, 277–272 BC

By the end of 277 the invaders had left Macedon, going north, or into Thrace, or across into Asia Minor. Those in Europe gorged on loot, and settled into relatively stable kingdoms at some distance from Macedon; those in Asia spent another decade ravaging the Asian lands. Eventually, from about 270, they were compelled to settle in the interior, but for the next 50 years and more bands of raiders were liable to break out. One of the marks of a successful king or ruler in Asia during the third century BC was to be able to boast that he had defeated a Galatian raiding band.

As in Macedon, the cities in Asia Minor were safe behind their walls, but the countryside, the fields, the villages, unwalled towns, country estates and anyone caught outside the cities, were in danger. Kyzikos suffered a ravaging of its lands,[1] unwalled Ilion was occupied and looted and damaged; Thyateira, Pergamon, Ephesos, Erythrai, Didyma, Miletos, Priene, Themisonion, Kelainai were all attacked and damaged.[2] Local defences were sometimes effective, and some cities paid ransom, but the main responsibility for combating the raids lay with King Antiochos. His Galatian war lasted several years, perhaps until about 270. The decisive battle, the 'elephant battle', was sometime between 275 and 270.[3]

The result of the Galatian invasion was to impose a decisive halt to any further expansion by the Seleukid state. Antiochos was fully occupied throughout the 270s in settling affairs in Asia Minor. In that period Antigonos was similarly settling in as king of Macedon. Ptolemy II was less bothered by internal problems but more satisfied with his international position, and in 275 celebrated extravagantly his kingship by a great parade in Alexandria;[4] that is, the Galatian invasions were decisive in finally forming the Hellenistic international world. The reunification of Alexander's empire, from Macedon to India, was still possible before they invaded. The damage they inflicted in Macedon and in Asia Minor compelled the kings they fought to concentrate on their own affairs, and so reduced their victims' wealth and strength that none was able to contemplate such an adventure again.

The fact that the kings who took up their offices between 282 and 277 were of the next generation after Alexander's contemporaries is crucial. The fathers, Seleukos, Ptolemy, Lysimachos, had all been born within a few years of Alexander and learned their early political skills in the time of Philip II and Alexander, first as pages at Philip's court, and then as commanders with Alexander; even Demetrios and Pyrrhos were evidently in thrall to Alexander's memory and achievements. These men could not help but be haunted by the possibility of the revival of the Macedonian empire which existed between 325 and 319, and their policies were directed at either seeking that reunification or resisting it. Their sons, born after Alexander's death, had no direct personal memories of such a political entity: their early political memories were of their fathers ruling as kings.

Ptolemy II, king of the most solidly established kingdom, showed no wish to extend his father's kingdom except in ways and areas designed to embarrass his rivals or to shore up his own defences. Antigonos Gonatas, despite his grandfather's and his father's ambitions and his own early experience of life at his grandfather's court (he was born about 319), and his clear and vocal loyalty to his father, never showed any ambition beyond maintaining control of Macedon and Greece; this applies even to his life before Demetrios' death; and a wrecked Macedon's condition precluded any adventurism. Antiochos gave up any claim to Macedon once Ptolemy Keraunos was dead. All three kings had to work hard to hold what they had, so that even if they had wished to conquer new lands, they hardly had the time or the opportunity to do so.

There was no predestined division of the empire into three kingdoms. The state Lysimachos ruled for two decades was stable until its last year or so, and western Asia Minor was the geographic base for a long series of states from the Late Bronze Age to the Byzantine Empire and on to the present Republic of Turkey. The Seleukid kingdom of Seleukos I and Antiochos I was always liable to lose control of Asia Minor; eventually it became the separate Attalid kingdom. One of the continuing tasks of Seleukid kings was to hold or regain Asia Minor; in the end it was beyond their strength. They attempted equally vainly to hold on to the east. Baktria was fully part of the kingdom only briefly, under Seleukos and Antiochos I; by about 260 it was effectively an independent state. Similarly the Ptolemaic kingdom was always liable to see either Cyprus or Cyrenaica, or both, become detached as separate independent kingdoms. Magas in Cyrenaica was an independent king all through Ptolemy II's reign.

These kingdoms were relatively extensive, but were never as powerful as they seemed. One basic reason for this was manpower. It was not until many decades had passed that either the Seleukid or the Ptolemaic states seriously involved the 'native' populations in their affairs, though both went out of their ways to conciliate the more powerful of their non-Greek, non-Macedonian subjects. In Babylonia a few Babylonians became city managers, or even local governors;[5] in Egypt the native priesthood was encouraged with concessions and grants and offices;[6] but these measures were not intended to involve the native elites in affairs, rather they were aimed at keeping them out of political and military matters. Seleukos I recruited Iranian cavalry – this is the only possible source for the large cavalry force he brought to the Ipsos campaign – but they seem to have been sent home soon after, and the Seleukids never had such a large cavalry force again.

For civil administration and military manpower all three kingdoms were reliant on Greeks and Macedonians, together with those of the native populations who could pass as Greek. (This required a knowledge of Greek and at least something of a Greek education.) For Macedon this was not difficult, but Macedon's limited geographical area also limited its population, and hence its civil and military power. The Ptolemaic and Seleukid kingdoms relied on immigration, and the natural increase among those immigrants' descendants. By 217 both kings could field armies of 70,000 men, though to do so both had to reach into the native populations and recruit from them – just, it was hoped, for the emergency.[7]

This complex of problems, centred on a restricted access to manpower, had been part of the new world even during Alexander's lifetime. The Seleukid kingdom was the most seriously affected. Macedon and Ptolemaic Egypt were compact states, relatively easy to defend because of their situations and borders, and they therefore required a less extensive military establishment than the Seleukids, but that state sprawled from India to Ionia, and had problems everywhere. Already in the reign of Seleukos I fragments became independent or semi-independent. He recognized the problem when he made his son king in the east, but there were other, less important or less accessible areas whose separation he ignored.

In northern Iran one of Alexander's Persian satraps, Atropates, founded the kingdom of Media Atropatene;[8] next door another mountainous area, Armenia, became independent under a line of satrap/kings beginning with Orontes, a former Akhaimenid governor.[9] Seleukos I's agreement with Chandragupta Maurya handed Arachosia to the Indian ruler, and this left Karmania and Gedrosia to themselves. By contrast Babylonia, the economic heart of the kingdom, was always loyal. As the news of the murder of Seleukos I spread, the kingdom virtually collapsed. Antiochos was kept busy in reclaiming his inheritance, notably in Asia Minor, and it was from Babylonia that he extracted much of the wealth he needed to finance his wars. An agonized Babylonian chronicle records the resulting poverty and hunger.[10] At about the same time, a fire at Persepolis probably indicates a local uprising, and there are stories of military rebellions suppressed by satraps; the later Seleukid kings held Persis only precariously.[11] They kept hold of Susiana, the next province to the west, but with Persis at least partly independent there was little chance of gaining access to the provinces further east.

In Iran, therefore, even as early as 280, the Seleukid kingdom was effectively reduced to Susiana, Persis and central Media, the lands along the old Royal Road from Babylonia to Baktria. In concentrating on their holdings in the west, the Seleukids lost control of much of the east; Baktria and the whole east became fully independent by 260, at first under the satraps Diodotos I and his son Diodotos II, and then under a whole series of kings.[12] A determined effort was made to fasten a grip on the remaining Iranian land by means of colonies, centred around Ekbatana, but this clearly came behind Baktria and Syria (and Asia Minor) as preferred destinations for the colonists.

In Asia Minor Antiochos was confronted with the enmity of a string of small but determined states along his northern border, and by the Galatian horde, and he became enmeshed in a long war to beat back the invaders. Perforce he accepted the independence of Bithynia, and the Northern League of cities and kingdoms. To these can be added Kappadokia, whose history is a blank between the war between Antigonos and the mid-third century; the Galatians eventually settled in part of it, and the rest emerged as an independent kingdom later on. The kingship – in the hands of yet another family descended from an Akhaimenid aristocrat – seems to have developed as a response to the threatening presence of the Galatians; the local era, implying a decisive event in the land's history, began in 255 BC.[13]

The basic reasons for the failure of the Seleukid kingdom to hold many marginal territories were, first, the lack of military manpower, and secondly, the constant pressure exerted by enemies, particularly the Ptolemies from Egypt. A constant watch had to be kept on the Ptolemaic frontier, liable to be the scene of war at almost any excuse. So on top of a scarcity of military manpower there was the need to concentrate much of it permanently in Syria, leaving less for use elsewhere.

Ptolemy II found he had gained more than he bargained for when he gave refuge to his sister Arsinoe II, the widow of Lysimachos and Ptolemy Keraunos. In Alexandria, she is said to have set about becoming the near-ruler of Egypt in compensation for losing Asia and Macedon. Ptolemy was already married to her stepdaughter, Arsinoe (I), who was soon evicted from the palace, and Arsinoe II then married her brother.[14] The intriguing abilities of her mother had clearly descended to Arsinoe; the Ptolemaic dynasty was thereby well set on its route to repeated intermarriage.

The strong will of Arsinoe is generally assumed to have required this marriage. Greeks were scandalized, and caustic comments came from poets and anecdotists,[15] who were punished by Ptolemy when he could reach them. But it takes two to marry, and Ptolemy knew what he was doing. His sister was a valuable woman with a much wider knowledge of the contemporary world than he had, after her earlier marriages. She could bring a fresh view to affairs, a view untainted by the flattery to which the Ptolemies were already subject, and which inevitably distorted their view of outside events. Above all Arsinoe could give advice on the situation in Macedon.

The marriage is also related to the problem of the royal succession. The marital and progenitive career of Ptolemy I had left a complex family situation, three wives and a variety of children. Ptolemy II was the son of the third wife, and his half-brothers might consider they had a better claim to the throne. Keraunos was dead, but Magas was independent in Cyrenaica. Ptolemy II had to consolidate the royal family into a unit. He gave refuge to Arsinoe's son Ptolemy, but kept him under control. He gave refuge to Arsinoe herself and controlled her by their marriage – which, on this interpretation, was his idea. Two of his half-brothers, or brothers, were executed in the 270s. He had children of his own by his first marriage, and Arsinoe II adopted them once she was married to her brother. Ptolemy had another sister, Philotera, who apparently never married; she was fully integrated into the family system though, and gave her name to at least three towns in the kingdom.[16]

The marriage of brother and sister was seen as a scandal, but it was also widely publicized and commemorated. Arsinoe appeared on coins either by herself or with her brother-husband. The two took the same surname, Philadelphos, and temples to them were built in Alexandria and Athens and other places. Arsinoe was commemorated and honoured when she died, but Philotera received the same honours. The whole process was Ptolemy II's deliberate exaltation of his immediate family above collateral members, so that challenges from other branches could not be convincingly made. It was another solution to the succession issue, one to put beside those of Seleukos I, Kassander, and the Argeads.

Antigonos Gonatas gained control of Macedon and Thessaly, the whole of his father's kingdom, but he did so by the use of Greek and Galatian mercenaries. His claim to rule was based on heredity and, more convincingly, on bringing peace to the ravaged land. Any acclamation by the Macedonian army was impossible and probably never occurred, and the Macedonians withheld their formal support for some time. Antigonos needed to keep on earning his kingship, but the longer he remained as king, the firmer his seat would be.

The danger in the short term was seen in 274. Pyrrhos had returned from his western expedition anxious to recover his old position in Epiros and Greece. He revived his claim to the Macedonian throne, dating from the aftermath of Demetrios' debacle, and invaded Macedon. There was the one battle between the kings, at a place called 'the Narrows', whose location is uncertain: Pyrrhos' forces defeated Antigonos' Galatians, and then the Macedonian phalanx crumbled and ran. Pyrrhos got as far as Aigai, the old capital.[17] The kings waited to see how the Macedonians would react; the Macedonians, meanwhile, waited to see who would win. Antigonos held the coastal towns, including the main cities, and his fleet. The stalemate broke when Pyrrhos allowed his Galatian mercenaries to loot the royal tombs at Aigai, thereby forfeiting the good opinion of the Macedonians.

He had no wish to besiege cities which could be easily supplied from the sea, and so retreated, leaving his son Ptolemy in charge; Antigonos, having done as little fighting as possible, quietly recovered all that he had lost. For the second time the cities had saved the kingdom, not the rural barons; Macedonian society had clearly been changed drastically by the events of the 270s.

Pyrrhos went off to the Peloponnese to attack Sparta on behalf of his friend Kleonymos, a claimant to the Spartan throne; King Areus and the Spartan army were away on a campaign in Crete, and no doubt Pyrrhos was aware of this. And yet Pyrrhos' attack on Sparta city was defeated by the resolution of the Spartans who were there, old men, women and boys, in a pitched battle. Gonatas moved in reinforcements by sea, to block his retreat. Driven away from Sparta by a Macedonian force and by the arrival of Areus and his army, he attempted to take Argos. One of his elephants got stuck in a narrow gateway and trumpeted the alarm, and during street fighting next day Pyrrhos was knocked out by a tile flung by an old woman sitting on a roof; one of Antigonos' soldiers finished him off.[18] He was Antigonos' opposite, dashing about from one fight to another where Antigonos deliberately avoided battles; he conjured up enemies on all sides, where Antigonos had doggedly aimed only at Macedon, and, having reached his goal, held on to it.

This was the last serious challenge Antigonos faced for Macedon. He employed mercenaries to drive out the Galatians, and avoided fighting Pyrrhos where possible, and so spared Macedon still further strains. His alliance with the Seleukid kingdom protected him internationally, and his fleet gave him partial control of the Aegean. His political interests were confined to Macedon and its immediate neighbours, and he acted as a traditional Macedonian king; he was not, as some must have feared, another Demetrios. He was the political heir of Kassander rather than his father or grandfather – he was a grandson of Antipater through his mother.

Antigonos was able to recover his dominant position in Greece, based on the control of Corinth, Peiraios, Chalkis and Demetrias, but he reduced his garrisons, and preferred to support friendly regimes in the cities rather than the unpopular garrisons. He left Boiotia alone and refrained from antagonizing the Aitolians. This was sufficient to satisfy him for the time being.

The Aitolian League, instrumental in saving the sanctuary at Delphi from the Galatians, came to control the Amphiktyonic League. This had been the means by which others, including Philip II, had attempted to dominate central Greece. By gathering many of the small local voting communities into their own league, the Aitolians succeeded rather better than Philip. This is the beginning of the Aitolians' great period. Their expansion was careful, relatively slow, and accomplished in the main by persuasion and consent, but it produced a compact state by the 250s. It succeeded in this because of the exhaustion of Macedon, and eventually the two states were bound to clash. Until Macedon recovered, both remained wary.[19]

The more distant enemy Antigonos faced was Ptolemy II, who may have financed Pyrrhos' attack on him in 274.[20] Ptolemy's enmity was based on naval competition in the Aegean, and on Antigonos' alliance with Antiochos. Antigonos' marriage with Phila, and the preceding agreement by which a firm boundary was set to the two kings' territories and areas of influence, solved all their mutual problems, which was the essential foundation for the alliance's continuation, since neither had designs on the other's lands.[21] In addition both kings were kept busy in the 270s with other problems, Antigonos in Macedon, with Pyrrhos, and in Greece, Antiochos with Asia Minor.

Antiochos had to fight bands of Galatians where he could find them. It took time to locate and catch them, and defeating them was never easy. Eventually he brought a large force of them into battle, in which his elephants provided a major winning weapon. This may have been as early as 275 or as late as 270.[22] The acceptance of responsibility for combating these raiders by the Seleukid king is interesting: he had inherited Asia Minor from his father, who had held it only a few months before his death. Antiochos was determined to hold on to this part of his inheritance, but it was not an easy task and cost rather more in terms of imperial control than perhaps was warranted.

The campaigns were confused and confusing, exactly the sort of situation Ptolemy II was adept at exploiting, but he seems on this occasion to have been pre-empted. His half-brother Magas, king in Cyrenaica, married the daughter of Antiochos and Stratonike, Apama, a signal that the kings were allied. This took place by 274; even during the Galatian war, Antiochos was active in anti-Ptolemaic diplomacy; he was now allied with Antigonos and Magas; Ptolemy's riposte may well have been to encourage Pyrrhos to attack Antigonos in 274. Magas made a grasp for the Egyptian kingship in 275, beginning a march on Alexandria from Kyrene, but a rising of the native Libyans forced him to turn back.[23] Ptolemy blamed Antiochos for the war, but was prevented from marching against either Magas or Antiochos by a mutiny among his Galatian mercenaries. When he put it down, he claimed a victory over the barbarians equivalent to that of Antigonos and Antiochos.[24]

The situation developed into a war in Syria between Ptolemy and Antiochos, beginning probably in 274, as a result of which Magas in Cyrenaica and the Galatians in Asia Minor had to be left largely alone. Antiochos made some conquests in Syria and Ptolemy had to fight hard to recover his losses. The kings made peace in 271 without any serious territorial changes taking place; Antiochos turned back north to give the Galatians another drubbing – the elephant victory was in the late 270s.

The Galatian invasion of Asia Minor protected the new kingdoms along the

north coast of Anatolia from being subdued by Antiochos and indirectly assisted
Magas maintaining his independence as king in Cyrenaica. Within Asia Minor
new emphasis was laid on other local powers, including the Macedonian lords:
Philetairos of Pergamon assisted in the fight against the invaders and this hoisted
him to a position of near-independence;[25] Antiochos' brother Akhaios settled in
Asia Minor and gained a position of local authority from which his descendents
later aspired to local kingship.[26] Meanwhile the Galatians settled in part of
Kappadokia, centred on such ancient towns as Ankyra and Gordion. The process
had thus continued of the slow disintegration of the great kingdoms, which was
to end in the first century BC by them being swallowed up by Rome or Parthia. In
place of two kingdoms, Macedon and Persia, in 335, there were at least nine states
in 270: Macedon, the Seleukid and Ptolemaic kingdoms, Bithynia, the Northern
League, Pontos, Armenia, Atropatene, the Galatians, and soon Baktria would be
independent; the process had only just begun.

Within the great kingdoms, attempts to enlist native support grew. In
Babylonia, local men were working in the administration. In Egypt, Ptolemy was
generous to the temples, and he announced victory in his war with Antiochos by
reporting that the statues of gods abducted by his enemies had been recovered,
an Egyptian formulation.[27] In Asia, the Greek cities honoured Antiochos for his
efforts to protect them from the Galatian raids. In Baktria, the Seleukid governors,
successors of Antiochos' work between 292 and 281, united Greeks and Baktrians
in their efforts to resist nomad incursions. In Macedonia, Antigonos' careful rule
contributed to a gradual acceptance of the new dynasty by the Macedonians, a
partnership which lasted for another century. The three greater kingdoms which
had emerged from the wreckage and confusion of Alexander's empire were now
firmly founded, each had a clear character of its own, and each had an operative
governing system, though the Macedonian version would take time to develop; all
of them looked solidly established for the foreseeable future. The new generation
of kings had ambitions of their own, but they were a good deal less disruptive
than those of their fathers, and these lesser ambitions were much less damaging to
their subjects' well-being, though this reduction was due more to an appreciation
of the limits of their resources than anything else.

The round of warfare which began with Magas' attempt on the Ptolemaic
throne in 275 and ended with the peace agreement between Antiochos I and
Ptolemy II in 271 demonstrated the kingdoms' limitations: none was any longer
capable of seriously damaging the others. The alliance of Antiochos II with Magas
is particularly significant, and shows that diplomatic manoeuvring was as crucial
an element in affairs as warlike preparations. If an attack was apprehended, the
potential victim had plenty of diplomatic resources available to distract the
attacker. That is, a balance of power now existed in the eastern Mediterranean,
just as it had in Greece before the Macedonian intervention in the affairs of

the city-states. Like all balances of power, survival depended on alertness and produced constant warfare, and eventually a single winner would emerge. There was no sign for the next two centuries that any king harboured a serious aim to recover the brief unity of Alexander's empire, with the possible exception of Antiochos III. All three kingdoms had solved that bane of Macedon, the hiatus at the death of a king, each in its own way, and their dynasties provided an ordered centre for the administration which kept the internal peace.

The unification of Alexander's empire was part of the world's political discourse for almost 50 years, from Alexander's return from India to the death of Seleukos Nikator. It proved to be impossible to realize that unity except for the brief period between 325 and the death of Antipater in 319, despite its near achievement by Antigonos and by Seleukos. The frustration of the idea of unity was due at first to the lack of imagination of the two dominating personalities of Antipater and Antigonos and that was above all due to their not having accompanied Alexander on the great campaigns in Baktria and India. These men then set the political agenda for the next 20 years: Antigonos looked to have the ambition to re-unify, but, like Antipater, he was really too old. Yet it was not age which stopped him, for Seleukos had the ambition still until his death in his late seventies. Nor was unity really blocked by the lesser ambitions of Kassander and Ptolemy and Antigonos Gonatas. In the end it was blocked by the inability of the Macedonian kingdom and people to rise to the task; the repeated refusal of the Macedonians to accept their imperial role was the real block to unity. Alexander's ambition was too great for his people.

World view III: 272 BC

In Greece, 272 marks the death in battle at Argos of King Pyrrhos, after which matters were much less disturbed and exciting. Pyrrhos' garrison in Taras surrendered to the Romans in the same year, which led to the Roman capture of the city, which they called Tarentum.[1] This marked the preliminary Roman unification of Italy, the moment at which another Great Power emerged on to the Mediterranean geopolitical scene, joining Ptolemy's Egypt, Macedon, the Seleukid empire, and, as it proved, Carthage. The actual unification of Italy was still fairly rudimentary, amounting to a series of annexations, alliances, and more or less brutal conquests over the previous 70 years, but it placed Rome in control of central and southern Italy for the next two centuries.

The new condition of Italy was recognized the year before when Ptolemy II initiated diplomatic contact with Rome.[2] Roman power had been growing for some time, but it is remarkable just how quickly the city had developed its confederation of Italy. In 360, in the first of these 'world views', Rome had been a single city; in less than a century it had become a great power – and in less than another century, it was to be the greatest Mediterranean power.

The Roman success was due in part to the repeated revivals and collapses of the Greek state of Sicily. Three times the Greek cities of the island had united into a powerful state, the third time under Agathokles between 313 and 289, and three times the hard-won unity scarcely survived the death of the ruler; if Sicily had continued to dominate south Italy, as it had under Dionysios I and II and then under Agathokles, it seems unlikely that Rome would have been able to penetrate southwards much beyond Campania.

Rome's success was also in part a consequence of the failure of the empire of Alexander. If Alexander had carried out the western expedition he was planning, one of his main purposes would be to establish his control over Sicily, so preempting Agathokles' kingdom. The island was the essential basis for power in the western Mediterranean, as Rome and Carthage both appreciated in their great contest between 264 and 202: the First and Second Punic Wars were in many ways wars for Sicily, and Rome's victory was decisive for its future power. The Roman embassy in Babylon in 323 will have gone home with news of Alexander's plans, and Rome at once would begin to expand its power. The two events may not have been as directly connected as that, but Alexander's death would be a relief to those in Rome with the strategic insight to understand his ambition. The break-up of his empire left the interventions from old Greece into the west to the Epirotes and the Spartans. Alexander of Epiros was almost successful, and Pyrrhos did his erratic best, but the interventions were never strong enough, and the local population and economic base in south Italy could not sustain a northward offensive; and there were mutual suspicions between the Greek cities, and suspicions invariably developed between rescuers and rescued. Pyrrhos' expedition between 280 and 275 only hastened the Roman conquest, the better to prevent any other armed arrivals.

Pyrrhos also clashed with Carthage, and his career emphasized the continuing disaster which was Greek Sicily. Agathokles had made himself king during the elevation process following Antigonus' self-proclamation,[3] and when he died his kingdom collapsed. The Greeks of the island had to be rescued by Pyrrhos from a likely Carthaginian conquest ten years later.[4] Sicily's political history was rather like Macedon's: at the end of one regime or king came a collapse, which had to be painfully recovered from.

The west had changed drastically since the last survey, for 319 'world view II'. The power and cohesion of the Greek centre in Sicily had proved far too fragile, and that of southern Italy far too weak; that of Carthage endured, surviving even an invasion of Africa by Agathokles, and that of Rome had grown spectacularly. The collapse of Greek Sicily provided an all too attractive area of combined wealth and weakness, a power vacuum into which its neighbours were inevitably drawn: the scene was set for the conflict of Rome and Carthage, a mutually absorbing conflict which would keep both of these powers out of the eastern Mediterranean for almost a century.

No such problems of internal conflict affected India. In 272 a new emperor of India, Asoka, took the throne, though he had to face competition from his brothers, and it was not for some time that he felt secure enough to be crowned formally.[5] Asoka was the third emperor of the Maurya family: Chandragupta the founder had seized control of the Magadhan kingdom and vigorously expanded it into the Indus Valley after Alexander's visit, and then rebuffed Seleukos' attempt to regain control there. He was succeeded by his son Bindusara in 297, who extended the empire into the south until only the southern tip of the peninsula and the region of Orissa called Kalinga were outside the empire; this was conquered by Asoka.

Asoka was not the eldest son of his emperor father – it was not just Macedonians who had these succession troubles. The problem at the top did not have serious effects elsewhere, but Asoka felt the need to demonstrate martial achievements by his conquest of Kalinga. Then he could settle down to a long and peaceful reign, during which he tried to push his people to be Buddhists. The imposition of a uniform religion as a means of assisting political unification was a problem the successors of Alexander did not have to face.

The western and eastern neighbours of the fragmented empire of Alexander had therefore developed into formidable powers of their own during the period of Macedonian warfare; to a large degree it was in reaction to Alexander's career of conquest and brutality that this happened. Rome's conquest and unification in Italy was undoubtedly eased by the continuing threat that, if the Italians remained divided, a conqueror would emerge from the east to do the job for them. Chandragupta Maurya is specifically said to have been 'inspired' by Alexander's career; the prospect of another Macedonian invasion of the Indus Valley would be quite enough to persuade the ravaged societies there to prefer his rule to that of the westerners; it is quite likely that the final seal on his new empire was applied by Seleukos' invasion, with its implied threat of even more killing and damage, and by Chandragupta's victorious defence.

In China the growth of Qin, the most westerly kingdom of the Warring States, continued. It owed its success to an effective system of government, its border position, which allowed it to expand and gave its army plenty of practice, and the deliberate ruthlessness of its rulers. It was a similar polity to Macedon, but had been compelled to develop an effective bureaucratic governing system by the intense competition of its equals. At the same time Rome established its early hegemony in Italy, Qin did the same in China. Between 311 and 293, some small states in the centre were annexed, and three of the larger were defeated in war. In 288, the lords of Qin and Qi agreed that each should be called emperor, and no others. Qi succumbed to a hostile alliance four years later, and Qin was left as the most powerful state in the Chinese system. Yet Qin directly controlled only a part of central China, and it would take another half-century of effort to bring the whole distracted country into unity.[6] The effectiveness of the governments in all the Chinese kingdoms is shown by their ability to construct long sections of wall to prevent attacks by neighbours, and by the regular mobilization of large parts of their populations into their armies. It would be impossible at 272 to discern the future course of Chinese history. The collapse of Qi in 284 could well be repeated in Qin. The one certainty was that warfare would continue. Like Rome in Italy, only one great power remained; if it survived, it would be the unifier and peace-bringer.

The break-up of Alexander's empire ended Macedonian expansion, and began the reduction of the territories under the rule of Macedonian kings as the border areas asserted their independence. This began in the Indian borderlands even before Alexander's death, and some parts of Iran and Anatolia were never part of the empire at all: these formed themselves into independent kingdoms. At the west, some of Philip II's conquests for Macedon were lost to Epiros in the 290s. Then the invasion of the Galatians eliminated Macedonian remnants in Thrace; and when the Galatians settled down, they took over a considerable section of Anatolia, so sheltering the new Anatolian states of the north and east behind them.

The unifications of India and Italy, and the potential unification of China, contrasted strongly with the failure of Alexander's empire. The difference was that Alexander's work was superficial, whereas the other processes were slow and careful and detailed. Alexander's attempts to recruit the Iranians to his imperial cause suggest that he appreciated the need to conciliate his new subjects and win their cooperation, and the move into independence of many Iranian regions showed his good sense in that. But he could not convince others. Alexander had essentially failed as an empire builder.

Conclusion

For two centuries from 550 BC, from the Bay of Bengal to the Atlantic Ocean, the Akhaimenid empire dominated the world. Its political influence reached well beyond its borders, into Greece and the western Mediterranean, deep into India, and it affected the lives and movements of the nomads of the Eurasian steppes. Its economic influence was as pervasive, perhaps more so. It was the centre of the civilized world – indeed, it *was* the civilized world, and anyone outside its borders was a barbarian. This included not just the nomads and the Arabs of the desert, but Greeks and Macedonians, Italians and Indians – though these did not necessarily agree with this classification.

Alexander's invasion was, to the Persians and to many of their subjects, a barbarian invasion, destructive, murderous and sacrilegious. In India, this was obvious even to the Macedonian soldiers, but it had been so regarded by the Persians, Babylonians and Baktrians all along. Those who welcomed Alexander's invasion were few: the Ionian Greeks, the Egyptians, possibly some of the Babylonians; to everyone else, his career was a disaster in one way or another. And Macedon suffered as well.

It is worth considering the events recounted in this book from the point of view of the victims, since the normal assumption is that Alexander was a hero, a military genius, that the Greeks and Macedonians had been victims of Akhaimenid aggression, and the results of his career of conquest beneficial. This is the viewpoint of the victors and their political and emotional heirs in Europe. Adopt the Persian point of view, and the landscape looks very different.[1]

It has always been difficult to isolate the heritage of the Akhaimenid state. Certain elements in the administration of the Seleukid kingdom can be traced back, but they consist mainly of provincial names and boundaries; their administrative systems were different. Local dynasties in the Near East – Pontos, Armenia, Kommagene, Atropatene – purported to trace their origins back to Akhaimenid times, but it is often an assertion only, not documented proof, and these are marginal areas, some of which were scarcely part of the Akhaimenid state at all. The real reaction of the empire's former subjects is to be seen in the fragmentation of the Iranian and Anatolian lands into independent states: this began as soon as Alexander was dead, or even before, and within 50 years his Macedonian successors controlled little more than half of Iran and less than half of Anatolia. The independence of the states along the north, from Bithynia to Atropatene, showed their detestation of Macedonian rule. Within a decade of 272, Baktria was also independent: a development foreshadowed by its stiff resistance to Alexander's invasion.

The conclusion must be that for the former subjects of the Akhaimenid empire the Macedonian conquest was a disaster, something they continued to detest after Alexander was dead, and they wished to escape Macedonian rule as soon as possible. There is some evidence, indeed, that numbers of Iranians left Iran, particularly for India, rather than accept Macedonian rule. This applied to aristocrats such as Barsaentes, the satrap of Arachosia, and to craftsmen whose skills were not required by Greek and Macedonian rulers. They took their skills and the Iranian artistic tradition eastwards, and elements of Iranian art can be detected in later Indian buildings.[2] This antipathy to Macedonian rule was not an attitude shared by all. The Egyptians seem to have been generally content with the Ptolemaic kings for a time. Their opportunities for dissent were few, and when the chance came, a formidable rebellion developed; its aim was independence. The Babylonians had never been particularly pleased to be Akhaimenid subjects; when the Seleukids showed themselves willing to respect their customs and their gods, and to pay handsomely for the upkeep for their temples and cities, they became generally content, even strongly supportive during Seleukos' and Antiochus' early wars.[3] That was after they had the experience of the alternative, which was rule by Antigonos.

The other victim of Alexander's career was his own kingdom, Macedon, to which we ought to add Greece. Alexander's expedition left Macedon substantially weakened, and its geographical position left it vulnerable to invasion from the north. It had suffered this repeatedly during the previous two centuries, and it was only in Philip II's reign that the kingdom became organized and led in such a way that its resistance to invasion was invariably successful. But the price of importing Greek military skills, as Philip did, was also to import Greek ideas and prejudices. Philip adopted the Greek concept of revenge for the Persian invasions, even though those invasions had greatly benefited Macedon. His acceptance of the idea implies a distortion of his kingdom's history and a wholesale acceptance of the Greek view of the past.

Philip's intentions in invading the Akhaimenid empire cannot be known, but Alexander aimed to conquer the world. Inevitably he failed. He also failed to give a proper thought to his kingdom, his primary responsibility. His failure to provide an heir was compounded by draining the kingdom of its manpower; both were made worse by his carelessness in dying young; he had doctors who knew what was wrong with him and he refused their ministrations. Perhaps he really did think he was a god.

He died in the midst of attempts to impose his authority on his empire, another task he ignored for too long. Even in this he was irresponsible, planning to sail off on a new expedition before the administrative work was properly done. He was incapable of delegating work and responsibility, even though the history of the next 40 years demonstrates that he commanded a group of officers of outstanding ability. He seems to have known he was out of his depth and was fleeing the problem. It is unlikely that his empire would have survived his absence in Arabia; it survived only a few years after his death.

Macedon reverted to its old preoccupations. The kingdom's rulers abandoned any attempts to dominate the Balkans. They intervened in Greece brutally, where both Philip and Alexander had used finesse and minimum force. The incipient unification of Greece represented by the League of Corinth was abandoned in place of Macedonian military domination, a condition not wholly beyond Macedon's powers, but one requiring repeated warfare.

For Greece, the result was as unpleasant as the same domination had been for Persia. Greek cities were repeatedly attacked, besieged, conquered, sacked – Thebes, Athens, Corinth, Sparta, Argos. They were garrisoned by Macedonian and mercenary soldiers, and much of their energy went into paying for their conquerors, and in finding ways to get rid of them. The constant struggle absorbed and wasted the energies of everyone, Greek and Macedonian alike.

The end came with the Galatians, who broke into and overran Macedon with appalling ease. The rural kingdom ceased to exist except as groups of scattered resisters living in cities. Royal authority only revived when Antigonus Gonatas recruited pirates and Galatians to drive other Galatians out. A warrior kingdom such as Macedon could not sink lower. It was the ultimate result of Alexander's expedition, which had meant that his homeland was unable to defend itself.

I have chosen to emphasize the negative aspects of the great expedition because it is often described as a time of excitement and achievement, with Alexander as hero. This is a view based on the interpretation adopted by the ancient sources, but other points of view are available. Moving away from Alexander shifts one's angle of vision, and paradoxically emphasizes the role of specific individuals. The absence of Antipater and Antigonos (and Demetrios) from the campaigns Alexander waged in Baktria and India was clearly important for their view of the empire. This was the hardest, most costly and nastiest fighting of Alexander's wars, and none of the men involved was unaffected by the experience. The Greek garrison/colonists whom Alexander left in Baktria twice attempted to escape from the country where he had marooned them; the succeeding Indian campaigns revealed Greco-Macedonian warfare at its worst, partly as a result of the hardships of the Baktrian fighting. Yet many of the participants were also inspired. India long remained a land of infinite attraction to the Greeks for its very exoticism, and Baktria exercised a great attraction, becoming the home of many thousands of Greek colonists, who transformed it into a land of cities; the 'thousand cities of Baktria' became proverbial.

Of the Macedonian lords who succeeded Alexander, several showed the same appreciation of the prospects of these eastern lands. The obvious one is Seleukos, but note also Stasanor, the satrap of Baktria, Peithon, the satrap of Media, who aimed to exercise a supervisory role over the easterners, and the satraps of the east who tended to be long in office. In Baktria, the only satrapy with anything approaching a viable list of governors, Stasanor was satrap from 320 until after 315 (having been satrap of Areia-Drangiana from 329 to 320); Seleukos' son Antiochos ruled it from 294 to 281; Diodotos and his son were successive satraps over a period of perhaps 40 years, beginning under Antiochus I, and eventually led the land into independence. These long periods of rule will have promoted stability, and were part of the reason for the Greek migration.

So, of the three men whose policies were directed at retaining or reviving the unity of the empire of Alexander, only Seleukos had direct experience of the east. This allowed him to recruit the cavalry and the elephants with which the Ipsos battle was won. From that time, 301, he also controlled the whole route to the east from the coast of Syria to Baktria along which the emigrants had to travel. He founded or enlarged ten cities in Syria and half a dozen in Iran, not to mention the great Seleukeia-on-the-Tigris. Colonization of these cities and lands by Greeks and Macedonians was a major part of his general policy. Of course, it was done for his own reasons, to develop a reliable and sizeable Greco-Macedonian population from which he could recruit an army and a civil service, but to do so he had to found cities, provide land, help with seeds, provide tax breaks, and so on. The law of unintended consequences then ensured that other results flowed from that policy.

The restoration of the unity of the empire after Antipater's death therefore required that one man be determined to take up the task, that he commanded a sizeable army, and that he controlled substantial wealth, but that he should also have experience and support from all parts of the empire. This meant the east as well as the centre (Baktria, Babylonia and Asia Minor) and Macedon. Of these, Macedon was crucial, because of its manpower, and because of the psychological charge still contained in the title 'King of the Macedonians', but the east was also necessary. Control of eastern manpower sources gave Seleukos his great strength. But neither Antipater nor Antigonos showed any interest. Antipater simply ignored the area. Antigonos could have tapped into that power source, and, if he had, Seleukos would never have had his chance, but he was content to have beaten Eumenes.

The real obstacle to the unity of the empire was therefore first of all the family of Antipater, the man himself, uninterested in anything outside Macedon, and Kassander, who took after his father in this as in much else; and secondly the family of Antigonos, none of whom saw the potential of the east. The potential of Macedon, even after Alexander, was shown by Demetrios' mobilization, though he characteristically threatened everyone, so that they all combined against him, even the people of Macedon. Even so, even if he had retained Macedon's support, he would have failed in the face of all the manpower of Asia and the east.

Antipater and Kassander reflected, in their policies, the prejudices and preferences of the Macedonians. Their reaction to Demetrios' plans, and their earlier antipathy towards Antigonos, showed their general antipathy to overseas adventures. They had no ideological imperative to restore the empire their king had conquered. Kassander's policy of resistance to the imperialism of Antigonos was thus a well-calculated articulation of what his subjects required. Seleukos appeared to have the capability to reunite the empire in 282–281, but his slowness in moving into Macedon rather suggests he knew he would have difficulty there.

The decisive factor in preventing reunification was partly the obdurate resistance of Ptolemy of Egypt, and partly the unwillingness of the Macedonians to exert themselves in the cause, but the major problem was that of the royal succession in Macedon. It bears repeating that the accession to power of Alexander on the killing of his father in 336 was the first time in two centuries that a royal succession in Macedon did not see a civil war or a collapse of the state, or both. Even then, Alexander had to drive off invaders and indulge in several murders to ensure peace. It is scarcely surprising that Alexander's own death resulted in civil war and political collapse. The problem was repeated on the deaths of Antipater, Kassander, Kassander's sons, Demetrios and Seleukos. Only the horrifying experience of the Galatian invasions and the careful manipulations and innovations of Antigonos Gonatas ensured that his dynasty succeeded in overcoming the problem for the next century.

The danger was clearly recognized by everyone else: Seleukos and Ptolemy organized their successions carefully, well in advance of their deaths. Antigonos the One-Eyed appointed his son king as soon as he took the title himself, and Antigonos Gonatas became king on his father's death as a matter of course. Lysimachos' dynastic disaster was an object lesson to all. The problem lay with the Macedonians. Kassander tried to appoint his successor, but his widow then interfered. The Macedonians whom Kassander ruled were those who had not gone overseas, the traditionalists who disliked any innovation. Only their experience of the Galatian invasion – another drastic winnowing process – finally compelled the abandonment of their indulgence in succession disputes. In the meantime they had, by their self-centredness and obduracy, effectively wrecked their own empire.

Notes

Notes to Introduction

1   See Cartledge (2004), 295–316.
2   The sources for Alexander are Diodoros, bk 17, Curtius, Plutarch, *Alexander*, Arrian and Justin.
3   Toynbee (1969), 421–86.

Notes to Chapter 1: Macedon 370–359 BC: a failing state

1   Hammond, Griffith and Walbank (1972), *A History of Macedonia* vol. 1, covers matters to 550 BC; also Borza (1990), chs 1 to 4.
2   Ibid., vol. 1; Hammond (1989), chs 1 and 2.
3   Boardman (1964), 236–39; Isaac (1986).
4   Knowledge of the Macedonian army before Philip is sparse, but judging by the innovations and improvements he made, it was as described here; Borza (1990), 125–6.
5   For Upper Macedon, cf. Borza (1990), 31–8.
6   Hammond in *Macedonia* 2.58–60 (on Amyntas; the basic source is Herodotos, *Histories*, 5.17–20),; and 2.98–102 (on Alexander I); also Errington (1990), 8–13; Borza (1990), 98–115.
7   Herodotos 5.22; Roos (1985), 162–8.
8   Strabo 7.326 and 9.434, based on Hekataios (sixth century BC), describes the area as Epirotis; Thucydides, late in the fifth century, calls it Macedonian.
9   Hammond in *Macedonia* 1.436–39.
10 Thucydides 2.99.2–4.
11 On the social 'structure' of Macedon, see Hammond in *Macedonia* 2.150; Errington (1990), 1–8.
12 Thucydides 1.98.1; Herodotos 7.107; Plutarch, *Kimon* 7.2–8.3; Isaac (1986), 19–26.
13 Meiggs (1972); Hammond in *Macedonia* 2.102–3 and 115–19; Errington (1990), 13–15.
14 There is no sign whatsoever at any time of a 'constitution' for Macedon; the kingdom was ruled by custom and personality; a body of law developed on the basis of precedent.
15 Thucydides 1.57.3; Aelian, *Varia Historia* 2.41; Plato, *Gorgias* 471 a–b; Hammond in *Macedonia* 2.115.
16 On the Assembly see Hammond in *Macedonia*, 2.160–2 and Hatzopoulos (1996).

17   Thucydides 2.99.2–100.3; I.G. I(3), 89; Hammond in *Macedonia* 2.115; Borza (1990), 135.
18   Hammond in *Macedonia* 2.115–36.
19   Hammond in *Macedonia* 2.137–41; Borza (1990), 161–6.
20   Hammond in *Macedonia* 2.146–7.
21   Borza (1990), 166–71.
22   Diodoros 14.7.6 (a hunting accident); Aristotle, *Politics* 1311b 8–35 (assassination by the king's lover).
23   Hammond in *Macedonia* 2.167–72; Errington (1990), 28–30; Borza (1990), 177–9.
24   Diodoros 14.92.3.
25   Hammond in *Macedonia* 2.172–6; Borza (1990), 182 and 296–7.
26   Ellis (1969), 1–8.
27   Xenophon, *Hellenica* 5.2.12–14.
28   Hammond in *Macedonia* 2.144–50.
29   Pausanias 7.25.6.
30   Thucydides, 1.114.3; Theopompos, *FGrH* 115, F 384.
31   Diodoros 15.9.2–3; this is sometimes condemned as a 'doublet' of the invasion of ten years earlier, but this time Amyntas is said to have recovered his kingship by his own efforts, a crucial difference from 393/391; Hammond in *Macedonia* 2.174–6.
32   Diodoros 15.19.2–5; Xenophon, *Hellenica* 5.2.12–22.
33   Diodoros 15.20.3–23.3; Xenophon, *Hellenica* 5.2.37–3.9 and 3.14–3.26.
34   Tod, *GHI* 129, an alliance dated to the mid-370s; Xenophon, *Hellenica* 6.1.11, noting Athenian reliance on Macedonian shipbuilding timber; Borza (1987), 32–52.
35   Errington (1990), 222–3 for a summary, with references.
36   Xenophon, *Hellenica* 5.3.1., 5.2.15; Diodoros 15.19.3.
37   Thucydides 2.100.
38   Tod, *GHI* 129.
39   Diodoros 16.2.2; Justin 7.9.1.
40   Diodoros 16.61.3–5.
41   Diodoros 15.67; Plutarch, *Pelopidas* 26.
42   Diodoros 15.71.1.
43   Hammond in *Macedonia* 2.192.
44   Aeschines 2.26–9; Diodoros 16.2.6; Nepos, *Iphikrates* 3.2.
45   Plutarch, *Pelopidas* 27.2–4.
46   Hammond in *Macedonia* 2.178.
47   Diodoros 15.77.5 and 16.2.4.
48   Justin 7.5.3, stating that Philip was hostage for three years; Borza (1987); Roesch (1984), 45–60; see also Hatzopoulos (1985), 247–57.
49   Diodoros 15.81.6; Demosthenes, *First Philippic* 4.4–5; Tod, *GHI* 149.
50   Demosthenes 2.14; Polyainos, 3.10.7 and 14.
51   Aeschines 2.30; Polyainos, 3.10.8.
52   Pseudo-Aristotle, *Oeconomicus* 2.22.
53   Polyainos 4.10.1.
54   Frontinus 2.5.19.
55   Diodoros 16.2.4–5.

56 Diodoros 16.2.4–6; Griffith in *Macedonia* 2.207–8.

57 Justin 7.4.5 and 8.3.10; Theopompos, *FGrH* 115, F 27.

58 Griffith in *Macedonia*, appendix 2.

59 Justin 7.5.6–9; *IG* II.3055; a statement by Satyros that Philip reigned for 22 years (he actually held power for 24), may suggest that he was regent for Amyntas for two years; Ellis (1971), 15–25; Griffith in *Macedonia* 2.702–4.

Notes to World View I: 360 BC

1 Ryder (1965).

2 Caven (1990); Sanders (1987).

3 Warmington (1964); Picard (1987).

4 Cunliffe (1988), chs 2 and 3.

5 Huergon (1973); Toynbee (1965); Cornell (1995).

6 Huergon (1973), 176–86; Cornell (1995), ch. 13.

7 Diodoros 16.69.1; Livy, *per.* 13 – the treaty is dated to 348 BC or thereabouts.

8 Livy 7.23–6.

9 Herakleides Pontikos, in Plutarch, *Camillus* 22.

10 Cook (1983); Weisehofer (1996), part I; Olmstead (1948).

11 It may have remained as overlord, as Macedon between 513 and 478: Vogelsang (1990), 93–110.

12 Cawkwell (2005), ch. 8.

13 Ibid, 1–29.

14 Cook (1983), 220–3; Weiskopf (1989); Moysey (1991).

15 Thapar (1966), ch. 3; Raychaudhuri (1996), part II, ch. 2.

16 Loewe and Shaughnessy (1999), 967–1032.

Notes to Chapter 2: The security of Macedon, 359–354 BC

1 Biographies of Philip: Cloche (1955), Cawkwell (1978), Ellis (1976) and Hammond (1994); Griffith in *Macedonia*, 2.203–721.

2 Justin 7.5.1; this item is universally ignored, except by Griffith in *Macedonia* 2.181; also Diodoros 16.2.2, though garbled.

3 Plutarch, *Pelopidas* 26; Diodoros 15.67; Aymard (1954), 15–36.

4 Athenaios 11.506f (a letter of Karystos of Pergamon).

5 Diodoros 16.3.3–4.

6 Diodoros 16.3.5–4.1; Heskel (1996), 37–56.

7 Diodoros 16.2.6; Griffith, *Macedonia* 211.

8 Diodoros 16.3.4.

9 Griffith in *Macedonia* 2.210 note, calls it an 'impossibility' that Philip had sufficient cash for these expenses, but he always spent freely, and was quite capable of emptying his treasury in a good cause; possibly Perdikkas had left it full.

10   Diodoros 16.4.3.

11   Diodoros 17.17.4–5; Milns (1966), 167–9.

12   Griffith in *Macedonia* 2.404–14; Hammond (1994), ch. 3; Cawkwell (1978), 30–5.

13   See discussion by Griffith in *Macedonia* 2, appendix 1.

14   e.g. Diodoros 16.4.3.

15   Andronicos (1970), 91–107.

16   The best discussion on this is Griffith in *Macedonia* 2.404–31.

17   Marsden (1969), 58–60, argues that 'torsion artillery' was invented in Macedon under Philip.

18   Diodoros 16.4.2.

19   Diodoros 16.4.4.

20   Diodoros 16.4.5–7.

21   The basic source is Satyros, *Life of Philip*, quoted by Athenaios 11.557a–b; see Tronson (1984), 116–26.

22   Satyros in Athenaios 11.557a; Justin 9.8.2 and 13.2.11 preserves some of the insulting descriptions of Philinna, but she is best seen as the daughter of an aristocratic Thessalian family; she was the mother of the later King Philip III Arrhidaios.

23   Diodoros 16.8.2; Demosthenes 1.8.

24   Sources here are difficult, mainly later allusions by Athenian orators, uninterested in accuracy: Griffith in *Macedonia*, 2.236–44, with the sources there noted; see also Ellis (1976), 63–4.

25   Tod, *GHI*, 158; Diodoros 16.2.3–4.

26   Diodoros 16.8.6–7; Griffith in *Macedonia* 2.246–50.

27   Diodoros 16.8.5; Griffith in *Macedonia* 2.244–6, 250–1.

28   Diodoros 16.22.3; Tod, *GHI* 157; Plutarch, *Alexander* 3.

29   Griffith in *Macedonia* 2.251, suggests that Lyppeios was dealt with by Philip later.

30   Griffith in *Macedonia* 2.252, thinks Philip led his army on a march along the Thracian coast; there is no evidence for this.

31   Diodoros 16.34.4–5; Justin 7.6.13–16; Strabo 7, frag. 22.

32   Diodoros 16.31.6, for the fall of Methone in 354, the loan of troops is argued to be in 355 by Griffith in *Macedonia* 2.220–30 and Ellis (1976), 74.

33   Collart (1937).

34   Strabo 7, frag. 37; Skymnos, *Geographi Graeci Minores* 1.221; Griffith in *Macedonia* 2.363.

35   Tod, *GHI* 159.

Notes to Chapter 3: The defence of the kingdom, 354–346 BC

1   Griffith, in *Macedonia* 2.650–1; Bosworth (1971), 93–105.

2   Dismissed by Hatzopoulos (1996), 327f, unconvincingly.

3   Hammond in *Macedonia* 2.156–7.

4   Ps.-Aristotle, *Oeconomikos* 2.22; Perdikkas' revenue from customs rose from 20 to 40 talents as a result of Kallistratos' innovations, a pathetically small amount for such a huge state, and it implies an economy which was virtually undeveloped.

5   Griffith in *Macedonia* 2.392–5.

6   Theagenes, *FGrH* 74 F 3; Hammond (1989), 157.

7   Stephanus of Byzantion, sv Herakleia.

8   Diodoros 8.44; Strabo 7, frag. 36; Pliny, *NH* 4.41.

9   The palace (Ps. – Skylax 66), and the royal treasury (Strabo 7, frag. 20) were there; even before Philip's reign it was the kingdom's largest city (Xenophon, *Hellenica* 5.2.13).

10 Justin 8.2.7–6.2; perhaps from Theopompos of Chios, who lived at Philip's court in the 340s.

11 e.g. Hatzopoulos (1996), vol. 2, nos 56–7, and 73 (Beroia).

12 Diodoros 16.35.1.

13 Diodoros 16.34.1; Demosthenes 21.183.

14 Polyainos 4.2.2.

15 Diodoros 16.35.1.

16 Diodoros 16.35.2; Polyainos, 2.38.2.

17 Diodoros 16.35.3–6; Justin 8.2.3–4; Griffith in *Macedonia* 2.273–7.

18 Diodoros 16.37.3; 38.1–2; Westlake (1935), chs 7 and 8; Griffith in *Macedonia* 2.278–9 and 285–95.

19 Theopompos, *FGrH* 115, F 81; Westlake (1935), 179–80.

20 Diodoros 16.38.1.

21 Theopompos, *FGrH* 115, F 249; Diodoros 16.34.3; Demosthenes 23.14.

22 Demosthenes 3.4; Griffith in *Macedonia* 2.281–5.

23 Olynthos is referred to as 'our friend' by Demosthenes in 352, so 353 probably saw the diplomatic change: Demosthenes 23.107–9; Griffith in *Macedonia*, 2.296–8.

24 A very obscure issue, evidenced by allusion and later references: cf. Griffith in *Macedonia* 2.298–304; Cawkwell (1962), 122–40.

25 Buckler (1996), 77–97.

26 Isocrates, *Philip*.

27 Ellis (1976), 92, makes Pammenes' expedition the inspiration for Philip; see also Fredericksmeyer (1982), 85–98.

28 cf. Griffith in *Macedonia* 2.484–9.

29 Demosthenes 1.13; Justin 8.6.5–6; Hammond (1967), 543–4.

30 Diodoros 16.52.9 and 53.2.

31 Philochoros, *FGrH* 328, F 49.

32 Plutarch, *Phokion* 12–14; Aeschines 3.84–6; Demosthenes 21.162 and 39.16; Cawkwell (1962); Brunt (1969), 245–65; Carter (1971), 418–29.

33 Diodoros 16.52.9; one of the former tyrants, Peitholaos, returned, and was given Athenian citizenship (Aristotle, *Rhetoric* 1.1410a).

34 Diodoros 16.52.9.

35 Diodoros 16.53.2–3.

36 Aeschines 2.12–4.

37 Ibid.

38 Athens was waking up to Philip's power, notably because of Olynthos: cf. Ellis and Milns (1970).

39 Strabo 7 F 55; Demosthenes 18.70.

40 Demosthenes 19. 163.

41 Diodoros 16.58.4–6; Pausanias 10.2.5–3.2.

42 Aeschines 2.79; Demosthenes 19.10.

43 Aeschines 2.132–5.

44 Aeschines 2.18.

45 Aeschines 2.82–4.

46 Ellis (1976), 114–16.

47 Aeschines 2.137.

48 The actual terms have to be extracted from the later speeches of Athenian orators: Griffith in *Macedonia* 2.338–41.

49 Markle (1974).

50 Aeschines 2.137.

51 Diodoros 16.59.3.

52 Aeschines 2.141.

53 Diodoros 6.60; Justin 8.5; Aeschines 2.142–4; Demosthenes 19.64–5.

54 Aeschines 2.140–2; Pausanias 10.2.2; Griffith in *Macedonia* 2.347, note 1, believes that 'Philip's decision … decided everything', but it seems that discussion was open.

Notes to Chapter 4: Cold war, 346–340 BC

1 Aeschines 2.139; Demosthenes 19.86–7.

2 Diodoros 16.69.7; Hammond (1966), 73–85.

3 Demosthenes 19.320; Westlake (1935), 190–1.

4 Griffith in *Macedonia* 2.523–7; Westlake (1935), 191–2.

5 Westlake (1935), 201–4; an intermediate organization, a decadarchy, may have existed between 344 and 342; Griffith in *Macedonia* 2.528–53 argued it never existed; even if it did, it was clearly ephemeral.

6 Diodoros 16.72.1; Justin 8.6.4–5.

7 [Demosthenes] 7.32.

8 Demosthenes 9.34 and 4.24–6.

9 Demosthenes 9.34.

10 Demosthenes 6.15–25.

11 Diodoros 16.44.1; Demosthenes 7 and 18, 136; Cawkwell (1978), 123–5.

12 Elis, Pausanaias 4.28.4 and 5.4.9; Demosthenes 19.294–60; Megara, Plutarch, *Phokion* 15.

13 Demosthenes 19.87; Brunt, 1969.

14 Philochoros, *FGrH* 328 F 158.

15 Cook (1983), 223–4; Olmstead (1948), 436–41.

16 Diodoros 16.44.1–2; Philochoros, *FGrH* 328 F 157.

17 Diodoros 16.52.2.

18 Diodoros 16.71.1–2; Griffith in *Macedonia* 2.554–66; Hammond (1994), 122–5; Ellis (1976), 166–8.

19 Satyrus in Athenaios 11.557a–b.

20 Diodoros 16.8.6.

21   Michel (1957), 389–91.
22   Demosthenes 8.50, 9.35, 10.60.
23   [Demosthenes] 7.2; Griffith in *Macedonia* 2.510–12.
24   [Demosthenes] 7.2.
25   Brunt (1969).
26   Aeschines 3.95–9; Griffith in *Macedonia* 2.549, note 3.
27   Demosthenes 12.12–15; Hypereides F 6–6; Plutarch, *Vita X Or.* 850a.
28   Aristotle, *Rhetoric* 2.1386 a 13.
29   Justin 9.1.2.
30   [Demosthenes] 12.3.
31   [Demosthenes] 12.16.
32   Demosthenes 12 (probably not wholly genuine).
33   Diodoros 16.74.1–76.3, 77.1; Justin 9.1.2–7.
34   Details are lost, but Philip's letter (Demosthenes 12) virtually acknowledged war's inevitability, and the Assembly clearly agreed. The precise moment of declaration is irrelevant: the conflict had been developing for years, and actual fighting had been going on for months.

Notes to Chapter 5: The conquest of Greece, 340–334 BC

1   Frontinus, *Stratagems*, 1.4.13.
2   Diodoros 16.77.3 is suggestive; Ellis (1976), 184–5; Griffith in *Macedonia* 2.580.
3   Justin 9.2.1–16; Frontinus, *Stratagems* 2.8.14.
4   Diodoros 16.60.2; see Ellis (1976), 123.
5   Demosthenes 6.22; Didymus, *In Demosthenis* 11.26–47; Philochoros, *FGrH* 328 F 56.6.
6   I have seriously shortened this issue; the main source is Aeschines 3; Griffith in *Macedonia* 2.585–7 and 717–19 has an exemplary full account.
7   Aeschines 3.129; Demosthenes 18.151–2.
8   Diodoros 16.84.2; Demosthenes 18.169–71.
9   Demosthenes 18.213–14; Aeschines 3.124–44; Justin 9.35; Diodoros 16.85.1; Plutarch, *Demosthenes* 18.3–4.
10   Aeschines 3.146.
11   Demosthenes 18.156–8.
12   Polyainos 4.2.8.
13   Diodoros 16.86.1–6; Polyainos, 4.2.2; Justin 9.3.9–10; Hammond (1938), 186–218; Pritchett (1958), 307–11.
14   Justin 9.4.6–7; Diodoros 16.87.3; Pausanias 9.18 and 9.65; Roebuck (1948), 73–91; Larsen (1968), 175–8.
15   *SVA* 402; Diodoros 18.56.7; Plutarch, *Alexander* 28.2; Pausanias 1.5.3 and 1.34.1; cf. Roebuck (1948).
16   Plutarch, *Aratos* 23 (Corinth); Diodoros 17.3.3 (Ambrakia).
17   Polybios 9.28.7; Pausanias 8.35.4; Livy 38.34.3; Theopompos *FGrH* 115 F 328; cf. Roebuck (1948); Griffith in *Macedonia* 2.615–18.

18 SVA 403; Tod, *GHI* 177; Diodoros 16.69.3; Justin 9.5.2–4; Larsen (1968); Roebuck (1948); Griffith in *Macedonia* 2.623–8.

19 Justin 9.5.5; Diodoros 16.89.2–3.

20 Diodoros 17.5.3–6.2; Cook (1983), 224–5; Olmstead (1948), 489–90.

21 Athenaios 13.557d (Satyros); Plutarch, *Alexander* 9.3–12.

22 Diodoros 16.93.6.

23 Diodoros 16.91.2; Justin 9.5.8–9.

24 Tod *GHI* 191 (Eresos); Arrian 1.17.10–11 (Ephesos).

25 Pausanias 5.20.9; Griffith in *Macedonia* 2.393–694.

26 Fredericksmeyer (1982), 85–98.

27 Aelian Aristides 38.715D.

28 Diodoros 16.93.1–94.4; Justin 9.6; Aristotle, *Politics*, 5.1311b.

29 Bosworth (1971).

30 The main conspiracy theorist is Badian (1963), 244–50. All biographies of Philip and Alexander consider the matter, all coming to different conclusions.

31 Ps. – Kallisthenes 1.26.

32 Hammond in *Macedonia* 3.1–9.

33 Justin 9.7.12; Pausanias 8.7.7; one may ignore the gory details (probably invented later) and yet accept Olympias' guilt.

34 Diodoros 17.5.1–2; Curtius 7.13; Justin 12.6.14.

35 Justin 12.6.14; Alexander as a force for terror: Green (1974), ch. 4; Bosworth (1988), 26–8.

36 Diodoros 17.4.1; Justin 11.3.1–2.

37 *SVA* 403 II; Diodoros 17.4.2–6; Justin 11.2.5; Plutarch, *Alexander* 14.1.

38 Arrian, 1.1.4.6–5.5; Diodoros 17.8.1.

39 Arrian 1.5.6–6.11.

40 Fuller (1958), 219–29.

41 Aeschines 3.239; Dinarchos 1.10 and 18.

42 Justin 11.2.8.

43 Diodoros 17.8.5–6.

44 Arrian 1.7.4–7; Diodoros 17.8.2; Hammond (1981), 57–62.

45 Diodoros 17.8.3–12.5; Arrian 1.7.7–8.7.

46 Arrian 1.9.9; Justin 11.3.8–10.

47 Diodoros 17.17.3–3; Green (1974), 156–9 tabulates the army clearly; see also Bosworth (1988), 259–66.

48 Diodoros 17.16.2.

49 Arrian 1.12.8–10; numbers are only approximate.

50 Arrian 1.11.6–12.1; Justin 11.5.10–12; Diodoros 17.16.4; Plutarch, *Alexander* 15.

51 Arrian 1.12.9–10; Diodoros 17.18.2.

52 Arrian 1.14.1–16.7; Diodoros 17.19.1–21.6; Justin 11.6.8–13; Plutarch, *Alexander* 16; the imprecision of the ancient sources hamper reconstruction: Bosworth (1988), 40–4; Fuller (1958), 147–54; Green (1974), 174–80; and Hammond (1981), 70–6 are all careful, and all different.

53 Arrian 1.17.1–2.

54 Sardis: Arrian 1.17.3; Diodoros 17.21.7; Plutarch, *Alexander* 17.1; Asander: Arrian 1.17.7.

55 Arrian 1.17.10–12.

56 Diodoros 17.22.1–4; Plutarch, *Alexander* 17.1; Arrian 1.18.3–19.6.

57 Arrian 1.20.1; Diodoros 22.5–22.1.

58 Arrian 1.20.5–23.5; Diodoros 17.24.4–25.5.

59 Badian (1966), 37–69, argues that they were not enrolled in the league, and certainly the absence of evidence encourages that view; Bosworth (1988), 250–8, agrees, but also notes that the cities' situation was 'anomalous'.

Notes to Chapter 6: The great campaign, 334–325 BC

1 Diodoros 17.24.2–3; Arrian 1.23.8; only to Karia, not Lykia.

2 Sardis, Arrian 1.17.7.

3 Cawkwell (2005), 1–29, notes that no Greek shows any knowledge of Persia beyond Susa.

4 Arrian 1.24.4 and 26.1–7; Nearchos, Arrian 3.6.6.

5 Arrian 1.29.1–5 and 2.1–3; Curtius 3.1.1–8.

6 Arrian 2.4.1–2.

7 Arrian 2.4.2; he may be Abistamenes (Plutarch, *Alexander* 18.3).

8 Diodoros 17.27.5–6, 29.1–3 and 31.3–4; Arrian 1.19.8 and 2.1.1–3; Tod, *GHI* 192; Badian (1966).

9 Arrian 2.7.3–11.10; Diodoros 17.33.1–34.7; Justin 11.9.1–10; see Fuller (1958), 154–62, especially.

10 Diodoros 17.48.2–5; Curtius 4.7.1–2, 27–33; Arrian 2.13.2–3.

11 Curtius 4.1.34–40; Burn (1952).

12 Arrian 2.20.1 (Arados) and 3 (Cyprus).

13 Curtius 4.1.35; Anson (1988), 471–7; Briant (1973), 47–71; Billows (1990).

14 Arrian 2.15.24.5; Curtius 4.2.1–4.21; Plutarch, *Alexander* 24–5; Diodoros 17.40.2–46.5; Justin 11.10.10–14.

15 First offer: Arrian, 2.14.1–9; Curtius 4.1.7–14; second offer: Arrian 2.25.2–3; Curtius 5.1–3; the sources vary; not all moderns accept these exchanges as authentic.

16 Arrian 2.25.4–27.7; Curtius 4.5.10–6.31; Plutarch, *Alexander* 25; Diodoros 17.48.7–49.1; Romane (1988).

17 Soli: Curtius 3.7.2; near Issos: Curtius 3.7.7.

18 A difficult area: Bosworth (1974).

19 Arrian 2.20.5; Curtius 4.3.11.

20 Administration: Arrian 3.5.2–7; Curtius 4.8.5; Alexandria: Arrian 3.1.5–22; Diodoros 17.52.1–5; Strabo 17.1.1.10; Vitruvius, 2 *praef*; Ammon: Arrian 3.4.4–5; Curtius 4.7.5–32; Callisthenes F 15; Strabo 15.1.35; Plutarch, *Alexander* 27.3; Diodoros 17.49.1–51.4.

21 Diodoros 17.62.5–6.

22 Arrian 2.13.5–6; Curtius 4.1. 39; Diodoros 17.48.1 and 62.6–63.4; Justin 12.1.4–11; Plutarch, *Agis* 3.

23 Arrian 3.8.1–15.6; Curtius 4.12.1–16.33; Justin 11.13–14; Diodoros 17.55.3–61.3; Plutarch, *Alexander* 31–3; Marsden (1964).

24   Engels (1979), app. 5.

25   Susa: Diodoros 17.66.1–2; Justin 11.14.8; Plutarch, *Alexander* 36.1; Arrian 3.16.6–7; Curtius 5.2.8–10; Persepolis: Diodoros 17.71.1–72.6; Curtius 5.6.9.

26   Arrian 3.16.10.

27   Diodoros 17.63.1.

28   Arrian 3.6.2–6; Curtius 4.8.15.

29   Diodoros 17.63.1–3; Plutarch, *Agis* 3; Curtius 6.1.1–16; Justin 12.1.4–11.

30   Arrian 3.19.5–8; Curtius 5.7.12.

31   Curtius 6.1.20.

32   Arrian 3.21.1–10; Justin 11.15.1–15; Curtius 5.9.2–12.25, an account informed by Curtius' acquaintanceship with Roman conspiracies and emperors.

33   The first was Mazaios, reappointed as satrap of Babylon.

34   Philotas and Parmenion: Arrian 3.26–27; Curtius 6.7.1–7.2.32; Diodoros 17.77–83; Plutarch, *Alexander* 48–9; Justin 17.5.1–8; Strabo 724; Kleitos: Arrian 4.8.1–9; Curtius 8.19–21; Plutarch, *Alexander* 51; Kallisthenes: Arrian 4.14; Plutarch, *Alexander* 55; Curtius 8.6.24; Badian (2000); Cartledge (2004), 67–75; Worthington (2003), 273–95, has a collection of extracts on the subject.

35   Alexander Lynkestis, for example: Curtius 8.1.5–9; Diodoros 17.80.2. All through the campaign Alexander met or captured Greeks and Macedonians who had joined the Persian side, or were envoys from Greek cities of the league to the Great King. His campaign in Asia was in part a continuation of the wars he and his father had fought in Greece.

36   Ehrenburg (1938), 52–61.

37   Arrian 3.25.3; Curtius 6.6.12–13.

38   Arrian bk 4; Curtius bk 7; Bosworth (1996); Holt (1989) and (2005). Tarn (1951) is dated and overtaken by later work, but worth reading nonetheless for its style and imagination.

39   Holt (2005), 107, suggests up to 120,000; of course, we cannot know.

40   11,200 infantry and 600 cavalry recruited in Arachosia, 19,400 infantry and 2,600 cavalry at Baktra: Curtius 7.3.4–5 and 10.11–12; Arrian 5.11.3 and 4.16.7; garrison: Arrian 4.22.3.

41   Fraser (1996).

42   Vogelsang (1990).

43   Arrian 5.25.1–29.3; Curtius 9.2.11–3.19; Plutarch, *Alexander*, 62; Diodoros 17.94.5.

44   Arrian 6.27.3; Curtius 9.10.19.

45   Arrian 6.9.11; Curtius 9.4.26–5.19; Plutarch, *Alexander*, 63; Diodoros 17.98.3–99.4; Justin 12.9.5–11; Plutarch, *Moralia* 327B, 343D–344D.

46   Arrian wrote an account of the Indian campaign, part surviving as *Indica*; Narain (1965), 155–65, is a useful corrective to Alexander-centred accounts.

47   Nearchos: Arrian, *Indica* 20–42; Leonnatos: Curtius 9.10.2 and 19; Arrian, *Indica* 23.5–6.

48   The journey: Arrian 6.22–6; Curtius 9.10.8–16; Plutarch, *Alexander*, 66; Diodoros 17.105.3–106.3; Arrian 5.25.1–29.3; the celebration: Curtius 9.10.23–9; Plutarch, *Alexander*, 67 Diodoros 17.106.1; Arrian 6.28.1–2.

49   Lock (1977), 91–107.

Notes to Chapter 7: The united empire, 325–319 BC

1 Curtius 9.10.21 and 29.
2 Arrian 6.27.3–5; Curtius 10.1.1–8.
3 Arrian 7.4.1; Plutarch, *Alexander* 68.7.
4 For views on Alexander's policy in Iran, see Bosworth (1980) and Hamilton (1987), 467–86.
5 Curtius 9.10.7; Arrian 6.27.3 and 6.
6 Arrian 4.18.3; Curtius 8.3.17.
7 Arrian 6.29.2 and 30.1–2.
8 Curtius 10.1.22–38.
9 Diodoros 17.108.6; Curtius 10.2.1; Badian (1961), 16–43.
10 Justin 13.4.11; Arrian 7.23.6 and 8; *OGIS* 570; Kleomenes' promotion is not certain.
11 Diodoros 17.106.3; Artaxerxes III had also done this after the Satraps' Revolt.
12 Diodoros 17.99.5–6; Curtius 9.7.1–11; Holt (2005), 111–12.
13 Arrian 6.27.3; Curtius 9.10.19 and 10.1.9.
14 Arrian 7.6.3–5; Bosworth (1980).
15 Arrian 7.6.2.
16 Arrian 7.4.4–8; Diodoros 17.107.6; Plutarch, *Alexander* 70; Chares, *FGrH* 125 F 4.
17 Diodoros 17.108.3.
18 Arrian 7.6.5.
19 Arrian 7.5.1–3.
20 Arrian 7.6.1; this was arranged before the Indian campaign. These troops had been in training for two years: Curtius 8.5.1, Plutarch, *Alexander* 47.3; Diodoros 17.108.1.
21 Arrian 7.12.4; Justin 2.17.9; Curtius 10.10.15; Heckel (1988).
22 Fraser (1996) concludes that Alexander founded just five cities (one of which is doubtful); he did leave large numbers of garrison troops scattered across Asia, and these are the source of the large number of later 'Alexandrias'.
23 Diodoros 17.109.1; Curtius 10.2.4–7; Justin 13.5.2–5. The purpose of the decree is not known; other suggested reasons include disposing of surplus soldiers (Green (1974), 451) or to plant Macedonian supporters within the cities (Bickerman, 1940).
24 Hypereides, *Epitaphios* 8. Oral reaction by Demosthenes and by a Spartan, Damis, was disparaging, but Athens established a cult, and envoys to Babylon in the spring of 323 crowned the king with gold, thus paying him divine honours.
25 Heckel (2006), 388.
26 Badian (1961).
27 Arrian 7.14.1–15.3; Diodoros 17.110.8, 111.5, 114.1–115.6; Justin 17.12.11–12; Plutarch, *Alexander* 72.
28 Arrian 7.19.6–20.2.
29 Arrian 7.24.4; Plutarch, *Alexander* 76; Diodoros 17.117.1–15; Justin 17.13.7.
30 Bosworth (1971), 112–36, which ends with the sentence: 'Complete proof is impossible, but the probability is that Alexander was murdered'– the absence of 'proof' and the word 'probability' undermine the whole thesis; also Doherty (2004) and Philips (2004). The basis is the 'Metz Epitome', for which see Heckel (1988) and later romances, for which see

Wolohojian (1969) and Stoneman (1991).

31 Though this is not a practice around which his life revolved, despite O'Brien (1992).

32 Arrian 7.26.3.

33 Diodoros 20.20.1; Justin 11.10.3; Plutarch, *Eumenes* 1.7.

34 Metz Epitome 70.

35 Plutarch, *Alexander*, 77.6.

36 Arrian, *Succ.* F 1; Curtius 10.6.1–7.9; Diodoros 18.2.1–4; I have drastically abbreviated this episode; Bosworth (2002), ch. 2; Errington (1970), 49–77.

37 Diodoros 18.3.1–3; Justin 13.4.10–23; Curtius 10.10.1–4; Arrian, *Succ.* 1.5–7; Dexippos, *FGrH* 100 F 8; Plutarch, *Alexander* 77.6.

38 Diodoros 18.4.8 and 7.1.9

39 Diodoros 18.4.8 and 7.1–9; Holt (2005), 116–17.

40 Diodoros 18.8.7–9.4.

41 Diodoros 18.11.1–12.4; Plutarch, *Phokion* 23; id., *Demosthenes* 27.

42 Diodoros 18.15.1–7; Justin 13.5.15–16; Arrian, *Succ.* 1.9.

43 Leonnatos: Plutarch, *Eumenes* 2.4–10; Diodoros 18.21.1 and 14.4–5; Justin 13.5.14.

44 Kleitos and the naval war: *IG* II (2), 398 and 493; Marmor Parium, *FGrH* 239, B 9 (Austin 21).

45 Arrian, *Succ.* 1.12; Plutarch, *Demosthenes* 28.2; id., *Phokion* 26.1; Diodoros 18.17.

46 *SVA* 415; Diodoros 18.18.3; Plutarch, *Phokion* 26–8.

47 Diodoros 18.24.1–25.3; Grainger (1999).

48 Diodoros 18.16.1–3; Arrian, *Succ.* F 1.11.

49 Diodoros 18.23.3–4; Arrian, *Succ.* F 1.20 and 24; Plutarch, *Eumenes* 3.4–5.

50 Diodoros 18.25.6, 28,2–6, 33.1–36.5; Arrian, *Succ.* F 1.25, 28–9; Justin 13.8.10; Pausanias 1.6.3; Strabo 17.1.8; Hauben (1977), 95–120.

51 Diodoros 18.29.1–32.4; Arrian, *Succ.* F 1, 26–27; Justin 13.8. 1–9; Plutarch, *Eumenes* 4–7.

52 Arrian, *Succ.* F 1.34–38; Diodoros 19.29.3.

53 Arrian, *Succ.* F 1.52; Diodoros 19.39.5–7.

54 Diodoros 18.48.

Notes to World View II: 319 BC

1 Arrian 7.1–2; Curtius 10.1.17–19; Diodoros 18.4.1–6.

2 Diodoros 18.4.6.

3 Diodoros 18.16.1–3.

4 Arrian 7.15.5: envoys from 'Bruttians, Lucanians and Etruscans'.

5 Toynbee (1965), 88–93; Morley (1996).

6 Archidamos: Plutarch, *Agis* 3.2; Diodoros 16.62.4 and 63.2; Theopompos; *FGrH* 259, 261; Alexander of Epiros: Livy 8.3.6, 17.9 and 24.4; Diodoros 16.5 and 18.90.2; Justin 12.2; Strabo 6.34.13–20.

7 Plutarch, *Timoleon*; Diodoros book 16; Talbert (1974).

8 Tillyard (1908); Finley (1969), 100–1; Meister, CAH VII.I, 384–411; cf. also Lewis (2000).

9 Arrian, *Succ.*, F 9.

10   Justin 15.4.
11   Raychaudhuri (1996), 234–40 and 591–3.
12   Suetonius, *Augustus* 18; Dio Cassius 51.16.
13   Loewe and Shaughnessy (1999).

Notes to Chapter 8: Antigonos the One-Eyed, 319–311 BC

1   Diodoros 18.48.1–3; Plutarch, *Phokion* 31.1 and *Alexander* 3.130. Hammond (1989), 255, ascribed his appointment to the Macedonian Assembly, but both sources make it clear that it was Antipater's appointment.
2   Errington (1977).
3   Diodoros 18.45.2–3.
4   Diodoros 18.52.5–8.
5   Diodoros 18.49.1–3; Plutarch, *Eumenes* 12.
6   Diodoros 18.61.1–3; Polyainos 4.8.2; Plutarch, *Eumenes* 13.2–4; Briant (1972).
7   Diodoros 18.4.1 and 1.6–9; Arrian, *Succ.* F 9.17–18; Pausanias 1.6.3.
8   Diodoros 18.26.49; Pausanias 1.6.3.
9   Diodoros 18.31.6; Arrian, *Succ.* F 9.28–9.
10   Diodoros 18.43; Appian, *Syrian Wars* 52.264; Arrian, *Succ.* 10.6; Wheatley (1995).
11   Diodoros 18.62.1–2.
12   Diodoros 19.12.2; 17.2.
13   Diodoros 19.14.1–8.
14   Diodoros 19.13.5.
15   Diodoros 19.18–34 and 37–44; Plutarch, *Eumenes* 14–17; Polyainos 4.6.13; Bosworth (2002), ch. 4; Billows (1990), ch. 3; Habicht (1997), 467–51.
16   *SVA* 403 III; Diodoros 18.56.1–57.1.
17   *SVA* 421; Diodoros 18.74.2–3.
18   Diodoros 18.75.1–2.
19   Justin 14.5.1–4.; Diodoros 19.11.1.
20   Diodoros 19.11.2.
21   Diodoros 19.11.4–9.
22   Diodoros 19.36.1–6 and 49.1–51.5.
23   Diodoros 19.52.4.
24   Diodoros 19.52.1.
25   Diodoros 19.44.1.
26   Diodoros 19.46.1–4.
27   Diodoros 19.48.1–4; Cloche (1955).
28   Diodoros 19.56.2–6; Grainger (1990b), 48–50.
29   Diodoros 19.56.1–3.
30   Diodoros 19.56.3.
31   Diodoros 19.48.8 and 56.5; Antigonos collected 10,000 more talents, from the treasury at Kyinda in Cilicia.
32   Diodoros 19.57.1–2.

33 This follows from the fact that he was in occupation when Antigonos returned.
34 Diodoros 19.58.1–5.
35 Diodoros 19.61.1–5; Simpson (1959).
36 Diodoros 19.60.1–61.3; Billows (1990), 114–16.
37 Diodoros 19.60.3–4 and 62.3–7.
38 Errington (1977) and Hauben (1973).
39 Diodoros 19.64.8.
40 Diodoros 19.64.3–6; Billows (1990), 461.
41 *IG* XI.4.1036 and XI.2.154a; Tarn (1913), appendix 5; Merker (1970), 141–60; Billows (1990), 220–5.
42 Diodoros 19.64.1–2.
43 Diodoros 19.77.2–4.
44 Holbl (2001), 26 (and references therein); Will (1964).
45 Diodoros 19.77.7.
46 Diodoros 19.79.6–7 and 80.3.
47 Diodoros 19.80.3–84.8.
48 Diodoros 19.85.5.
49 Diodoros 19.86.1–2.
50 Diodoros 19.5.2–4.
51 Diodoros 19.91.1–4; Grainger (1990b), 72–5.
52 Diodoros 19.93.4–7.
53 Diodoros 19.87.1–3.
54 Diodoros 19.92.1–4.
55 Diodoros 19.100.3–7.
55 Diodoros 19.105.1–4; *SVA* 428; *OGIS* 5 (Austin 31).
57 This is the burden of the article by Simpson (note 35).
58 Bosworth (2002), ch. 3, concludes that available manpower was reduced; also Bosworth (1986), 1–12; and Adams (1996).

Notes to Chapter 9: The new king, 311–306 BC

1   Diodoros 20.19.2.
2   Diodoros 20.19.5.
3   Diodoros 20.20.–4 and 28.1–4; Billows (1990), 140–1.
4   Diodoros 20.21.1–3.
5   Launey (1949–1950).
6   Diodoros 20.27.1–3.
7   Diodoros 20.37.1–2.
8   Alexander IV: Diodoros 20.105.2 (Kassander put the blame on the jailer); Herakles: Diodoros 20.28.3; Kleopatra: Diodoros 20.37.3–6; Whitehorne (1996), ch. 5.
9   As in a chronicle compiled in Babylonia (Austin 158), and in the dating formulae used in papyri in Egypt.
10 Diodoros 19.92.5

11 Plutarch, *Demetrius* 7.2.

12 Polyainos 4.9.1.

13 Grainger (1990b).

14 e.g., *SVA* 433 between Ptolemy and Antigonos and 434 between Ptolemy and Kassander.

15 Billows (1990), appendix 3, no. 106.

16 Justin 41.4.1; Billows (1990), appendix 3, no. 136.

17 Pliny, *NH* 6.18.

18 Seleukos' work in Baktria is being teased out gradually: see Sherwin-White and Kuhrt (1993), and comments on it in *Topoi* 4, 1994; Holt (1989) and (1999).

19 Diodoros 18.21.7–9 and 20.40.1–42.5; Will (1964).

20 Holbl (2001), 25–7.

21 Hatzopoulos (1996) works backwards from the administrative system of the Antigonid kings after 270, but is not convincing: see Borza (1999), 44–8. Kassander used the informal, personal system of rule he had inherited from his father.

22 The Ptolemaic administration is much studied, because of the wealth of papyri providing evidence: a useful brief summary is in Bagnall and Derow (2004), 285–8.

23 Billows (1990), ch. 7.

24 Holbl (2001), 26–7; on Alexandria, Fraser (1972).

25 Fraser (1996).

26 Tarn and Griffith (1952), 145–50; Avi-Yonah (1978).

27 For Babylonia, see Kuhrt and Sherwin-White (1994) which supplements their 1993 edition.

28 Refoundation of Thebes: Diodoros 19.53.2; Kassandreia: Diodoros 19.52.2; Thessalonika: Strabo 7 frags 21, 24, 25, 27.

29 Strabo 7 frag. 51; Pliny, *NH* 4.10.37.

30 Diodoros 20.9.1; Pausanias 1.9.8.

31 Antigoneia in Syria: Diodoros 20.47.5; for Antigonos in Asia Minor, cf. Billows (1990), 296–8; Smyrna: Strabo 14.1.37.

32 Appian, *Syrian Wars* 57–8; the date of the city's foundation is uncertain; it is referred to in Babylonian sources as the 'city of kingship', but this is ambiguous.

33 Eusebius, *Chronographia* 1.249; Arrian 7.2 9 and 2.5; see Eddy (1961) for a most interesting interpretation of these stories.

34 Plutarch, *Demetrios* 8.3–12; Diodoros 20.45.1–46.4; Polyainos 4.7.6; Habicht (1997), 65–73.

35 Diodoros 20.46.4–52.6; Polyainos 4.7.7; Plutarch, *Demetrios* 16–17.

36 Diodoros 20.53.1–2; Plutarch, *Demetrios* 17–18; Billows (1990), 157–60; Gruen (1985), especially 253–7.

Notes to Chapter 10: Antigonos' failure, 306–298 BC

1 Alexander IV was believed to be alive until 307/306 by the compiler of a local chronicle in Babylonia (S. Smith, 1924), but that only means the compiler did not know of his death. Tomb III at Vergina (ancient Aigai), containing the cremated remains of a child supposedly

aged between 11 and 14 has been identified as that of Alexander (Hammond, 1982), but certainty is impossible, as is the date of the funeral: 306 seems a good guess.

2 Plutarch, *Demetrios* 17; Diodoros 20.53.1–2.

3 Pausanias 1.15.1 and 1.26.3; Habicht (1997), 74–5.

4 Plutarch, *Demetrios* 19; Diodoros 20.73.1–76.7; Hauben (1975/6).

5 Hauben (1977).

6 *SVA* 442; Plutarch, *Demetrios* 21–2; Diodoros 20.81–8 and 91–100.

7 Holbl (2001), 20, dates this to 306 – before Antigonos' attack; Billows (1990), 59, to early 304.

8 In 305/304, according to the Babylonian chronicle.

9 Lund (1992), 156–7, gives 304, without discussion; on all this, cf. Gruen (1985).

10 Hammond in *Macedonia* 3.174.

11 Plutarch, *Demetrios* 10.3.

12 Gruen (1985); Burstein (1974), 80.

13 Plutarch, *Demetrios* 23; Diodoros 20.100.5–6.

14 Demetrios in Athens: Plutarch, *Demetrios* 24; in the Peloponnese: Plutarch, *Demetrios* 25; Diodoros 20.102.1–7; an alliance between Athens and Sikyon was one result of Demetrios' work: *SVA* 445.

15 Plutarch, *Demetrios* 25; Diodoros 20.46.5. The 'charter' of the league is preserved in a fragmentary inscription from Epidauros: Robert (1946), 15–23; this league and the inscription are widely discussed; *SVA* 446.

16 Diodoros 20.106.1–2.

17 SVA 447; Diodoros 20.106.3–5; Plutarch, *Demetrios* 28.2; Justin 15.2.15–17.

18 Diodoros 20.110.2–6.

19 Diodoros 20.10.1–2.

20 Diodoros 20.109.1–2.

21 Lund (1992), for sources for this paragraph.

22 Holt (1999), 21–9.

23 *SVA* 441; Strabo 15.2.9; Justin 15.4.20; Tarn (1951).

24 Grainger (1990b), chs 6 and 7; the numbers are disputed, but Seleukos certainly had a much larger elephant park than Antigonos, who had 83 in 306, and probably fewer in 301.

25 Strabo 15, 724 and 16.752; Plutarch, *Alexander* 52; Plutarch, *Demetrios* 28; Bar-Kochva (1976), 76–7.

26 Billows (1990), 175–77; Diodoros 20.107.2–5.

27 Diodoros 20.113.4.

28 Diodoros 20.113.1.

29 Diodoros 20.111.1–2.

30 Diodoros 20.113.1–2.

31 Billows (1990), 178.

32 Diodoros 20.113.2.

33 Diodoros 20.112.1–4.

34 See the map in Billows (1990), 464.

35 Plutarch, *Demetrios* 28–9; Bar-Kochva (1976), 106–7; Billows (1990), 181–2.

36 Plutarch, *Demetrios* 30.

37 Plutarch, *Demetrios* 20.2–4.

38 Terms have to be deduced from the later possessions of the kings: Diodoros 21.1.5; Justin 15.4.21–22; Plutarch, *Demetrios*, 28–31.

39 Plutarch, *Demetrios* 31; Robert (1945), no. 44; Seibert (1967).

40 Based on Grainger (1990a).

41 Eusebius, *Chronographia* 2.119.

Notes to Chapter 11: New kings for Macedon, 298–291 BC

1 Habicht (1997), 81–5.

2 Robert (1945), no 44.

3 Billows (1995), 81–109.

4 Errington (1990), 134–7.

5 Diodoros 21.2.1–3.

6 Pausanias 9.7.2; Eusebius, *Chronographia* 1.231.

7 Porphyry, *FGrH* 260 F 3.5.

8 Habicht (1997), 85–7.

9 Plutarch, *Pyrrhos* 4.6–5.1; Pausanias 1.11.5.

10 Plutarch, *Pyrrhos* 9.2; Diodoros 21.4.

11 Plutarch, *Pyrrhos* 5.1–14.

12 Plutarch, *Demetrios* 33.

13 Plutarch, *Demetrios* 32.

14 Plutarch, *Demetrios* 35.

15 Plutarch, *Demetrios* 33.

16 Habicht (1997), 85–7.

17 Habicht (1997), 86–7; Plutarch, *Demetrios* 33; Polyainos 4.7.5 and 3.7.1.

18 Plutarch, *Demetrios* 34; Thonemann (2005).

19 Plutarch, *Demetrios* 35; SIG 368.

20 Plutarch, *Demetrios* 36 and *Pyrrhos* 6; Pausanias 5.7.3; Diodoros 21.7.

21 Plutarch, *Pyrrhos* 6; Hammond in *Macedonia* 3.214–215; Justin 10.1.8.

22 Plutarch, *Demetrios* 36.4–37.15.

23 Plutarch, *Demetrios* 37.2. This is one of the clearest examples of the Assembly's role in a succession, and is in part the basis of the theory of its very existence.

24 Plutarch, *Demetrios* 37; Justin 16.2.4.

25 *SVA* 460.

26 Plutarch, *Demetrios* 39; Polyainos 4.7.11.

27 Plutarch, *Demetrios* 39.

28 Ibid.

29 *SVA* 463.

30 Plutarch, *Demetrios* 39.

31 Ibid; Diodoros 21.14.

32 Plutarch, *Pyrrhos* 6; Justin 16.1.9; Porphyry *FGrH* 260 F 3.3; Lund (1992), 45–9.

33 Plutarch, *Demetrios* 39.

34   Lund (1992), 82; Burstein (1974).

35   For Lysimachos' situation, see Lund (1992), 91–5.

36   Plutarch, *Demetrios* 38; Appian, *Syrian Wars* 59–61.

37   The date of Antiochos' appointment was between 294 and 291 BC; the connection with the marriage, and so with the conquest of Kilikia from Demetrios, would suggest the earlier part of that period: Holt (1999), notes 12 and 13.

38   Holt (1999), 26–9; the nomad invasion is postulated by Tarn (1951), 116–18, and elaborated by J. Wolski in several studies.

Notes to Chapter 12: King Demetrios and his enemies, 291–285 BC

1   Plutarch, *Demetrios* 40.1–2, and *Pyrrhos* 7.3.

2   Plutarch, *Demetrios* 40.1.

3   Newell (1927); Hammond in *Macedonia* 3.226–7.

4   Diogenes Laertius 2.140

5   McNicoll (1997).

6   Plutarch, *Demetrios* 43.2–7 and *Pyrrhos* 10.3; these figures are accepted by Walbank in *Macedonia* 3.226, ignored by Errington (1990) and Will, *CAH* VII, 1, ch. 4.

7   Plutarch, *Demetrios* 43.2.

8   Plutarch, *Demetrios* 42.

9   Plutarch, *Demetrios* 41.2 and *Pyrrhos* 7.4–10.

10   Plutarch, *Demetrios* 42.3 and *Pyrrhos* 10.1–4.

11   This alliance is required by the situation and by the events of the next years.

12   Lund (1992), 96–8.

13   Plutarch, *Pyrrhos* 11.1.

14   Plutarch, *Demetrios* 44.3; *IG* 12.7.50b (Austin 219).

15   Shipley (2000), ch. 3.

16   See Grainger (1990a) for examples; the conclusions apply in interior Asia Minor, Iran and Baktria as well as Syria.

17   Shear (1978); but the consensus now is that the revolt took place in 287; cf. Osborne (1979), 181–94.

18   Polyainos 4.12.2; Plutarch, *Demetrios* 44 and *Pyrrhos* 11; Trogus, *Prologue*, 16; Justin 16.2.1–2; Pausanias 1.10.2.

19   Plutarch, *Demetrios* 45.1.

20   Seibert (1970), 337–51.

21   Shear (1978); Habicht (1997).

22   Plutarch, *Pyrrhos* 12.1.

23   Shear (1978); Plutarch, *Pyrrhos* 12.8.

24   Plutarch, *Demetrios* 46, perhaps equating Demetrios' march with that of Mark Antony.

25   Plutarch, *Demetrios* 46–7.

26   Plutarch, *Demetrios* 47–9.

Notes to Chapter 13: The last chance for the empire, 285–281 BC

1   Plutarch, *Pyrrhos* 12.

2   Plutarch, *Pyrrhos* 12.8

3   Antigonos' strength is not clear, some thousands of soldiers and tens of ships at least; his problem, as Tarn (1913), 113, notes, was not so much manpower as the money needed to pay his troops.

4   Plutarch, *Pyrrhos* 12.9–2; Justin 16.3.1–2; Pausanias 1.10.2.

5   Seibert (1967), 72–7.

6   Hazzard (1967), 140–58.

7   Appian, *Syrian Wars* 63.

8   Burstein (1974); Lund (1992), 75, 88, 98.

9   Plutarch, *Demetrios* 46; Justin 17.1.1–4; Trogus, *Prologue* 17; Strabo 13.4.1–2; Memnon, *FGrH* 434, F 5.6; Pausanias 1.10.3.

10 Robert (1959), 172–9.

11 Lund (1992), 181–98.

12 Memnon, *FGrH* 434, F 5.7; Justin 17.1.7; Pausanias 1.1.3.

13 Justin 17.1.6.

14 Justin 17.1.7.

15 Strabo 13.4.1 C 623; Pausanias 1.8.1; Memnon, *FGrH* 434, F 5.1.6.

16 Justin 17.1.1–4.

17 Plutarch, *Demetrios* 51.

18 Plutarch, *Demetrios* 52–53.

19 Holbl (2001), 27, dated this death to 'winter of 283/282'; the coronation of Ptolemy II took place on 7 January 282: Holbl (2001), 35.

20 282 is only a possible date; Holbl (2001), 36, implies 282.

21 Polyainos 6.12.

22 Ibid, 4.9.4.

23 Keil (1902).

24 Pausanias 1.10.5.

25 Trogus, *Prologue* 17.

26 Memnon, *FGrH* 227a, 9–14.

27 Memnon, *FGrH* 226a, 14–22.

28 Justin 24.2.

29 Ibid; Memnon, *FGrH* 226b, 14–33.

30 Memnon, *FGrH* 226b, 1–14.

Notes to Chapter 14: New kings, and disaster, 281–277 BC

1   Memnon, *FGrH* 226.6.1–14.

2   Memnon, *FGrH* 434 F 8.4–6; Justin 24.1.8–2.1.

3   Justin 17.2.14.

4   Justin 17.2.15 and 24.1.8; Seibert (1967), 102; this was Pyrrhos' fifth marriage; the names of neither mother nor daughter are known.

5   Justin 17.2.9–10.
6   Memnon, *FGrH* 227a.4–6.
7   Trogus, *Prologue* 24; Justin 24.2–5.
8   Justin 17.2.4–8 and 24.2.1–3.10; Justin's inconsistencies are explained as differing stages of affairs at Kassandreia: Heinen (1972), 81–3; Walbank in *Macedonia* 3.247–8.
9   Trogus, *Prologue*, 24.
10 *OGIS* 55 (Austin 270).
11 Justin 17.2.1.
12 Smith (1924), 150–9.
13 *OGIS* 219 (Austin 162).
14 H. Heinen, *CAH* (3) VII, 1, 415–16; Grainger (1990b), 196–7.
15 Polybius 2.4.1.
16 Justin 24.1.
17 Austin 259, *I. Didyma* 12.
18 Justin 25.1.1.
19 Justin 24.1.8.
20 Strabo 12.3.8; Allen (1983), 14.
21 Appian, *Syrian Wars* 63.
22 *SVA* 465; the league's formation was apparently stimulated by the quarrel with Seleukos: Memnon, *FGrH* 226a.14–22.
23 Arrian 1.4.6; Strabo 310.
24 Justin 32.3.8.
25 Pliny, *HN* 31.53.
26 Pausanias 1.19.4.
27 Nachtergael (1977), 8, n. 7.
28 Pausanias 10.19.6–7.
29 Justin 24.4.6–11; Memnon, *FGrH* 434 F 8.8; Diodoros 22.3.
30 Eusebius, *Chronographia* 1.235; cf. Walbank in *Macedonia* 3, appendix 3.
31 The best attempt is by Nachtergael (1977).
32 Justin 24.5.12.
33 Justin 25.1.2.
34 Diodoros 22.51–52; Trogus, *Prologue* 25; Polyainos 2.29.1; Fuks (1974), 51–81.
35 Justin 24.6.1–4; Diodoros 22.9.1; Pausanias 10.23.11–14.
36 Appian, *Illyrian Wars* 3.
37 Trogus, *Prologue* 25; Justin 25.1–2; *SIG* 207.
38 Walbank in *Macedonia* 3.257.
39 Polyainos 4.6.18.
40 Polybius 4.46.
41 Memnon, *FGrH* 434 F 11.
42 *SVA* 469.
43 Livy 38.16.6–7.
44 Hatzopoulos (1996), vol. 2, has the evidence for the administration, but most come from the Antigonid period; of the few which are earlier, most are from cities such as Amphipolis, hardly a typical Macedonian place.

Notes to Chapter 15: The new world, 277–272 BC

1   Launey (1944), 217–36.
2   Mitchell (1993), 13–20; also Grainger (1990b), 205; for the settlement of the Galatians in Kappadokia, see Moraux (1957), 56–75, and H. Heinen, *CAH* VII, 1, 423.
3   Worrle (1975) argues for 270 rather than 275 based on this one inscription. Bar-Kochva (1973), 1–8, concluded it was 'shortly after April 272'.
4   Rice (1983), now dated 275 by Foertmeyer (1988), 90–104.
5   Sherwin-White and Kuhrt (1993), 147–61; the numbers of Babylonians recruited was, however, always small.
6   Holbl (2001), ch. 3.
7   Polybius 5.65–79; Bar-Kochva (1976), 128–41.
8   Strabo 11.13.1; Schottky (1989).
9   Diodoros 19.23.3 and 31.19.5; Sherwin-White and Kuhrt (1993), 15 and 192–4.
10 Smith (1924), 150–9 (Austin 141).
11 Sherwin-White and Kuhrt (1993), 29–30 and 76–7.
12 Holt (1999).
13 Heinen, *CAH* CII, I, 426.
14 Theokritos XVII.131; Pausanais 1.7.1; Memnon, *FGrH* 434, F 8.7; Seibert (1967), 81–5.
15 Sotades in Athenaios 14.621a–b, for example; Sotades was murdered for his verses.
16 Burstein (1982), 197–212.
17 Plutarch, *Pyrrhos*, 26.5–9; Pausanias 1.13.2; Justin 25.3.5; Diodoros 22.11.1.
18 Plutarch, *Pyrrhos* 26–34.
19 Grainger (1999); Scholten (2000).
20 Tarn (1913), 263–4 and 444–5, not been widely accepted; but Ptolemy had much to gain, Pyrrhos was an old associate of the Ptolemies, and Ptolemy was interested in reducing Antigonos' power.
21 *Vita Aratoi*; Diogenes Laertius 7.1.8; Grainger (1990b), 207–8.
22 See note 3.
23 Pausanias 1.7.1–21; Polybius 2.28.1–2.
24 Pausanias 1.7.2; Callimachos 4.185–7; Laubscher (1987).
25 *OGIS* 798 (Austin 231); cf. Launey (1944).
26 Worrle (1975) (Austin 168).
27 Smith (1924), 150–9 (Austin 141).

Notes to World view III: 272 BC

1   Zonaras 8.6.13.
2   Livy *per.* 14; Dionysios of Halicarnassus 20.14; Dio Cassius 10, frag. 4; Justin 18.2.9.
3   Diodoros 20.54.1; K. Meister, *CAH* VII, 1, 405.
4   Plutarch, *Pyrrhos* 22–27.
5   Thapar (1997), 25–8.
6   Loewe and Shaughnessy (1999), 632–41.

Notes to Conclusion

1   Cawkwell (2005) for the fifth and fourth centuries BC.
2   Wheeler (1968).
3   Smith (1924) (Austin 163): Babylonian suffering but no resentment.

Bibliography

Adams, W. L. (1996) 'In the wake of Alexander the Great: the impact of conquest on the Aegean world', *Ancient World* 27, 29–37.

Adams, W. L. and Borza, E. N. (eds) (1982) *Philip II, Alexander the Great and the Macedonian Heritage*, Washington DC.

Alexandre le Grand, Image et Realité (1976) Fondation Hardt, Geneva.

Allen, R. E. (1983) *The Attalid Kingdom*, Oxford.

Andronicos, M. (1970) 'Sarisa', *BCH*, 94, 91–107.

Anson, E. M. (1988) 'Antigonos, Satrap of Phrygia', *Historia* 37, 471–7.

Ashley, J. R. (1998) *The Macedonian Empire, The Era of Warfare under Philip II and Alexander the Great, 359–323 BC*, Jefferson NC.

Avi-Yonah, M. (1978) *Hellenism in the East*, Jerusalem.

Aymard, A. (1954) 'Philippe de Macedoine ôtage à Thèbes', *REA* 5, 15–36.

Badian, E. (1958) 'Alexander the Great and the unity of mankind', *Historia* 7, 425–44.

— (1961) 'Harpalus', *JHS* 81, 16–43.

— (1963) 'The Death of Philip II', *Phoenix* 17, 244–50.

— (1966) 'Alexander the Great and the Greeks of Asia', in Badian, E. (ed.), *Ancient Society and Institutions, Studies Presented to Victor Ehrenburg on his 75th Birthday*, Oxford, pp. 37–69.

— (2000) 'Conspiracies', in Bosworth, A. B. and Baynham, E. J. *Alexander the Great in Fact and Fiction*, Oxford.

Bagnall, R. S. (1976) *The Administration of the Ptolemaic Possessions outside Egypt*, Leiden.

Bagnall, R. S. and Derow, P. (2004) *The Hellenistic Period: Historical sources in Translation*, 2nd edn, Oxford.

Bar-Kochva, B. (1973) 'On the sources and chronology of Antiochos I's battle against the Galatians', *Proceedings of the Cambridge Philosophical Society* 119, 1–8.

— (1976) *The Seleucid Army*, Cambridge.

Baynham, E. J. (1998) *Alexander the Great*, Ann Arbor MI.

Bellinger, A. R. (1963) *Essays in the Coinage of Alexander the Great*, New York.

Bernard, P. (1967) 'Ai Khanum on the Oxus: a Hellenistic city in Central Asia', *Proceedings of the British Academy* 53, 71–95.

— (1994) 'L'Asie centrale et l'empire séleucide', *Topoi* 4, 473–511.

Bevan, E. R. (1902) *The House of Seleucus*, vol. 1, London.

— (1927) *History of Egypt under the Ptolemaic Dynasty*, London.

Bickerman, E. (1938) *Institutions des Seleucides*, Paris.

— (1940) 'La lettre d'Alexandre le Grand aux bannus grecs', *REA*, 53, 25–35.

Billows, R. A. (1990) *Antigonos the One-Eyed and the Creation of the Hellenistic State*, Berkeley and Los Angeles CA.

— (1995) *Kings and Colonists: Aspects of Macedonian Imperialism*, Leiden.

Boardman, J. (1964) *The Greeks Overseas*, Harmondsworth.

Borza, E. N. (1987) 'Timber and politics in the ancient world: Macedon and the Greeks', *Proceedings of the American Philosophical Association*, 131, 32–52.

Borza, E. N. (1990) *In the Shadow of Olympos, the Emergence of Macedon*, Princeton NJ.

— (1999) *Before Alexander, Constructing Early Macedonia*, Claremont CA.

Bosworth, A. B. (1971) 'Philip II and Upper Macedon', *CQ*, NS 21, 93–105.

— (1971) 'The Death of Alexander the Great: rumour and propaganda', *CQ* NS 21, 112–36.

— (1974) 'The Government of Syria under Alexander the Great', *CQ* NS 24, 46–64.

— (1980) 'Alexander and the Iranians', *JHS* 100 1–21.

— (1986) 'Alexander the Great and the decline of Macedon', *JHS* 106, 1–12.

— (1988) *Conquest and Empire*, Cambridge.

— (1996) *Alexander and the East*, Oxford.

— (2002) *The Legacy of Alexander*, Oxford.

Bosworth, A. B. and Baynham, E. J. (eds) (2000) *Alexander the Great in Fact and Fiction*, Oxford.

Bouche-Leclercq, A. (1903–1907) *Histoire des Lagides*, 4 vols, Paris.

— (1913–1914) *Histoire des Seléucides*, 2 vols, Paris.

Briant, P. (1972) 'D'Alexandre le Grand aux Diadoques: le Cas d'Eumènes de Kardia', *REA* 74, 32–73 and 73, 43–81.

— (1973) *Antigone le Borgne*, Paris.

— (1978) 'Colonisation hellénistiques et populations indigènes; la phase d'installation', *Klio* 60, 57–98.

Brunt, P. A. (1969) 'Euboea in the Time of Philip II', *CQ*, NS 19, 245–65.

Buckler, J. (1996) 'Philip II's designs on Greece', in Wallace, R. W. and Harris, E. M. *Transitions to Empire, Essays in Greco-Roman History 360–146 BC in Honor of E. Badian*, Norman OK, 77–98.

Burn, A. R. (1952) 'Notes on Alexander's Campaigns 332–330', *JHS* 72, 81–4.

Burstein, S. M. (1974) *Outpost of Hellenism, the Emergence of Heraclea on the Black Sea*, Berkeley and Los Angeles CA.

— (1982) 'Arsinoe II Philadelphos: a revisionist view', in Adams, W. L. and Borza, E. N. (eds) (1982) *Philip II, Alexander the Great and the Macedonian Heritage*, Washington, DC, pp. 197–212.

Cantor, N. (2005) *Alexander the Great, Journey to the End of the Earth*, New York.

Carter, J. M. (1971) 'Athens, Euboea and Olynthos', *Historia* 20, 418–29.

Cartledge, P. (2004) *Alexander the Great, the Hunt for a New Past*, London.

Cartledge P. and Spawforth, A. (1989) *Hellenistic and Roman Sparta, a Tale of Two Cities*, London.

Cary, M. (1951) *A History of the Greek World, 323–146 BC*, 2nd edn, London.

Caven, B. (1990) *Dionysios I, War-Lord of Sicily*, New Haven CT.

Cawkwell, G. L. (1962) 'The Defence of Olynthos', *CQ*, NS 12, 122–40.

— (1978) *Philip of Macedon*, London.

— (2005) *The Greek Wars*, Oxford.

Chamoux, F. (1956) 'Le roi Magas', *Revue Historique* 216, 18–34.

Chaniotis, A. (2005) *War in the Hellenistic World*, Oxford.

Cloche, P. (1955) *Un Fondateur d'Empire*, St Etienne.

— (1957) *Demosthènes et la fin de la démocratie athénienne*, Paris.

Collart, P. (1937) *Philippes, Ville de Macedoine*, Paris.

Cook, J. M. (1983) *The Persian Empire*, London.

Cornell, T. J. (1995) *The Beginnings of Rome*, London.

Cunliffe, B. (1988) *Greeks, Romans and Barbarians, Spheres of Interaction*, London.

David, E. (1981) *Sparta between Empire and Revolution (404–243 BC)*, Salem NH.

Davis, N. and Kraay, C. (1973) *The Hellenistic Kingdoms: Portrait Coins and History*, London.

Dodge, T. A. (1890) *Alexander*, Boston.

Doherty, P. (2004) *Alexander, Death of a God*, London.

Eddy, S. K. (1961) *The King is Dead*, Lincoln NB.

Edson, C. (1958) 'Imperium Macedonicum: the Seleucid Empire and the literary evidence', *Classical Philology* 53, 153–70.

Ehrenburg, V. (1938) 'Pothos', in *Alexander and the Greeks*, Oxford, pp. 52–61.

Ellis, J. R. (1969) 'Amyntas III, Illyria and Olynthos, 383/2–380/379', *Makedonika* 9, 1–8.

— (1971) 'Amyntas Perdikka, Philip II, and Alexander the Great', *JHS* 91, 15–25.

— (1976) *Philip II and Macedonian Imperialism*, London.

Ellis, J. R. and Milns, R. D. (1970) *The Spectre of Philip*, Sydney.

Engel, R. (*c.*1978) *Untersuchungen zum Machtaufstieg des Antigonos I Monophthalmos*, Kallmunz.

Engels, D. W. (1979) *Alexander the Great and the Logistics of the Macedonian Army*, Berkeley and Los Angeles CA.

Errington, R. M. (1970) 'From Babylon to Triparadeisos: 323–320 BC', *JHS* 90, 49–77.

—(1977) 'Diodorus Siculus and the chronology of the early Diadochoi, 320–311 BC', *Hermes* 105, 478–504.

— (1990) *A History of Macedonia*, Berkeley and Los Angeles CA.

Ferguson, W. S. (1911) *Hellenistic Athens, an Historical Essay*, London.

Finley, M. I. (1969) *Ancient Sicily to the Arab Conquest*, London.

Flower, M. A. (1994) *Theopompos of Chios, History and Rhetoric in the Fourth Century BC*, Oxford.

Foertmeyer, V. (1988) 'The dating of the Pompe of Ptolemy II Philadelphus', *Historia* 37, 90–104.

Fontana, M. J. (1960) *Le lotte per la successione di Alessandro Magno dal 323 al 315*, Palermo.

Fox, R. L. (1973) *Alexander the Great*, London.

Fraser, P. M. (1972) *Ptolemaic Alexandria*, 3 vols, Oxford.

— (1996) *Cities of Alexander the Great*, Oxford.

Fredericksmeyer, E. A. (1982) 'On the final aims of Philip II' in Adams, W. L. and Borza, E. N. (eds) *Philip II, Alexander the Great and the Macedonian Heritage*, Washington DC, pp. 85–98.

Fuks, A. (1974) 'Patterns and types of social-economic revolution in Greece from the fourth to the second century BC', *Ancient Society* 5, 51–81.

Fuller, J. F. C. (1958) *The Generalship of Alexander the Great*, London.

Funck, B. (1974) 'Zur Innenpolitik des Seleukos Nikator', *Acta Antiqua academiae scientiarum Hungaricae* 22, 505–20.

Garland, R. (1987) *The Piraeus from the Fifth to the First Century BC*, Ithaca NY.

Grainger, J. D. (1990a) *The Cities of Seleukid Syria*, Oxford.

— (1990b) *Seleukos Nikator*, London.

— (1999) *The League of the Aitolians*, Leiden.

Grant, M. (1990) *The Hellenistic Greeks from Alexander to Cleopatra*, new edn, London.

Grayson, A. K. (1975) *Assyrian and Babylonian Chronicles*, Locust Valley NY.

Green, P. (1974) *Alexander of Macedon*, Harmondsworth.

— (1990) *Alexander to Actium*, Berkeley and Los Angeles CA.

Griffith, G. T. (1935) *The Mercenaries of the Hellenistic World*, Cambridge.

Griffith, G. T. (ed.) (1996) *Alexander the Great, the Main Problems*, Cambridge.

Grimal, P., Bengtson, H., Caskel, W., Derchain, P. and Smith, M. (1968) *Hellenism and the Rise of Rome*, London.

Gruen, E. S. (1985) 'The Coronation of the Diadochoi', in Eadie, J. H. and Ober, J. (eds), *The Craft of the Ancient Historian, Essays in Honor of Chester G. Starr*, Lanham MD, pp. 253–71.

Habicht, C. (1997) *Athens from Alexander to Antony* (trans. C. L. Schneider), Cambridge MA.

Hadley, R. A. (1974) 'Royal propaganda of Seleucus I and Lysimachus', *JHS* 94, 50–65.

Hamilton, J. R. (1973) *Alexander the Great*, London.

— (1987) 'Alexander's Iranian policy', in Will, W. and Heinrichs, J. (eds), *Zu Alexander der Grosse, Festschrift G. Wirth*, Amsterdam, pp. 467–86.

Hammond, N. G. L. (1938) 'The two battles of Chaeronea (338 BC and 86 BC), *Klio* 3, 186–218.

— (1966) 'The kingdoms in Illyria, *c.*400–167 BC', *Annual of the British School at Athens* 61, 73–85.

— (1967) *Epirus*, Oxford.

— (1981) *Alexander the Great*, London.

— (1982) 'The evidence for the identity of the royal tombs at Vergina', in Adams, W. L. and Borza, E. N. (eds) (1982) *Philip II, Alexander the Great and the Macedonian Heritage*, Washington DC.

— (1983) *Three Historians of Alexander the Great*, Cambridge.

— (1989) *The Macedonian State, its Origins, Institutions, and History*, Oxford.

— (1994) *Philip of Macedon*, London.

Hammond, N. G. L., Griffith, G. T. and Walbank, F. M. (1972, 1976, 1988) *A History of Macedonia*, 3 vols, Oxford.

Hatzopoulos, M. B. (1985) 'La Béotie et la Macedoine à l'époque de l'hégémonie thébaine: le point de vue macedonien', in *La Béotie Antique*, Paris, 247–57.

— (1996) *Macedonian Institutions under the Kings*, Meletemata 22, Athens.

Hauben, H. (1973) 'On the chronology of the years 313–311 BC', *American Journal of Philology*, 4, 256–67.

— (1975/6) 'Antigonos' invasion plan for his attack on Egypt in 306 BC', *Orientalia Lovaniensia Periodica* 6/7, 267–71.

— (1977) 'Rhodes, Alexander, and the Diadochi from 333/2 to 304 BC', *Historia* 26, 307–39.

— (1977) 'The first war of the Successors (321 BC)', *Ancient Society* 8, 85–120.

Hazzard, M. A. (1967) 'The regnal years of Ptolemy II Philadelphus', *Phoenix* 41, 140–58.

Heckel, W. (1988) *The Last Days and Testament of Alexander the Great*, Historia Einzelschriften 56, Stuttgart.

— (2006) *Who's Who in the Age of Alexander the Great*, London.

Heinen, H. (1972) *Untersuchungen zur Geschichte des 3 Jahrhunderderts v. chr. Zur Geschichte der Zeit des Ptolemaios Keraunos und zur Chremonidischen Krieg, Historia* Einszelschriften 20, Wiesbaden.

Heisserer, A. J. (1980) *Alexander the Great and the Greeks, the Epigraphic Evidence*, Norman OK.

Heskel, J. (1996) 'Philip II and Argaios: a pretender's story', in Wallace, R. W. and Harris, E. M., *Transitions to Empire, Essays in Greco-Roman History 360–146 BC in Honor of E. Badian*, Norman OK, pp. 37–56.

Holbl, G. (2001) *A History of the Ptolemaic Empire*, London.

Holt, F. L. (1989) *Alexander the Great and Bactria*, Leiden.

— (1999) *Thundering Zeus*, Berkeley and Los Angeles CA.

— (2003) *Alexander the Great and the Mystery of the Elephant Medallions*, Berkeley and Los Angeles CA.

— (2005) *Into the Land of Bones*, Berkeley and Los Angeles CA.

Huergon, J. (1973) *The Rise of Rome to 264 BC*, London.

Isaac, B. (1986) *Greek Settlements in Thrace*, London.

Karttunen, K. (1997) *India and the Hellenistic World*, Helsinki.

Keil, B. (1902) 'Korou Pedion', *Revue de Philologie* 26, 257–9.

Kuhrt, A. and Sherwin-White, S. (eds) (1987) *Hellenism in the East: the Interaction of Greek and non-Greek Civilisation from Syria to Central Asia after Alexander*, Berkeley and Los Angeles CA.

Kuhrt, A. and Sherwin-White, S. (1994) 'The transition from Achaemenid to Seleucid rule in Babylonia: revolution or evolution?', *Topoi* 4, 311–27.

Larsen, J. A. O. (1968) *Greek Federal States*, Oxford.

Laubscher, H. P. (1987) 'Ein ptolemaischer Gallierdenkmal', *Antike Kunst* 30, 131–54.

Launey, M. (1944) 'Un épisode oublié de l'invasion galate en Asie Mineure (278/7 av. J.-C.)', *REA* 46, 217–36.

— (1949–1950) *Recherches sur les Armées Hellénistiques*, Paris.

Leveque, P. (1957) *Pyrrhos*, Paris.

Lewis, S. (2000) 'The tyrant's myth', in Smith, C. and Servanti, J. *Sicily from Aeneas to Augustus*, Edinburgh, pp. 93–106.

Lock, R. (1977) 'The Macedonian army assembly in the time of Alexander the Great', *Classical Philology* 72, 91–107.

Loewe, M. and Shaughnessy, E. L. (eds) (1999) *The Cambridge History of Ancient China, from the Origins of Civilisation to 220 BC*, Cambridge.

Longega, G. (1968) *Arsinoe II*, Rome.

Lund, H. S. (1992) *Lysimachos, a Study in Hellenistic Kingship*, London.

McNicoll, A. (1997) *Hellenistic Fortifications from the Aegean to the Euphrates*, rev. N. P. Milner, Oxford.

Markle, M. M. (1974) 'The strategy of Philip II in 346 BC', *CQ*, NS 24, 253–68.

Marsden, E. W. (1964) *The Campaign of Gaugamela*, Liverpool.

— (1969) *Greek and Roman Artillery, Historical Development*, Oxford.

May, M. F. (1939) *The Coinage of Damastion*, Oxford.

Mehl, A. (1986) *Seleukos Nikator und sein Reich*, Louvain.

Meiggs, R. (1972) *The Athenian Empire*, Oxford.

Merker, I. L. (1970) 'The Ptolemaic officials and the League of the Islanders', *Historia* 9, 141–60.

Michel, H. (1957) *The Economics of Ancient Greece*, Cambridge.

Milns, R. D. (1966) 'Alexander's Macedonian cavalry and Diodoros XVII, 17, 4', *JHS* 86, 167–80.

Mitchell, S. (1993) *Anatolia, Land, Men, and Gods in Asia Minor*, Oxford.

Moraux, P. (1957) 'L'établissement des galates en Asie Mineure', *Istanbuler Mitteilungen*, 56–73.

Morkholm, O. (1991) *Early Hellenistic Coinage*, Cambridge.

Morley, N. G. G. (1996) *Metropolis and Hinterland, the City of Rome and the Italian Economy 200 BC–AD 200*, Cambridge.

Mossé, C. (1973) *Athens in Decline, 404–86 BC* (trans. J. Stewart), London.

— (2004) *Alexander, Destiny and Myth* (trans. J. Lloyd), Edinburgh.

Moysey, R. A. (1991) 'Diodoros, the satraps and the decline of the Persian Empire', *Ancient History Bulletin* 5, 111–20.

Muller, O. (1973) *Antigonos Monophthalamos und 'das Jahre des Könige'*, Bonn.

Nachtergael, G. (1977) *Les Galates en Grèce et les Sotéria de Delphes*, Brussels.

Narain, A. K. (1957) *The Indo-Greeks*, Cambridge.

— (1965) 'Alexander and India', *Greece and Rome*, 2nd series, 12, 155–65.

Newell, E. T. (1927) *The Coinages of Demetrius Poliorcetes*, Oxford.

O'Brien, J. M. (1992) *Alexander the Great, the Invisible Enemy*, London.

Olmstead, A. T. (1948) *History of the Persian Empire*, Chicago IL.

Osborne, M. J. (1979) 'Kallias, Phaidros and the revolt of Athens in 287 BC', *Zeitschrift für Papyrologie und Eigraphik* 25, 181–94.

Pearson, L. (1983) *The Lost Histories of Alexander the Great*, Chico CL.

Perlman, S. (ed.) (1973) *Philip and Athens*, Cambridge.

Philips, G. (2004) *Alexander the Great, Murder in Babylon*, London.

Picard, G. C. and Picard, C. (1987) *Carthage* (trans. D. Collon), London.

Préaux, C. (1987) *Le Monde Hellénistique*, 2 vols, 2nd edn, Paris.

Price, M. J. (1991) *The Coinage in the Name of Alexander the Great and Philip Arrhidaios*, London.

Pritchett, W. K. (1958) 'Observations on Chaeronea', *American Journal of Archaeology* 62, 307–11.

Raychaudhuri, H. (1996) *Political History of Ancient India*, with a commentary by B. N. Mukherji, Oxford.

Rice, E. E. (1983) *The Grand Procession of Ptolemy Philadelphus*, Oxford.

Robert, L. (1945) *Le sanctuaire de Sinuri près de Mylasa: I Les inscriptions grecques*, Paris.

— (1946) *Hellenica, Recueil d'épigraphie de numismatique et d'antiquités grecques*, 2nd edn, Paris.

— (1959) 'Les inscriptions grecques de Bulgarie', *Revue de Philologie* 38, 172–9.

Roebuck, C. (1948) 'The settlements of Philip II with the Greek states in 338 BC', *Classical Philology* 3, 73–91.

Roesch, P. (1984) 'Un décret inédit de la Ligue Thébaine et le flotte d'Epaminondas', *Revue des Etudes Grecques*, 97, 45–60.

Romane, P. (1988) 'Alexander's siege of Gaza', *Ancient World* 18, 21–30.

Roos, P. (1985) 'Alexander I in Olympia', *Eranos* 83, 162–8.

Ryder, T. T. B. (1965) *Koine Eirene*, Oxford.

Sachs, A. J. and Wiseman, D. J. (1954) 'A Babylonian king list of the Hellenistic period', *Iraq* 16, 202–12.

Sanders, L. J. (1987) *Dionysios I of Sicily and Greek Tyranny*, Beckenham.

Savill, A. (1990) *Alexander the Great and his Time*, 2nd edn, New York.

Schlumberger, D. (1969) 'Triparadisos', *Bulletin du Musée de Beyrouth* 22, 147–9.

Schober, L. (1981) *Untersuchungen zur Geschichte babyloniens und der oberen Satrapien von 323–303 V. Chr.*, Frankfurt.

Scholten, J. B. (2000) *The Politics of Plunder*, Berkeley and Los Angeles CA.

Schottky, F. F. (1989) *Media Atropatene und Gross Armenien in hellenistischer Zeit*, Bonn.

Schwenk, C. J. (1985) *Athens in the Age of Alexander*, Chicago IL.

Sedlar, J. W. (1980) *India and the Greek World*, Totowa NJ.

Seibert, J. (1967) *Historische Beitrage zu den dynastischen verbindungen in hellenistischer Zeit*, *Historia* Einzelschriften 10, Wiesbaden.

— (1970) 'Philokles, Sohn des Apollodoros, König der Sidonier', *Historia* 19, 337–51.

Seyrig, H. (1988) 'Seleucus I and the foundation of Hellenistic Syria', in Ward, W. A. (ed.), *The Role of the Phoenicians in the Interaction of Mediterranean Civilisations*, Beirut, pp. 53–63.

Shear, T. L. (1978) *Kallias of Sphettos and the Revolt of Athens in 286 BC*, *Hesperia* Supplement 17, Princeton NJ.

Sherwin-White, S. and Kuhrt, A. (1993) *From Samarkhand to Sardis*, London.

Shipley, G. (2000) *The Greek World after Alexander 323–30 BC*, London.

Simpson, R. H. (1954) 'The historical circumstances of the peace of 311 BC', *JHS* 74, 25–31.

— (1959) 'Antigonos the One-Eyed and the Greeks', *Historia* 8, 385–409.

Smith, L. C. (1961) 'The chronology of Books 18–22 of Diodorus Siculus', *American Journal of Philology* 82, 283–90.

Smith, S. (1924) *Babylonian Historical Texts*, London.

Stark, F. (1958) *Alexander's Path*, London.

Stoneman, R. (ed.) (1991) *The Greek Alexander Romance*, London.

Talbert, R. J. A. (1974) *Timoleon and the Revival of Greek Sicily, 344–317 BC*, Cambridge.

Tarn, W. W. (1913) *Antigonos Gonatas*, Oxford.

— (1951) *The Greeks in Bactria and India*, 2nd edn, Cambridge.

Tarn, W. W. and Griffith, G. T. (1952) *Hellenistic Civilisation*, 3rd edn, London.

Thapar, R. (1966) *A History of India*, vol. 1, Harmondsworth.

— (1997) *Asoka and the Decline of the Mauryas*, 2nd edn, Oxford.

Thompson, D. (1988) *Memphis under the Ptolemies*, Princeton NJ.

Thonemann, P. (2005) 'The tragic king: Demetrios Poliorketes and the city of Athens', in Hekster, O. and Fowler, R. (eds), *Imaginary Kings*, Stuttgart, pp. 63–85.

Tillyard, H. J. W. (1908) *Agathocles*, Cambridge.

Toynbee, A. J. (1965) *Hannibal's Legacy*, vol. 1, Oxford.

— (1969) *Some Problems of Greek History*, Oxford.

Tronson, A. (1984) 'Satyros the Peripatetic and the marriages of Philip II', *JHS* 104, 116–26.

Vogelsang, W. (1987) 'Some remarks on Eastern Iran in the late Achaemenid Period', in Sancisi-Weedenberg, H. (ed.), *Achaemenid History I, Sources, Structure and Synthesis*, Leiden.

— (1990) 'The Achaemenids and India', in Sancisi-Weedenberg, H. (ed.), *Achaemenid History IV, Centre and Periphery*, Leiden, pp. 93–110.

Vogt, J. (1971) 'Kleomenes von Naukratis, Herr von Agypten', *Chiron* 1, 153–7.

Walbank, F. W. (1981) *The Hellenistic World*, London.

Warmington, B. H. (1964) *Carthage*, Harmondsworth.

Wehrli, C. (1969) *Antigone et Démétrios*, Geneva.

Weisehofer, J. (1996) *Ancient Persia* (trans. A. Azodi), London.

Weiskopf, M. (1989) 'The so-called "Satraps Revolt", 366–360 BC', in *Historia* Einszelschriften, Stuttgart.

Westlake, H. D. (1935) *Thessaly in the Fourth Century B.C.*, London.

Wheatley, P. (1995) 'Ptolemy Soter's annexation of Syria 320 BC', *CQ*, NS 45, 433–40.

Wheeler, M. (1968) *Flames over Persepolis: Turning Point in History*, London.

Whitehorne, J. (1996) *Cleopatras*, London.

Wilcken, U. (1967) *Alexander the Great* (trans. G. C. Richards), New York.

Will, E. (1964) 'Ophellas, Ptolémée, Cassandre et la chronologie', *REA* 66, 320–33.

— (1967) 'La Cyrenaïque et les partages successifs de l'empire d'Alexandre', *Antiquité classique* 29, 369–90.

— (1979) *Histoire politique du Monde Hellénistique*, 2nd edn, Nancy.

Wolohojian, A. M. (1969) *The Romance of Alexander the Great by Pseudo-Callisthenes*, New York.

Wood, M. (1997) *In the Footsteps of Alexander the Great*, London.

Worrle, M. (1975) 'Antiochos I, Achaios der Altere und die Galater', *Chiron* 5, 59–87.

Worthington, I. (2003) *Alexander the Great, a Reader*, London.

Index